Céline Fallet

The Princes of Art

Painters, sculptors, and engravers

Céline Fallet

The Princes of Art
Painters, sculptors, and engravers

ISBN/EAN: 9783337168643

Printed in Europe, USA, Canada, Australia, Japan

Cover: Foto ©Thomas Meinert / pixelio.de

More available books at **www.hansebooks.com**

THE OLD MASTERS.

THE

PRINCES OF ART:

PAINTERS, SCULPTORS,

AND

ENGRAVERS.

TRANSLATED FROM THE FRENCH

BY

MRS. S. R. URBINO.

BOSTON:
LEE AND SHEPARD.
1883.

Entered according to Act of Congress, in the year 1870, by
S. R. URBINO,
in the Office of the Librarian of Congress, at Washington.

ELECTROTYPED AT THE
BOSTON STEREOTYPE FOUNDRY,
19 Spring Lane.

University Press: John Wilson & Son, Cambridge.

INTRODUCTORY.

THE FINE ARTS.

A FEW remarks upon the Fine Arts may not be out of place in a work like this, which treats of the lives and productions of eminent artists.

All sorts of works are arts, properly speaking, and those in which the mind is mostly engaged, are the fine arts. The more mechanical are those of unquestionable utility, and the perfection to which they are carried constitutes the measure of civilization, of industry and wealth, of a people. The others, although their chief object is embellishment, not only render him who cultivates them with success illustrious, but also the city where he was born, and the nation to which he belongs.

"The fine arts," says an ancient author, "are the children of genius; nature is their model, and taste their teacher. Simplicity ought to form their chief characteristic, for they become corrupted when they degenerate into luxury and show. Our own feelings lead to correct judgment in the fine arts: they lose their effect if they speak only to the mind, but they triumph when they touch the heart."

Architecture, Sculpture, Painting, Engraving, Music, and Poetry, are known under the name of fine arts.

ARCHITECTURE.

Architecture is the art of building. As soon as man felt the need of sheltering himself from the injurious effects of the air, and defending himself against ferocious animals, he sought to construct a habitation. Therefore it is evident that the origin of architecture dates back to the earliest times. The Bible says that Cain built a city, after the death of his brother Abel, and it mentions the cities of Nineveh and Babylon, founded by Nimrod the hunter, great grandson of Noah. The Egyptians perfected the art; but the Greeks were the first to unite the rules of this art, form a method, and furnish fine models to posterity.

The Tuscans, the Romans, then the French and the Italians, had celebrated architects, and constructed magnificent monuments. Every nation, according to its taste or genius, added to, or took from what had already been done. These changes originated the different orders, which are distinguished by the proportions and various ornaments of the columns which sustain or beautify large buildings.

The Greeks had three orders of architecture: the Doric, Ionic, and the Corinthian. Solidity is the characteristic of the Doric order: it is used in many public edifices, where delicacy and ornament would be out of place.

The Corinthian order was invented by Callimachus. It is said that this artist, passing near a tomb, was struck by the fine effect produced by the elegant leaves of the acanthus encircling a basket, which had been placed in their midst. The artist resolved to make use of the ornament thus indicated by Nature and since that time; two rows of acanthus leaves, at the top of a column, mark the Corinthian order.

The Ionic holds the middle place between the simplicity of the Doric and the elegance of the Corinthian. The temple of Diana, at Ephesus, which passed for one of the seven wonders of the world, was of this order.

The Tuscan is less ornamented, and is the simplest of the orders. The Composite, on the contrary, is even more ornate than the Corinthian, but is less esteemed, by masters in art, than the beautiful architecture of the Greeks.

The Gothic order, of which the old churches are the finest examples, is of more recent creation, and differs from the antique in its proportions and ornaments. This species of architecture unites sublime simplicity with incomparable boldness. Its distinctive sign is its high and sharply pointed-arches, which seem to bear the prayers of the faithful heavenward.

SCULPTURE.

Sculpture is the art of reproducing palpable objects by means of solid materials; its origin is lost in the night of ages.

At first, the sculptor exercised his talent upon clay or wax, flexible substances, and more easily worked than wood or stone. According to the Greeks, the first sculptor was a potter of Sicyon, and his daughter the first designer, because she traced the profile of her betrothed upon the wall, and the potter obtained the solid portrait of his future son-in-law by filling the spaces between the charcoal outlines with clay, and then baking it.

However, there is nothing to justify the pretension of the Greeks, and it is probable that the instinct of imitation with which man is endowed would have caused him to make similar discoveries in various places. Afterwards more venturous persons sought to render their works durable, and began to chisel in the hard wood of the lemon, cypress, palm, olive, and ebony. Finally they used ivory, stones, and metals: marble became the most esteemed, on account of its solidity, and the fineness and polish of its grain.

The Egyptians are cited among the first people who

cultivated the art of sculpture. They raised a colossal statue to preserve the memory of King Mœris, and of the queen, his wife, for having constructed a lake destined to assure the fertility of the country. A piece of Egyptian statuary was the work of many artists, each one occupying himself with a specialty, and the union of these different parts forming a remarkable whole.

If the Greeks were really the inventors of sculpture, it made very little progress among them for a long time, as nothing which they produced before the travels of Dædalus in Egypt merits attention as a work of art. Dædalus studied many years under Egyptian masters: on his return to Greece he opened a school which produced able artists and fine works. Sculpture, like other arts, was, after a time, perfected by the Greeks, and the masterpieces of Myron, Lysippus, and Phidias are considered, even now, as the most perfect statuary. This judgment might be considered partial, if the moderns, who have produced such admirable works, had not made use of the antiques, we will not say as models, but as guides, in teaching that true beauty consists in the imitation of nature.

The fine arts, friends of peace and liberty, lost their brilliancy with the subjugation of Greece by the Romans. The masters of the world, knowing little of art, did not think of preserving the works left by celebrated painters and sculptors. As the Romans neither knew nor appreciated other laurels than those gained in war, they did not, at first, envy Greece (which they had conquered and reduced to a province of their vast empire) the title it had long borne of the home of the fine arts; but when they realized that there was another glory than that of imposing their yoke upon nations, they made their capital an asylum for the learned and for artists.

Sculpture, however, did not long flourish at Rome. After having prospered under Augustus, it was neglected by his successors. The protection which it obtained from Nero was injurious, rather than beneficial, because the merit of a piece of statuary, according to this prince, consisted in its bulk; and he always found a statue of gigantic proportions admirable.

The arts, which had declined during the struggles of the Roman empire, did not find the impetus necessary for their recovery until towards the end of the thirteenth century. The most brilliant epoch of sculpture was that in which Julius II. and Leo X. occupied the pontifical throne, when the immortal genius of Michael Angelo shone forth.

Stone, wood, and bronze are the materials most generally employed by sculptors; among stones, marble, as we have already observed, is preferred.

The artist, to whom some great work in marble is confided, commences by making a model of the statue or group which he undertakes in clay; but as this shrinks in drying, the first effort is not satisfactory, and he remoulds it in plaster; in this mould he runs a new plaster model, from which he takes his measures. After having chipped off the grosser parts of the marble which he is about to use, and given it something of the form to be represented, he begins the earnest part of his work, and brings forth from the insensible mass a head which seems to think, members which seem ready to move, a heart which apparently throbs with grief, hope, or joy. He patiently handles the chisel, and then removes the traces of his labor; with the file he takes away the lines and roughness of the marble, so that nothing remains to do but to polish it.

Stone is sculptured like marble, but the instruments used are not so strong, and one is obliged to have at hand moistened plaster, and the dust of the stone on which he is working, to fill up cracks and cover defects.

Wood is used for small models, and sometimes for works of importance. Carvings in wood, of which magnificent specimens are found in many ancient churches, and in some old castles, have come into favor after having been long neglected, and the carved chests and armorial bearings of our ancestors, arm-chairs artistically wrought, and tables with ornamented legs, have become real objects of luxury — thanks to fashion, which, this time, is in the right.

The wood of the oak and chestnut are used for large carvings, the pear and the service tree for smaller ones, and the linden tree, and the box for more delicate works. It is necessary to have the wood thoroughly dry before using, to prevent its cracking.

Besides wood, stone, and marble, bronze is also used to reproduce the features of illustrious warriors, of great artists, and of the benefactors of mankind, and so transmit them, as well as memorable events, to posterity.

The art of liquefying metals was known to the ancients, but it is thought that they seldom used it for casting large pieces of sculpture. However, it is said that Myron, a celebrated Greek sculptor, who lived about the year 442 before Christ, cast a cow, in bronze, so perfectly, that animals themselves were deceived by it. Lysippus of Sicyon, who rendered himself illustrious about a hundred years afterwards, and who was selected to make statues of Alexander the Great, as Apelles was to make portraits of him, cast one of the statues in bronze, which was, we are assured, of a marvellous beauty. It came into the possession of the Emperor Nero, who valued it highly; but being only of bronze, he wished to have it covered with a layer of gold. The attempt was unsuccessful; the noble work of Lysippus was spoiled in taking off its rich covering. We would here observe that this great sculptor left no less than six hundred pieces of statuary, all worthy of note. Among them were, besides the statue of which we have spoken, those of Socrates, of Alexander as a child, and one of Apollo, forty cubits in height, known as the Apollo of Tarento.

The Romans also cast their sculptures in metal, for example, the bronze statue of Marcus Aurelius; but that statue, like those of Cosmo de Medici, at Florence, and of Henry IV., at Paris, was cast in different pieces. The equestrian statue of Louis XIV. was the first colossal group made by one casting; and when we consider that it weighed more than thirty thousand kilograms (sixty thousand pounds), we can understand the admiration and astonishment caused by the success of the casting.

Bronze is a mixture of small grains of copper and zinc, which, by fusion acquire a degree of solidity superior to all other metals.

PAINTING.

PAINTING is an art which represents all visible objects, upon a smooth surface, by means of lines and colors. Like all other arts, it was imperfect at its beginning. The principal features of a figure were drawn, and it was long after these first essays that colors were employed. At first only one color was used for each sketch; afterwards four — blue, red, black, and yellow.

Painting remained almost stationary in Egypt, where it was anciently cultivated, while it attained a high degree of perfection in Greece. Zeuxis, Parrhasius, Timanthes, Protogenes, and Apelles acquired great celebrity by their admirable compositions.

This art was highly esteemed among the Romans; but they could not dispute the palm with Greece. When the vast empire which they had subdued was crushed by the fury of the barbarians, painting appeared to be forever buried in its immense ruins. It was not until towards the middle of the thirteenth century that it began to rise again. Cimabue, a Florentine painter and architect, came from Constantinople to Italy, where he acquired great reputation, after having studied under the Greek masters. Charles I., King of Naples, honored him with his favor; and his example having been followed by other sovereigns of Europe, the number of artists increased, and painting awoke from the lethargy in which it had slumbered for centuries.

The first paintings were in distemper and fresco: painting in oil was not discovered until 1350.

They used some kind of glue with their distemper colors, and painted upon plaster, wood, skins, cloth, and strong paper. This kind of painting is durable when protected from dampness; it has the advantage of producing good effect, and not changing color.

The word *fresco* (fresh) is Italian, so called because this painting is done upon freshly plastered or stuccoed walls. Colors which have been submitted to the action of fire, and earths of a dry nature, only are used, as others would be injured by the action of the lime. Fresco lasts longer than any other kind of painting, and for this reason it has been chosen to decorate places exposed to the air.

Three things are necessary for fresco painting, — the sketch, the cartoons, and the plastering. Of the latter, two coats are used; the first, which is upon the stone, should be of coarse sand, and present a rough surface, in order that the second coat, composed of mortar, well-prepared lime, and fine river sand, may stick to it. The painting is done upon the second coat of plastering, which is laid on as needed, for if dry, the fresco will be unsatisfactory. The colors are mixed with water, and must be used freely, or the painting will not be durable. The great masters have generally left magnificent frescoes. It is to be regretted that all colors cannot be used in this kind of painting; there are shades which it is found impossible to represent.

The sketch is the rough draft of the work which the painter is planning. In fresco, the sketch is usually much smaller than the picture is intended to be: this sketch ought not only to represent the subject in all its parts, but also to indicate its colors; the artist is obliged to have it before his eyes, and to observe it carefully, if he wishes to give to his work that harmony which constitutes its beauty.

The cartoons for fresco painting are composed of many leaves of thick paper stuck together. Upon these the painter designs as much work as he can do in a day; and when the plastering, upon which he ought to work, has taken the requisite degree of solidity, he applies the cartoon, and traces the drawing with a pointed instrument; then, when all the lines are traced upon the wall, he begins to paint.

In Oil Painting all the colors are ground, and mixed with drying oil. This kind of painting offers the greatest advantages for vivacity, the mixture of tints, and delicacy of execution. Besides, it permits the artist to devote more time to his work, and give it a better finish, to retouch it, and take away whatever displeases him, without effacing all that he has done.

Painting in oil was, at first, done upon boards, then upon copper, finally upon canvas or taffeta: the use of canvas has been perpetuated to the present time.

Miniature painting resembles distemper painting, inasmuch as the colors are mixed with water and size, or other glutinous matter. Miniatures are painted upon fine-grained paper, or wood, prepared for the purpose; but ivory is generally preferred. This kind of painting requires much patience and great care, particularly in the gradations of color and finishing touches. A glazing, similar to varnish, is usually applied to preserve them.

Another kind of painting, called Mixed Painting, is made from the stippling of the miniature and the bolder manner of the distempter style; it is equally good for large or small pictures. The most delicate parts are finished by stippling; force and character are given by bold strokes. Correggio has left two magnificent pieces done in this manner.

The Pastel is a kind of painting in which crayons of different colors take the place of the hair pencil. These crayons are made of a paste (*pasta*), and formed into little rolls while soft.

Pastel is considered the easiest kind of painting, because one can leave the work and take it up again at convenience. Common tinted paper, pasted on thin board, is generally used. The picture, when finished, is put under glass, which protects the colors, and gives them an agreeable gloss.

The Mosaic is a painting composed of small stones, of different colors. There are beautiful fragments of mosaic, of very ancient origin, in Rome, and other cities of Italy. The artist, who wishes to make a mosaic, must have the picture which he will imitate before him, and cartoons of the exact size of his work. The little stones which he uses, are assorted according to their shades of color, and placed in baskets, or boxes, from which he can easily take them. The stones should have a flat and even surface, without brilliancy or polish, because if they reflect the light it is difficult to distinguish their colors. After having traced his cartoons with a point upon the plaster designed to be used, the artist dips the stones into a liquid mortar, and disposes them as their forms and colors require. This kind of painting ought to last as long as the wall upon which it is done.

Camaieu is a mode of painting in which there are but

two colors, or black and white only; thus the paintings which represent basso-relievos of marble or stone are camaieux. When the ground work is yellow, the French call it *cirage;* when gray, as upon the windows of some old churches, *grisaille.*

In painting, the word *school* means the union of artists who have learned their art from the same master, and who adhere to the principles given by the founder of the mode he uses. Great schools do not bear the name of the master, but of the country which he has rendered illustrious.

The Byzantine school, founded at Byzantium, by Greek artists, reanimated the taste for the arts in Italy. These ancient painters have left very few pictures, yet those few are very marked in style. Painting was then in its infancy. They represented only long and straight figures, like columns, all having the same attitude and the same physiognomy, or, rather, having no physiognomy. Great ignorance of the rules of drawing, of anatomy, of perspective, and of chiaro-scuro is manifested in all the works which have come from this school.

After the Byzantine comes the Italian school, which, on account of the great number of artists it has produced, is subdivided into the Florentine, Roman, Venetian, Lombardic, Bolognese, and Neapolitan.

Of these the Florentine is the oldest; it is celebrated for vivid and fruitful imagination, bold, correct, and graceful pencilling, and a style which is noble, and often sublime. Cimabue was the founder of this school, but Leonardo da Vinci and Michael Angelo are considered as its masters.

The Roman school may be traced nearly to the same epoch as the Florentine; it is distinguished by a poetical charm, by purity, and admirable sweetness, and an easy and elegant touch, while it is correct and learned. Perrugino is the father of the Roman school, but Raphael is its glory. The only reproach which can be made of the painters of this school, is their having somewhat neglected coloring.

The Venetian school, at the head of which stand Titian and Paul Veronese, is renowned for admirable coloring, knowledge of chiaro-scuro, a graceful and lively style, and a seductive imitation of nature. But if the Roman school can be reproached for not having studied coloring, in which the Venetian excelled, the latter can be reproached for having somewhat neglected drawing, in which the Roman painters are so correct.

The Lombardic school, which recognizes Correggio as its founder, has a right to be proud of its pure drawing, its taste, its fine composition, its soft and easy pencilling, and its noble and graceful manner.

The Bolognese school, founded by Francis, produced no great artists at first, but the Carracci built it up; if it did not attain the glory of the preceding schools, it was distinguished for science of composition, purity of drawing, truth of coloring, and understanding of chiaroscuro. Domenichino and Guido, pupils of the Carracci, contributed much to the celebrity of this school.

The Genoese school, which is not wanting in boldness and grace, has not produced any of the eminent men whose names form an epoch in the history of Art.

The Neapolitan school boasts of Salvator Rosa; but this great artist, who originated prodigies, had a manner peculiar to himself, which no other painter was capable of imitating.

The Spanish school, which has often been classed with the Neapolitan, produced Ribera, Velasquez, and Murillo. The name of the last suffices to illustrate it. Perfect drawing, elevated thoughts, brilliant imagination, a firm touch, a remarkable imitation of nature, something proud, poetic, and bold, distinguish the Spanish school.

The German school represented objects with their imperfections, and not as artists usually like to see them: it was skilful in coloring, but stiff in design; its figures wanting in expression, and its drapery in gracefulness and taste. However, some masters of this school have avoided those errors with which connoisseurs reproach German painting in general. Albert Durer is the glory of this school.

The Flemish school is of very ancient origin; but it did not become celebrated until towards the middle of the fourteenth century, when Jean Van Eyck, surnamed

Jean of Bruges, invented oil painting; and it was not at the height of its brilliancy until long after, under Rubens and Van Dyke, who are ranked among the first painters in the world. Easy pencilling, a profound knowledge of the mixing of colors, of chairo-scuro, a fine finish, with much grace and truthfulness, are the distinctive characteristics of the Flemish style.

The Dutch school recommends itself by similar qualities; but it has produced more painters of landscapes, or of interior scenes, than of history. Its most celebrated artist is Rembrandt, who, like Salvator Rosa, has, as yet, had no imitator.

Through the study of the masters of all countries, the French school has formed a manner which it would be difficult to define, but which has not the less become its own and original style. The grace, elegance, and spirit which characterize this nation are constantly visible, and genius often shines in its paintings. The French school excels in noble style and in history. Poussin and Sueur have best illustrated it.

Of all the schools of which we have spoken, the French is the only one which can be proud of its living artists: other schools have nothing more than recollections; for, after having shone with splendor in Italy, Flanders, and Spain, art has fallen into decay, and is now waiting for some great genius, gifted with power to resuscitate the glory of the past.

The French school is subdivided into many others,

which have received the names of their several masters — the school of Poussin, the school of Le Brun, &c.

The English school dates back but one century, and affects a peculiar character. Hogarth, one of the most celebrated among English painters, was a remarkable satirist, rather than a great painter; but there are at present many artists who are an honor to England, where the fine arts will, without doubt, soon be cultivated with as much success as commerce and manufactures.

ENGRAVING.

ENGRAVING is the art of representing the lights and shades of visible objects upon hard substances, by means of drawing and cutting. The art of engraving upon crystal, glass, and precious stones was known to the ancients; and although they may have engraved their inscriptions and their laws upon bronze and marble, they never thought to reproduce upon metal the pictures which they were desirous to transmit to posterity.

This discovery was reserved for the moderns. A Florentine goldsmith, named Maso Finiguerra, passes for the inventor of engraving; and it was by chance that he learned the advantages which art could derive from it. While chiselling gold and silver, he noticed that the melted sulphur, which he used, preserved the impression of the drawings which he had traced upon the metal, and reproduced them upon paper, the sulphur having taken off the black which was found in the lines made upon the gold or silver. He spoke of his discovery to one of his companions, who engraved a small picture upon copper, and took a number of copies from it. This invention passed into Flanders, and many painters of talent used it to make themselves known in Europe.

Engraving, which appeared in France in the time of Francis I., was perfected during the following reigns, and brought to honor by the greatest of artists.

Engraving is done upon wood, shell, and copper, either with a graver or the use of aquafortis. The graver is good for portraits; the aquafortis is preferable for small works, and gives them a lightness and finish not easily attained with the graver.

ARCHITECTS AND SCULPTORS.

PHIDIAS.

Phidias, who was born at Athens, about five hundred years before Christ, devoted himself to the study of sculpture. Great genius and assiduous labor permitted him to realize wonders, and so carry the art, then in its infancy, to a high degree of perfection. Having acquired a reputation by some fine pieces of statuary, his fellow-citizens demanded of him a statue of Minerva, and at the same time required one of Alcamenes, who was also celebrated as a sculptor. These two statues were to be submitted to the judgment of competent persons, and the most beautiful was to be placed upon a column which the city should erect. A great reward was promised to the victor, but this was the least consideration to the two artists, equally jealous of glory and honor. They commenced their work, and each sought to secure the prize by displaying all the resources of his talent.

On the day of trial the two statues were removed to the public square, in presence of the judges, and a crowd assembled to salute the happy victor. When the cloth which concealed the *Minerva* of Alcamenes was raised, they uttered a cry of surprise and admiration; they had never seen anything more beautiful, more pure, or more finished than this statue, which they almost believed to be living. Phidias, as calm as if he had not heard the praises given to Alcamenes, showed his work in his turn. The Athenians had expected something better from the talent of Phidias; his *Minerva* appeared to be only a kind of rough model; and thinking this negligence of the sculptor was a mark of disdain, they broke into loud expressions of disapprobation. The partisans of Phidias were quiet, those of Alcamenes gave vent to their joy.

The judges commanded silence, and, after another examination, and a short deliberation, they felicitated Alcamenes, and believed it a duty to recommend to Phidias to work with more care, not doubting, they said, that with time and patience he might, at a future day, succeed in equalling his rival. The crowd, by their approval, manifested that they held the same opinion as the judges; and Alcamenes, filled with delight, approached to receive the prize awarded him. But Phidias, instead of retiring, sad and confused, advanced towards the tribune reserved to the jury, and asked permission to address one question to the illustrious members of which it was composed.

"Is it not at the top of a column that the statue preferred is to be placed?" he asked, when permission was granted him to speak.

"Without doubt," was the answer.

"Then would it not be well to see the effect produced by these statues from its height, before giving judgment?" said Phidias.

Every one was struck by the justice of this idea, and the machines, destined to raise the Minerva, having been already prepared, the trial was made at once. The statue of Alcamenes, seen from a distance, lost all the fascination which it owed to the perfection of its details and its admirable finish; while that of Phidias, which had at first shocked the spectators by its massive and abrupt appearance, took a character of grandeur and majesty which astonished them. It was no longer possible to make a comparison between the two statues, and as each one wished to atone for his involuntary injustice, Phidias was proclaimed victor, with great enthusiasm.

From that time this celebrated sculptor had no more rivals; not only were his genius and ability recognized, but also his profound knowledge of all that pertained to his art.

The war between the Greeks and Persians broke out soon after, and the latter, proud of the superiority of their forces, hoped they could easily crush the Greeks, who had the audacity to attempt to defend themselves.

Before the battle of Marathon, they had prepared a block of marble, of which they wished to make a monument, destined to perpetuate the remembrance of their victory. But they had reckoned without considering the courage of their enemies, the enthusiasm which centuples armies, the love of country which inspires the feeblest hearts with heroism; they were completely beaten; and the marble intended as a trophy fell into the hands of the Athenians, who transported it to their city, and placed it at the disposition of Phidias. The sculptor made of it a Nemesis, the goddess of vengeance. The work was as much admired as the ingenuity of the idea; and the Nemesis was preserved as one of the dearest and most glorious of *souvenirs*.

Phidias was afterwards engaged to make a colossal statue of Minerva for the Parthenon,— a famous temple dedicated to that goddess. He made a Minerva twenty-five cubits high, so beautiful that, although of gold and ivory, the richness of the materials was its least merit. People came from all parts of the country to contemplate this masterpiece of statuary; and Phidias, laden with wealth and honors, was the object of the respect and admiration of his countrymen; but the Athenians, so justly considered the most fickle people in the world, soon forgot how much they were indebted to the glory of this great man, and, naturally jealous of all superiority, they vexed and irritated him until he became tired of their unreasonable demands and injustice, and yielded to thoughts of vengeance, which he had hitherto repelled.

He could revenge himself only as an artist. He understood too well how proud the Athenians were of possessing his statue at the Parthenon,— the richest piece of sculpture in all Greece,— not to hesitate upon the punishment he intended to inflict upon them. He had no thought of destroying this work, upon which he had wrought with so much love; but, sure of his own powers, he determined to endow some other city with a statue still more beautiful. Having formed this resolution, he quitted the ungrateful place of his birth, and travelled through Greece, meditating upon the work which he would execute wherever he should take up his abode.

The Helenes, who knew of his rare merit, received him with great honors, and he consented to remain some time in their city, engaging to leave a *souvenir* of his sojourn. They were delighted to furnish all that he required, without even asking him what he intended to do. Sensibly affected by this confidence in his talent, he decided to seek no farther for a home in which he would place his most beautiful work, and undertook his statue of *Jupiter Olympus*. The *Minerva* of the Parthenon was forgotten, or at least only occupied the second rank among the valuable works of this sculptor; and public admiration placed the *Jupiter Olympus* among the seven wonders of the world.

The Athenians repented of their ingratitude when

they saw this masterpiece,— the greatest work of art,— and begged Phidias to make something as remarkable for them; but their flattery and supplications were of no avail: the sculptor, certain of not being surpassed, laid down his chisel, never to resume it.

The name of Phidias has remained one of the greatest, not only of Greece, but of the world. The first of sculptors, he studied Nature to reproduce it, and knew how to imitate it in all its grace and beauty; and when he wished to represent Divinity, it was done with so much majesty, grandeur, and power, that, in the words of an ancient author, his chisel seemed to have been guided by Divinity itself.

PRAXITELES.

Praxiteles flourished about three hundred and sixty-five years before Christ, that is to say, about a century after Phidias. Endowed with great genius, he realized all that the most ambitious and most devoted artist could desire. Marble seemed to become animated under his chisel, and nothing could give an idea of the ravishing beauty of his works. Those whom he permitted to visit his studio, remained in ecstasy before the first piece of statuary offered to their view; feeling sure that it would be impossible to see anything better, they were disinclined to look farther. When Praxiteles had succeeded in attracting their attention to another group, they forgot the first, and finally remained uncertain to which they could give preference. Such embarrassment was considered by the sculptor as his greatest triumph; it was to him the proof of a pleasure seldom enjoyed by the greatest artists, whose genius is generally fitful, while he was ever master of his own.

The famous Phryne, having obtained permission to choose, from among the works of the celebrated sculptor, that which she liked best, found it so difficult to decide, that she asked the advice of Praxiteles himself. The artist avoided giving her an answer; he did not wish to deceive her, and did not care to give up his best piece. But Phryne was not to be discouraged. As cunning as she was beautiful, she resolved to obtain by stratagem that which had been refused her.

One night, Praxiteles was aroused from sleep by the cry of fire; and, springing up, he rushed, half dressed, from his chamber.

Phryne, who feigned to have come in with those who were about him, begged him to calm himself, saying, "It is only your studio which is on fire."

At these words, Praxiteles, who feared more for his works than for himself, ran towards the place designated, crying out, "Quick, quick, my friends! Save my Satyr and my Cupid! Perhaps it is not too late! Alas, I am lost if the flames have destroyed them!"

Phryne learned what she wished to know: she stopped

Praxiteles, and avowed that it was only a trick which she had played, in order to draw from him his secret, and requiring the performance of his promise, demanded his Cupid. Praxiteles had been so much frightened at the thought of losing his studio, that he received the acknowledgment of Phryne as good news; and in the height of his joy, forgave her the injury she had done him, and allowed her to take away the *chef-d'œuvre* which he had designated as his choice.

Another statue of Love, made to replace the first, was the boast of the ancients, as incomparable; then came a statue of Phryne, a Venus, which equalled it, and a second Venus, more perfect still. This last statue was, for a long time, in the possession of the inhabitants of Cnidos: they regarded it as an inestimable treasure.

Praxiteles gloriously pursued his career, and gave to each of his numerous works the seal of grandeur, truth, and grace which caused them to be sought as the most perfect statuary. He studied nature patiently, and knew how to embellish it without making it lose anything of its life and its simplicity.

It is said that the famous statue of Love, by Praxiteles, was possessed by Isabella of Este, grandmother of the Dukes of Mantua. She had also a Cupid by Michael Angelo. One day, when she received, at Pavia, M. de Foix and President de Thou, sent to Italy by the King of France, the conversation turned upon the arts; and the princess, at the request of the two noble strangers, showed them the work of Michael Angelo. They viewed it with admiration, and thanked Isabella, saying, it was impossible to see anything more beautiful. The princess smiled; and conducting them into her cabinet, invited them to look at another statue, likewise representing Love. They were greatly surprised to find this last much superior to the one they had been praising, and looking at each other, were at a loss to find words to express their enthusiasm.

"Michael Angelo is the king of modern sculpture," said Isabella, "but Praxiteles is the divinity of ancient art."

It is by the study of the antique that the genius of the greatest artists, both painters and sculptors, has been developed. The antique is the surest rule for beauty and truth; and although all the pieces of sculpture which the ancients have left us are not equally perfect, all have the character of grandeur and simplicity, which prevents connoisseurs confounding them with modern works. As to those of Phidias, of Praxiteles, and many other Greek sculptors, they are distinguished by sublime taste, correct and sprightly execution, and elegant outlines; combining a happy charm of the most beautiful in nature, noble expression, great variety, a sobriety in ornament which rejects artificiality, and, finally, a majesty, which excludes neither simplicity nor grace.

POLYCLETUS.

After Praxiteles came Polycletus, who carried art to a higher point of glory than it had before attained. He was born at Sicyon, a city of Peloponnesus, in the year of the world 3760, and soon became known by his magnificent productions. He took pleasure in teaching the principles of sculpture to the great number of pupils whom his reputation had drawn to him. Wishing to leave to all these young artists, formed by his care, a model, to which they could have recourse when his advice failed, he caused the best formed men that could be found to be brought to him; and, selecting that which was irreproachable, in each of them, he formed a statue in which all the proportions of the human body were so perfectly observed, that people came from all parts, not only to admire, but to consult it. This *chef-d'œuvre* was named *The Rule*, first by Polycletus, and afterwards by the learned, and by connoisseurs.

Like most of the Greek painters, this able sculptor exposed the productions of his chisel to public criticism, and, like Apelles, he met more than one shoemaker who pretended to go beyond his last. Wishing to give a lesson to these ignorant people, who thought they knew, and allowed themselves to judge, of everything, he made over a statue, which had been submitted to the examination of the crowd, according to the various advice which had been given him, and composed a similar one, taking only the rules of art and his own genius for his guide. Having finished the two, he exposed them both to the public, and awaited the effect which they should produce.

The beholders could not find sufficient praise for the last, or sarcasm for the first, which they by no means attributed to the great Polycletus. The sculptor then showed himself to the people, and said,—

"The statue at which you rail is your own work, that which you admire is mine."

Turning towards his disciples, he added, "Never forget that a capable artist ought to listen to criticism, as an advice which can be useful to him, but not as a law which he is to follow.

LEONARDO DA VINCI.

Leonardo da Vinci was born at the castle of Vinci, near Florence, in 1452. His father, notary of the Seigniory of Florence, gave him an excellent education, and had the pleasure of seeing its advantages. There was never a mortal more richly endowed than Leonardo: a fine figure, robust constitution, superior intelligence, great force of character, prodigious memory, and a pleasant disposition, made him all that a parent could wish.

He learned, with great facility, history, geography, mathematics, architecture, drawing, and music; he seemed to understand the elements of these sciences, even before they were explained to him, and after having studied some time, puzzled his teachers by questions which they found it difficult to answer. He was not only the first in his studies, but none of his schoolmates could equal him in expertness, in strength, or in good humor. He always went from recreation to labor without regret, and considered the dryest studies as a succession of pleasures, the variety of which amused him.

Arithmetic, geometry, and mechanics afforded him much gratification, and, singular to say, he was passionately fond of poetry. When he had finished his studies, he continued to write poetry, practise music, and also painting. His father expected that he would succeed him in the office of notary; but when he perceived the young man's taste for art, he allowed him to select the career most agreeable to him. Leonardo was undetermined, when Andrea del Verrochio, a celebrated painter of Florence, and friend of his family, having seen some of his sketches, advised him to devote himself to painting, and invited him to work in his studio. Leonardo accepted the invitation, and soon became one of Master Andrea's best pupils.

This painter, being much hurried to finish a picture, representing the Baptism of Jesus Christ, thought he might trust Leonardo to assist him in his work, and, reserving the principal figures for himself, left the head of an angel, which, if it should be inferior to the rest of the composition, would not be noticed. So thought Verrochio; but what was his surprise, when the connoisseurs, to whom he showed his work, and who complimented him upon it, expatiated particularly upon the head of the angel, which, according to their ideas was much superior to anything which Andrea had hitherto done! Verrochio, at first astonished, was afterwards filled with chagrin at seeing himself surpassed by a very young man; and, unwilling to be only the disciple of his pupil, he broke his pallet, burned his pencils, and swore that he would never paint again. It is said that he faithfully kept his oath.

The friends of Andrea were much surprised at his resolution; but it was easily explained, on finding that the part of the picture on which they had bestowed such high encomiums, had been painted by Leonardo da Vinci. The young artist began to enjoy a certain reputation as soon as the anecdote became known. A Virgin, which he afterwards painted, placed him in the rank of the first painters of his time, and his name was celebrated throughout Italy before he had attained his twentieth year.

The Seigniory of Florence, wishing to offer a present of a set of hangings in silk and gold, such as was made in Flanders, desired Leonardo to compose the cartoon for it, and this cartoon, representing Adam and Eve in the garden of Eden, was found magnificent.

Although busily occupied with painting, Da Vinci did not neglect the other arts; he composed odes, sonnets, and songs, and set them to music; and, not content with the musical instruments in use, he invented a new one. While engaged with music and poetry, he plunged into the most complicated calculations, or pursued the solution of a problem, before which the most skilful mathematicians had recoiled.

Much assiduity to labor enabled him to carry on these different occupations; but he preferred painting, and that he might succeed, he was indefatigable in the study of nature. Flowers, animals, landscapes, and the physiognomy of man, above all, were the objects of his attention. If he saw a person with a characteristic face, or some odd attraction, a lame beggar, or an artisan in merry humor, while walking through the streets of Florence, he followed him long enough to observe, particularly, what had appeared extraordinary in the individual, and then, returning home, he drew it from memory.

He also went to see thieves on their way to prison, and condemned people going to punishment; then, turning from these pictures of affliction, he left the city, and entered into conversation with the shepherd, the laborer, and the brown harvest woman, returning home after her day's toil. He often invited peasants and common people to visit him; he offered them drinks, and took his place among them; and in order to excite their mirth, he related jocose stories, and when he saw them bursting with laughter, he took his pencil and reproduced the contortions which he considered most striking.

He was well paid for the pictures that he painted, besides receiving more orders than he could fill; so that, at an age when young people are hardly capable of supporting themselves, his house was furnished as well as that of the richest gentleman in Florence, and valets, pages, and horses awaited his orders.

His wit, his elegant manners, his taste in everything relating to dress, introduced him into the best society, by whom he was chosen as the leader of fashion. When a noble Florentine desired to give a splendid entertainment, he never failed to consult the brilliant artist, and Leonardo always invented some detail which gave the charm of novelty to the feast. If any important work was undertaken for public utility; if it was a question of constructing a bridge, digging a canal, opening a road, or building an edifice, the advice of Leonardo was sought, and his plans were sure to be the best.

Thus labor and pleasure divided the time of Da Vinci; and it passed so rapidly, that he had attained the age of forty years, without having found leisure to travel through the rest of Italy, as he had intended to do from the commencement of his career as an artist. However, he resolved to break in upon his cherished habits, and bidding adieu to his dear and beautiful Florence, much saddened by his departure, he went to Milan. The Duke Ludovico Sforza received him with all the honors due to his great reputation, and forced him to accept an apartment in his palace. At first, he went from time to time into Leonardo's studio, to see him paint; afterwards, fascinated by the sprightly and interesting conversation of the artist, he remained there whole days.

He loved Leonardo as much as he admired him, and, being passionately fond of music, he resolved to convoke an assembly of all the amateurs who were willing to take part in it. Vinci warmly approved the project, and asked the duke's permission to dispute the palm with the musicians who should answer to his appeal. Ludovico, who had not yet heard Leonardo, was surprised at such a request; he knew that the painter understood music, but he did not believe him able to compete in the assembly.

On the day of the feast, Leonardo carried an unknown instrument, which he had invented and made. It was a kind of lyre, shaped like a horse's skull. This was examined with much curiosity, and some secretly smiled at it; but when Leonardo touched the instrument, their laughter ceased: never had they heard a softer or more sonorous melody, and the musicians who had come with the hope of obtaining the prize, declared themselves vanquished. His triumph was crowned by the improvisation of some couplets, for which he composed the music while sitting amid the frantic applause of the audience, to the great satisfaction of the duke.

After this victory, Leonardo wished to leave Milan, but Ludovico, by entreaties and manifestations of the most sincere friendship, succeeded in detaining him. Magnificent entertainments, given almost every evening by the duke, afforded the illustrious painter ample opportunity to exercise his double talent of poet and musician, and there was not to be found, in all Italy, a man more admired than Leonardo da Vinci.

He passed whole days in his studio, pursuing his study of painting, or in the cabinet of the prince, who made him director of all the works to be done in the state, and who was pleased to hear him treat of serious and difficult things, with the same facility that he turned a madrigal or composed an elegy.

It was at the earnest entreaty of the Dominicans to paint a picture for their convent, that he consented to ornament their refectory with a fresco, representing the Lord's Supper. This magnificent composition, which has been so often reproduced by engraving, is everywhere known, and regarded as the masterpiece of Leonardo da Vinci.

The painter has chosen the moment in which Jesus Christ, taking his last repast with his disciples, addresses them with the words, "Verily, I say unto you, one of you shall betray me." Surprise, grief, and indignation are painted upon the faces of the disciples, whose eyes seem to interrogate their divine Master with a poignant curiosity, and the wish to reassure him, by the protestation of an unceasing love and unchangeable devotion. Each face, in the picture, has a wonderful expression, but it happened to Leonardo da Vinci, as to Timauthes with his picture of *Iphigenia:* after having given the most admirable character to the heads of the eleven faithful disciples, fearing that he could not make that of Jesus Christ sufficiently beautiful, noble, and divine, he left his fresco unfinished.

The prior of the convent, not understanding the scruple of the artist, who was waiting for the inspiration to complete his sublime work, or who did not care for it, was so anxious to see the completion of the fresco, which all Milan had contemplated with enthusiastic admiration, that he hurried and teased Leonardo to finish it quickly. The painter excused himself from so doing; the prior redoubled his importunities, and even went so far as to threaten to compel him. Then Leonardo set himself to work. The head of Judas, as well as that of Christ, remained to be done, and he began with the former, making it the portrait of the abbé, and giving it the most hateful and false expression it is possible to imagine. As to the head of Christ, he contented himself with sketching it, leaving to the imagination of the spectators that which he recognized as impossible to express. It is difficult to say what is most to be admired in this large composition,— the spirit, the nobleness, the elegance of the whole, or the truth, and finish of the most trifling details.

After having produced this *chef-d'œuvre* of painting, Leonardo, who was also skilled in the difficult art of sculpture, undertook the gigantic statue of Duke Francis Sforza, which crowned his reputation. It was impossible for him to think of leaving Milan, Ludovico could not do without him; and nothing that he could have asked in another country was spared. But war came to set the illustrious artist at liberty: Louis XII. drove out Ludovico Sforza, and Leonardo had the pain of seeing the French archers aim at his beautiful statue of Duke Francis in their daily exercises. He left Milan, and returned to Florence, to the great joy of his fellow-countrymen, who had sympathized in all his success.

To show himself worthy of the reception which was given him, Leonardo shut himself in his studio, and some weeks after his return to Florence placed before the public a cartoon, representing Christ, the Virgin, and St. Anne. All Florence crowded about this poetic picture, and Leonardo was proclaimed the first painter in the world. Soon after he painted the picture of Mona Lisa, wife of Francesco del Giocondo; and this splendid portrait, so well known as the *Joconda*, added to his glory. This picture is in the Louvre — it is of extraordinary loveliness, and of exquisite finish. The painter worked at it four years, and pronounced it still unfinished.

The grand council of Florence intrusted him with the reconstruction of the Council Hall, and, when the building was finished, they begged him to decorate it with some pictures, to which he consented. He thought he should have to paint many frescoes in it, not dreaming that there was an artist in Italy who would dare to enter into competition with him; but Pierre Soderini, the bearer of the holy standard, who possessed some of Michael Angelo's sculpture, and knew him to be very able in drawing, proposed to the young man to take charge of the sides of the hall. Michael Angelo, who loved to attempt that which others considered impossible, accepted the offer of Soderini.

Each of these two artists secretly prepared his cartoons, and then submitted them to the judges chosen to examine them. They found those of Leonardo superb, and they were so. The artist had represented the defeat of Nicolo Piccinino in the war of Pisa, and the Florentines allowing their arms to be chopped off rather than deliver up the standards which they had promised to defend. His friends had already pronounced him the victor, when, at the sight of Michael Angelo's cartoons, a murmur of astonishment was heard, which was soon changed into enthusiastic acclamations. The drawings of Leonardo remained a *chef-d'œuvre*, but there was something so sublime, so striking, so new, that, by this attempt of the young sculptor, Leonardo found himself equalled if not surpassed. What the examiners and the public felt could not be concealed from him; but if he had a doubt of the triumph of his young rival, a cruel word, incautiously spoken, would have undeceived him. One of the members of the grand council whispered in the ear of his neighbor, "Leonardo is growing old."

Leonardo is growing old! The illustrious artist could never forget this judgment, which engraved itself in the very depths of his heart. He found no consolation in the remembrance of all his past glory. He doubted the sincerity of the homage with which he had been surrounded; he doubted the friends who endeavored to encourage and calm him; he doubted everything, even his own talent. The order, given by the council, for having the cartoons of Leonardo, as well as those of Michael Angelo, exposed, as the best models which could be given to young artists, afforded no alleviation to his chagrin; he imagined that his fellow-citizens, habituated to regard him as an eminent painter, dared not deprive him of an honor of which they did not conscientiously consider him worthy.

The troubles which befell Florence prevented the two great artists from executing these paintings, and Leonardo went to Rome, where he painted several fine pictures. But he did not remain there long. He visited some of the other cities of Italy, and Cæsar Borgia, having invited him to Pavia, retained him there by appointing him general engineer.

War drove him from Pavia, as it had driven him from

Milan. He returned to his country, where a new disappointment awaited him. Cardinal de Medici, who had become Pope, under the name of Leo X., desired to endow Florence with a beautiful edifice; and forgetting, without doubt, that Leonardo da Vinci was as able an architect as painter, ordered Michael Angelo to come to the city, to construct the façade of San Lorenzo.

Michael Angelo again! It was, then, true, Leonardo da Vinci was old; they no longer dared to confide any important work to him. Leo X., the enlightened pontiff, the intelligent friend of arts, shared the same opinion as the members of the council of Florence! The artist, who had stood so long unrivalled, became discouraged: he set aside his pallet, abandoned his plans, neglected his chisel; even music had no power to divert him. He became so melancholy that his life was in danger, when Francis I., who had seen his works, and who understood his grief, invited him to his court.

The wars, from which Florence had suffered, had ruined Leonardo: after having been one of the greatest of artists, and one of the most brilliant lords of the country, he was reduced to a position of mediocrity, which, for a man accustomed to every luxurious enjoyment, was almost misery. He gratefully accepted the invitation of the king, and bade adieu forever to the beautiful sky under which he was born. Francis I. received him with every mark of joy and affection, and the court imitated the monarch, so that if Leonardo could have forgotten the past, he would have been happy in France.

He commenced several pictures for the king; but being old, and suffering, he could not work assiduously, and had not the time necessary for their completion. With the resignation of a Christian, he prepared himself for the end which he saw approaching. Francis I. often came to see him during his illness. Although Leonardo thanked him for his attentions, he did not pride himself upon them, because, in the face of death, he appreciated what men so much esteem, according to its true value. He was very independent in his conversations with the king, whether he related the history of his life, or passed judgment on his own works, or those of his contemporaries. Before his death, he asked pardon of God and of men for not having made better use of the genius which he had received from on high. Perhaps if this great man had been able to conquer his inconstant humor, he would have made greater progress in art than those who have astonished all Italy.

When Leonardo felt that his strength was failing, and that his life, like the flame of a candle, was about to be extinguished for want of aliment, he asked for the holy sacrament.

The king, being informed of the condition of the illustrious old man, hurried to see him for the last time. Leonardo tried to rise to salute Francis I., who, pressing his hand, seated himself at the bedside. The sick man related what had passed to the king, spoke of his confidence in God, and of the celestial joy which filled his soul. A convulsive shudder, the precursor of death, seized him while he was speaking. Francis rose, and held his head, to relieve him. Leonardo cast a look of ineffable gratitude upon the king, and died in his arms, at the age of seventy-five years.

This great man was sincerely regretted by the court of France, and the news of his death created much sensation in Italy. He had deceived himself: his fellow-countrymen, while rendering justice to the genius of Michael Angelo, knew that the name of Leonardo da Vinci would ever be one of the most glorious of Italy.

MICHAEL ANGELO BUONAROTTI.

Michael Angelo was born the 6th of March, 1474, at the castle of Caprese, in the territory of Arezzo. His father, Ludovico Buonarotti, then governor of Caprese and Chiusi, descended from the illustrious family of the Counts of Canosa. He thanked Heaven for giving him a son, who should sustain the honor of his name, and succeed him in one of the first offices of his country. It is said that Ludovico, in thinking of the future welfare of his son, did not limit his wishes simply to the position which had satisfied his own ambition. The affection and pride natural to parents lead them to foresee a much more brilliant career for their children than they have themselves enjoyed.

But with whatever glory Ludovico ornamented the brow of his new-born child, of whatever fame for his family he dreamed, as he sat by the cradle of the little one, the reality was to far surpass his hopes. Only this glory and this fame were not to come from the expected source. Who would know anything of the name of Buonarotti at the present day if Michael Angelo had been governor or chief standard-bearer? No one: while encircled by the aureola of genius, his name will be known to remotest ages.

Ludovico, having finished the term of his magistracy, left Caprese, to reside at his possessions in Settignano, where the child grew free as air, and happily passed his first years in the midst of workmen employed in working the stone with which Settignano abounded. It seemed to Michael Angelo that this life would always last; and he was not only surprised, but disquieted, when his father told him that the time had come for him to commence his studies; and he almost died of annoyance, when, instead of liberty, of open air, of the sun, the songs of the birds, the noise of the workmen's tools, he found only silence, and the monotonous lessons of a severe master, at the house of Francesco d'Urbano.

He begged his father to permit him to return to the pleasant life which he had heretofore led. Ludovico replied by telling him of the grave duties with which he would be charged at a future day, and tried to inspire the child with brilliant hopes, which he was incapable of understanding. Michael Angelo bore his chain with sadness. However, among the pupils who were a little older than himself was one who helped him to be patient while living with Francesco.

This comrade, named Granacci, had a taste for drawing, and passed his holidays in the shop of Master Dominico Ghirlandaio, one of the renowned painters of the time. The reader must not be surprised that we use the word *shop* — it was the manner of designating the studio of an artist.

Granacci, having found that his young companion much preferred a pencil, a brush, or a chisel, to books, promised to bring him drawings, and provide him with colors, that he might amuse himself with them from time to time. He kept his word; and from that hour forth, Michael devoted himself to the long hours of study and labor, to which he was obliged to submit, since he could draw and paint during the time for recreation.

One day Granacci offered to take Michael Angelo to Ghirlandaio's. To see the studio of a painter had for a long time been one of his most ardent wishes. He gladly accepted the offer, and followed Granacci, his heart beating with an unknown emotion.

"Master," said Granacci, "this is my comrade, whom I have so often mentioned, and here is his work."

As he spoke, he presented an engraving, illuminated with extreme care by Michael Angelo, who, not satisfied with the simple work of a colorist, had added to or subtracted from the work of the engraver, with a taste and discernment far beyond his age. He was not twelve years old.

It is the glory of Dominico Ghirlandaio to have been the teacher of Michael Angelo, but he was a man of talent. He perceived, at once, that the boy was a genius. After having examined the engraving which Granacci showed him, he extended his hand to Michael Angelo, and said to his pupils,—

"Here, gentlemen, is an artist who will surpass you, and all those who call themselves painters at the present day."

At this prediction all eyes were turned upon Buonarotti, who blushed deeply, and almost repented that he had yielded to the solicitations of his comrade.

"You must quit your other studies, my child," said Ghirlandaio, "and become my pupil."

That was precisely what Michael Angelo desired; but Ludovico Buonarotti never would give his consent to his son's leaving the college for the shop of Ghirlandaio, as he modestly told the master, who, smiling with the thought of having among his pupils a child of such hopeful promise, encouraged him, and agreed to go with him to his father.

Ludovico learned, with more chagrin than astonishment, that he could make nothing of Michael Angelo but a dauber and a mason. Little affected by what Ghirlandaio told him of the glory of the arts, he again tried to reason with his son; but seeing that his efforts were utterly useless, he attempted to touch his pride.

"So," said he, "your decision is made? You give up the career which I intended to open to you? You wish to be a painter?"

"A painter and a sculptor; yes, my father," replied the child.

"And you wish to study with Master Ghirlandaio?"

"Yes, my father."

"Very well! Master Ghirlandaio, I give up my son to you. Hereafter he belongs to you, as an apprentice, or a valet, as you please: you will keep him for three years, and you will pay me the sum of twenty-four florins for his services."

The pride of Michael Angelo revolted at this proposition: heir of the noble family of Canosa, he could not brook the idea of becoming a hired servant to the painter whom he wished for his teacher. But if he refused the conditions, he would be obliged to give up all idea of being an artist. He waited in silence until Master Ghirlandaio should accept the offer of his father, which he did, without hesitation; and, the bargain concluded, he followed him, forgetful of the humiliation imposed upon him, in his joy at recovering his liberty.

As the apprentice of Dominico, the young Buonarotti

soon surpassed all the other pupils, and the master himself. It happened, more than once, that he corrected the models which were given him to copy, and Ghirlandaio never reproached him for it: he was a conscientious man, and recognized superior talent in the child, of which he was so far from being jealous, that he was proud of it.

The fellow-pupils of Michael Angelo did not share the sentiments of Ghirlandaio. This uncommon talent cast them into the shade, and his proud and unsocial character was disagreeable to them. They took pleasure in humiliating and tormenting him under all circumstances; and the disdain with which Michael Angelo revenged himself for their ill treatment exasperated them still more.

From railleries and annoyances, they proceeded to blows; and Michael Angelo, who was only thirteen years old, was nearly killed by a certain Torrigiani, who, with one blow of his fist, broke the bone and cartilage of his nose. But if the superiority of Buonarotti excited the envy of his enemies, it was also his consolation. He avoided these wicked companions, and becoming all to himself, charmed his isolation by labor.

He was not fourteen, when, after having copied a small picture belonging to a friend of his master, he conceived the idea of keeping the original and returning the copy, which he smoked a little, to give the varnish the appearance of antiquity. Neither Dominico nor his friend perceived the substitution, and Michael Angelo was obliged to tell them of it, to get back his picture.

At this period Lorenzo di Medici, surnamed the Magnificent, an enlightened protector of art, established a museum of painting and of sculpture in his palace, and in the gardens of St. Mark, at Florence, where he was at great expense in collecting the most precious works of ancient art.

Dominico Ghirlandaio obtained permission for his pupils to visit and copy these *chefs-d'œuvre*, and Michael Angelo was not the last to take advantage of it. But while his fellow-pupils were admiring the beautiful paintings in the halls of the palace, he, who had always preferred sculpture to painting, remained in the garden, where a great number of workmen were employed in preparing blocks of stone and marble, which skilful artists should transform into statues, and where were the ancient pieces destined to serve them as models.

Some of the workmen, whom he had known at Settignano, authorized him to make use of a block of marble, and gave him some tools: he chose the head of a fawn among the models, and set about copying it. He returned the next morning, and several successive days, almost entirely abandoning Master Ghirlandaio. The head of his model had been so much injured by time, that the nose and mouth were almost entirely wanting. However, this difficulty did not stop Michael Angelo:

although he had never received a lesson, he finished his fawn, the mouth of which he made half open, as in a burst of laughter, showing the tongue and all the teeth.

This done, he examined it, to be sure that he had forgotten nothing, when he perceived a man at a short distance from him, who appeared to be contemplating his fawn with great attention.

"So! so!" said Michael Angelo to himself, without noticing the observer, "it seems to me that I have made out pretty well."

"Will you allow me to make an observation?" said the stranger.

"Certainly, if it is just," answered Buonarotti.

"You shall judge of it."

"Speak then."

"Your fawn is old, is it not?"

"That is easily seen."

"Not so easily as you think. The forehead is old, but the mouth is young. As for me, I have never met an old man who had all his teeth."

The criticism was just. Buonarotti broke two of his fawn's teeth, and hollowed the gum a little, before leaving the garden, in his turn. However, he did not wish to take away his work, thinking that perhaps he should find something to retouch in the morning.

But the next morning his fawn had disappeared! Michael Angelo vainly sought for it on all sides, and finally, perceiving the man who had spoken to him the evening before, and supposing that he might have taken it away, he went to him, and asked him if he knew where it was.

"I do know," answered the unknown, "and if you will follow me, I will show it to you."

"And you will give it back to me?"

"No, I wish to keep it."

"And by what right? let me ask. I made it; it seems to me that I ought to have it."

"Never mind; do not be angry. If you absolutely desire it, I will return it," said the amateur, smiling.

Michael Angelo, reassured by this promise, followed him into the interior of the palace, and even into the apartments of the duke, where he saw his fawn.

"O, give me back this rough sketch quickly," cried he; "the prince would be angry if he saw it among so many masterpieces. But who are you, sir, that you allow yourself such jokes?"

"Who am I?" replied the prince, for it was he; "I am your protector and your friend. Henceforth you shall dwell in my palace, you shall eat at my table, and be treated as one of my sons; because you cannot fail to become a great artist, Michael Angelo Buonarotti."

Michael Angelo, filled with joy, ran to announce this news to his father. Ludovico had refused to see his son since the day he entered the house of Ghirlandaio; but now, the young man, proud of the reception the prince had given him, forced his way past the sentinel, and into his father's cabinet. He threw himself on his knees to relate what had happened, and obtain pardon.

Ludovico could hardly trust his senses; but Michael Angelo led him to the palace, where Lorenzo the Magnificent was waiting for them. The prince repeated to the father what he had said to the son, and offered him whatever place he might choose, as a proof of the interest he took in Michael Angelo.

Ludovico was too joyful to be ambitious: he asked only a place in the custom-house, which Lorenzo granted, saying,—

"You will always be poor, Signor Buonarotti; you are too modest."

"I do not wish for a place that I cannot fill worthily," replied Ludovico; and besides, I shall always be sufficiently exalted for the father of a mason."

Notwithstanding the glorious future predicted to Michael Angelo, Ludovico still regretted that he had not wished to be a magistrate.

Lorenzo the Magnificent did all he had promised, and the talent of young Buonarotti made immense progress under his kind protection. But scarcely had he time to finish two or three statues, when the death of Lorenzo crushed his hopes.

Piero di Medici neither inherited the taste of his father for the arts, nor his affection for Michael Angelo, who left the palace, and retired to the convent of the Holy Spirit. The prior, in admiration of his talents, had offered him accommodations, where he could devote himself to the study of anatomy, — a study absolutely necessary to the sculptor. Michael Angelo gratefully accepted the offer. He studied the muscles, fibres, and frames of the dead bodies placed at his disposition, with such extreme care, that in a short time they were no longer secrets to him. As a manifestation of his gratitude to the prior, he offered him the first fruit of his new studies, — a Christ, in wood.

One day, Piero di Medici, remembering the young sculptor, whom he had seen at his father's table, sent for him. He had an order to give him, an order worthy of such a prince. A thick snow covered the earth; Piero had it heaped up by workmen, and then directed Michael Angelo to make a colossal statue of it. The artist obeyed, regretting more than ever his noble and generous protector, Lorenzo the Magnificent.

Florence was soon freed from the government of Piero, who possessed no one of the qualities so much admired in his father, to balance his faults. A revolution took place in 1494, and Piero was driven from the territory of the republic.

The respect which Michael Angelo owed to the memory of Lorenzo prevented him from declaring against Piero; he therefore quitted Florence at the commencement of the troubles. He went to Venice, where he was not known. Finding no employment, and his means failing, he next went to Bologna.

There he was arrested, because he went through the streets without wearing red wax on his thumb nail, in compliance with a singular order imposed upon strangers, of which he was ignorant. It was impossible for him to pay the fine to which he was condemned, and he would, without doubt, have languished in prison, if a gentleman, by the name of Aldobrandi, had not interposed, and taken him to his home.

By the mediation of this gentleman he obtained employment, and acquitted himself so well, that a Bolognese sculptor, furious with jealousy at the sight of such masterly work, threatened to stab him.

As soon as peace was established, Michael Angelo returned to his own country, and made his celebrated statue of Love. Some say that when the Love was finished, Michael Angelo broke one of its arms, and caused it to be sold as an antique; others think that the sculptor would not have mutilated his own work, but that the dealer, who paid but thirty crowns for it, practised the trick, by means of which he resold it for two hundred ducats. However it may be, the statue, by Michael Angelo, was regarded as one of the finest works of antiquity, until, the arm being found, the deception was discovered.

The Cardinal de St. George invited Michael Angelo to come to Rome, and gave him a lodging in his palace. The reputation of the young artist had preceded him, and he was soon fully occupied.

The statue of Bacchus, which is one of the most beautiful in the gallery at Florence, was his first work.

The Bacchus was very much admired, but when the group *della Pietà* appeared, the enthusiasm of the Romans knew no bounds. The grief of Mary, receiving her crucified Son in her arms, had never been more touchingly expressed; the dead Christ had never been more truthfully and more beautifully represented; and no one had ever attained the sublime expression and the marvellous finish which are admired in the *Descent from the Cross* of Michael Angelo.

However, there are some critics who reproach the sculptor for having made the Mother as young as the Son; but what is there, however perfect, that has not been criticised?

The magnificent group *della Pietà*, so pure in design, so perfect in grace, so marvellous in finish, that artists despair of equalling it, made for the Cardinal de Villiers, ambassador of Charles VIII. to Pope Alexander VI., is to be seen at St. Peter's, in Rome.

After the war, Michael Angelo yielded to the solicitations of his friends, and returned to Florence. Piero Soderini engaged him to make a colossal statue of David. The sculptor displayed the same talent and genius as heretofore, in the production of a *David*, which drew forth bursts of applause from an admiring public. Soderini could hardly contain himself for pride and joy, for he thought, poor standard-bearer, that if this gigantic statue was faultless, the artist owed it to him, Piero Soderini. It happened that Soderini, being admitted the first to see the new *chef-d'œuvre*, deigned to show himself satisfied; he dared, however, to venture an observation — the nose of David appeared to him too large.

Michael Angelo, of whose impetuous temper we have already spoken, impatiently heard his unjust criticism; he was on the point of railing at him for his ignorance, but, calming himself, he applauded the remark of his visitor, and throwing a handful of marble dust on the nose, he pretended to give it two or three strokes of the chisel; and wiping off the dust, he turned to Soderini, who congratulated him, as, in his opinion, nothing more was wanting.

Leonardo da Vinci, who was then known as the first painter of Italy, and of the world, had been engaged to fresco a part of the Council Hall. Soderini proposed to Michael Angelo to take charge of the other part, which he accepted.

Leonardo chose for his subject the defeat of Piccinino, general of the Duke of Milan, and the heroic valor of the old soldiers, who allowed their wrists to be cut off, rather than surrender the standards, which they wished to carry to Florence. Michael Angelo was to paint an episode of the war of Pisa. But for this artist, whose knowledge of anatomy surpassed that of all other painters, to be condemned to represent soldiers encased in heavy armor, was to yield the palm which he wished to contest; but his genius helped him to overcome this difficulty.

He took for his subject a circumstance which he remembered in the history of the war of Pisa. The Florentine soldiers, overcome with heat, were bathing in the Arno, without foreseeing an attack, when cries of alarm resounded, the Pisans were coming. Michael Angelo put so much purity, strength, and expression in his drawing of the army, thus surprised, that the day on which he presented his cartoons to the judges to be examined was for him a day of triumph. Florence extolled the new star which shone in its heaven, and began to feel more proud of Michael Angelo than of its great painter, Leonardo da Vinci.

The cartoons of the two illustrious artists remained exposed for the admiration of the curious, and for the study of young artists; neither Michael Angelo nor Leonardo being able at that time to execute the frescoes of which they had made the designs.

All the painters in Italy wished to see these wonderful drawings; and although Leonardo's cartoons were of exceeding beauty, those of Michael Angelo, whose name was, as yet, partially unknown, caused a much more lively sensation. He was unanimously proclaimed the master of art, and the most brilliant reputation faded before his.

But Michael Angelo had enemies, who, favored by

the troubles which agitated the last days of the Florentine republic, destroyed his cartoons. The public voice accused the sculptor Baccio Bandinelli of the crime.

Baccio Bandinelli had talent, but he could not compete with the inimitable Michael Angelo. Instead of accepting the second place, he suffered himself to be led away by jealousy and hatred, and to use every means in his power to impede the career of artists superior to himself, particularly that of Michael Angelo.

No sooner was Pope Julius II. seated upon the pontifical throne, than he sent for the great artist, whom he received with every demonstration of honor, and ordered him to make a statue.

"Try," said he, "to make this work worthy of Julius II. and of Michael Angelo."

A compliment thus framed was very flattering to Buonarotti: he answered it by making a colossal statue, which held a sword in one hand, while it blessed the world with the other. Michael Angelo designed to place a book in the hand, but Julius, who was more warlike than religious, decided to have a sword. This statue was cast in bronze, and placed upon the portal of St. Petrone, where it remained until 1511, when it was broken by a mob.

Julius II. was so much pleased with this first work of Michael Angelo, that he resolved to employ him on something great, which should transmit the name of the Pope and the artist to posterity. He therefore ordered him to make a monument for his tomb, and thinking it unnecessary to give him any instructions about it, left him to follow his own plans.

Michael Angelo projected a gigantic monument, which should be ornamented with forty statues, and magnificent basso-relievos. Julius II. was delighted with the idea, and desired the sculptor to set about his work immediately.

Michael Angelo, filled with joy at finding himself understood and appreciated, set out for Carrara. He wished to select the marble himself, as nothing could be too beautiful for this incomparable mausoleum. Thanks to the great number of workmen he employed, thanks to the ardor which his presence inspired, the work was accomplished in a very short time; and the marble having arrived at Rome, Michael Angelo thought only of realizing the sublime conceptions of his genius.

Julius II. had told the sculptor to address himself immediately to him when he was in need of money, and had ordered the doors of the Vatican to be always open to him. When Michael Angelo returned from Carrara, he wished to see the Pope, to obtain money to pay the people whom he had employed. To his great surprise he was refused entrance to the palace. His enemies had been working against him in his absence, and the Pope had forbidden that he should be admitted. Michael Angelo, knowing his own worth, was indignant at such an affront, and said to his informant,—

"Should his holiness need me, and ask for me, tell him that I am no longer an inhabitant of Rome!"

Two hours after he was on his way to Florence. No sooner had the Pope heard of his departure, than, feeling what he had lost by listening to calumniators, he sent five couriers, one after another, to recall the fugitive. But Michael Angelo refused to listen to them. Julius ordered them to bring him back, whether he would or not: he resisted more than ever, and threatened to kill the first one who dared approach him. He was so resolute in his threats that the cavaliers turned back.

Michael Angelo was received with open arms by the standard-bearer of Florence, who knew nothing of the cause of his prompt return. But the next day Soderini changed his tune: he had received a letter from the Pope, in which his holiness threatened to ruin Florence, and excommunicate him, if he did not force Michael Angelo to return to Rome.

Julius II., prompt in keeping his word, advanced towards Florence at the head of an army, taking Bologna on his way. Hearing this, Soderini called Michael Angelo, telling him that if he did not wish the destruction of his fellow-citizens, to leave Florence quickly, and go as far as possible, to avoid the anger of the Pope.

Michael Angelo followed the first of these counsels, which might pass for an order; but he thought not of fleeing for a moment; on the contrary, he took the road to Bologna, and resolutely went to Julius II. This boldness pleased the Pope, whose anger suddenly ceased: he extended his hand to the sculptor, ordered him for the second time to make his statue, and wished him to hurry, that he might not delay with the tomb.

Jealous people again tried to bring Michael Angelo into discredit, but they could not succeed: Julius knew him, and was not to be prejudiced against him. However, there are more means than one of injuring an artist; and when Michael Angelo's enemies saw that what they said had little influence upon the Pope, they adopted another plan. Their object was to prevent the great sculptor from immortalizing himself by the construction of the tomb of Julius II., and they conceived the idea of boasting of Buonarotti's talent for painting, so as to inspire the Pope with the desire of having some pictures by Michael Angelo, and thus cause him to postpone the execution of the Mausoleum.

They did not fail in their calculations. When the statue of Julius II. was completed, Michael Angelo returned to Rome, impatient to undertake the great work of which he had thought so much. The Pope received him in the most friendly manner; but when Michael Angelo wished to take his orders for the work which he was to commence, Julius II. said that he had chosen him to decorate the arched roof of the Sistine Chapel.

Michael Angelo imagined that he had misunderstood,

but the pontiff expressed his wish more strongly : he did not care about sculpture, he wished some of his paintings. Buonarotti endeavored to resist, declaring, as was the truth, that he had made cartoons for the Council Chamber of Florence, but that he had never painted ; and that he thought he was getting too old to commence his apprenticeship as a painter. At length he besought Julius to revoke his order ; but all that he said only augmented the desire of the Pope to see his sculptor as a painter ; and the artist, understanding that his will was unchangeable, resolved to obey.

The architect Bramante had taken the chief part in this plot, formed against Michael Angelo, to turn Julius II. from the idea of raising his own Mausoleum. Bramante d'Urbin, the uncle of Raphael Sanzio, feared the influence that Buonarotti exercised over the Pope might injure a young artist who had just come to Rome. He knew little of the character of Michael Angelo, who could suppose him capable of depreciating the merits of an artist like Raphael : Michael Angelo was too sure of his own talent to be jealous of that of others. Julius II. showed him the paintings of the young Sanzio, he frankly praised their beauty, and predicted a happy future to him who was the author of them ; but Bramante, anxious to see Buonarotti in the second rank, succeeded in bringing him into competition with Raphael.

Whatever it might cost Michael Angelo to put off to a future time the execution of the poem in marble, for which all the personages, created in his imagination, awaited only to be brought forth under his chisel, he had too much strength of character to allow himself to be cast down. He shut himself up in the Sistine Chapel, and declared that no one should see his pictures until they were finished. He sent to Florence for some of his friends, who were artists, among others Granacci, his old college and studio friend, and begged them to let him see them paint in fresco, because he was entirely ignorant of this style of painting, or of the preparation of the plaster necessary for it.

When he had satisfied himself, he dismissed his friends, and destroyed all that they had done. He remained alone in the chapel, refusing any assistance whatever, even in preparing the lime, mixing colors, &c.

One can hardly conceive of his courage and patience in surmounting all difficulties, transcribing and producing in painting the sublime thoughts which he had, until then, brought out in marble. On the other hand, the impatient pontiff tormented him, by continually urging haste. Notwithstanding Michael Angelo never lost a minute, he promised to be still more industrious; but Julius II. would not wait until the artist was ready to have his work exposed to public view, but ordered the scaffolding to be taken down before the ceiling was half finished.

All Rome wished to see the painting of Michael Angelo. The crowd was most enthusiastic in its bursts of applause, and Julius II. embraced the painter, saying, —

"I knew very well that the envy of your enemies would prepare a new triumph for you."

Michael Angelo resumed his labor, and in twenty months had finished the frescoes, whose beauty strikes those who visit the Sistine Chapel with astonishment and admiration. It is said that the artist, having been obliged to look up so much while painting, could never afterwards look down without pain.

By his wish, the architect San Gallo, one of his enemies, estimated the price of his work; and he received fifteen thousand ducats.

But Michael Angelo aspired to another recompense — permission to commence the Mausoleum of Julius II. without delay, which was granted him. The Pope, who fully appreciated the genius of this great man, honored him with sincere friendship, which, however, did not prevent him from being, at times, extremely rough. It is said that one day, Michael Angelo having dared to sustain a different opinion from that of Julius upon a question of art, he raised the cane, upon which he supported his tottering steps, to strike him. Michael Angelo, who would not have tolerated such violence from any person whatever, remained calm before his protector and friend. Julius, ashamed of having suffered himself to be carried away by anger, asked pardon of Buonarotti.

The most perfect harmony existed between these two great men, both of them proud and imperious: the one conscious of his power, the other of his genius. The Mausoleum was commenced, and the Pope, old and suffering as he was, went from time to time to see his sculptor working upon the marble, under which he was to repose. One day Michael Angelo waited for him. He came not: he was dead!

His favorite artist wept bitterly, and never forgot him. Wishing to show a last testimony of gratitude, he redoubled his zeal, that the tomb, which he had been forced to leave so many times, might be finished, to receive the noble ashes which it was destined to cover. But the new pontiff, Leo X., wishing to endow his native country, Florence, with remarkable monuments, ordered the sculptor to that city, to construct the façade of the Library of San Lorenzo.

Michael Angelo was then forty years of age, and had never attended to architecture; but he knew that he must obey; and, bidding adieu to his beautiful models, he set out for Florence.

He was deprived of the glory of finishing this work also, and ordered to Carrara, to select marble for some statues which he was commanded to make.

During his sojourn in Florence envy recommenced its work; and as it would have been as easy to deny the existence of the sun as the genius of Michael Angelo, they attacked his probity. Leo X., although of eminent mind and generous heart, listened an instant to this calumny, and ordered the sculptor to leave Carrara, and procure the blocks which he needed from Tuscany.

Buonarotti opened new quarries, and made roads to take the marble to the sea; then he returned to Florence; but Leo X. had given up the idea of finishing San Lorenzo, and Michael Angelo, discovering in the Pope's conduct towards him the work of base jealousy, which had for a long time pursued him, resolved that he would never reappear at the court of Rome.

Adrian VI., who succeeded Leo X., did not protect Michael Angelo, any more than his predecessor had done. But his reign was of short duration, and the Cardinal di Medici, called to the pontifical throne, under the name of Clement VII., honored him with his protection, and sustained him against the heirs of Julius II., among whom was the Duke d'Urbin, who threatened to stab the artist, if he did not immediately commence working on the Mausoleum. Michael Angelo, little frightened by the threat, returned to Florence, which was at the time a prey to new troubles. A popular faction had driven away the Medici.

Michael Angelo, who had little cause to be pleased with the nobles, and whose generous instincts carried him irresistibly towards the poor and oppressed, remained neutral as long as strangers did not threaten his country; but when undisciplined hordes, from all parts of Europe, were directed against Florence, at the instigation of the Medici, Michael Angelo, already sculptor, painter, and architect, became an engineer.

As commissary general of the fortifications of Florence, he, with twelve thousand combatants, defended the city, during eleven months, against an army of thirty-five thousand men. Michael Angelo roused the courage of the people, with as much success as he repaired the breaches made in the walls by the enemies' cannon. During these eleven months he performed prodigies of audacity and valor, and he alone gave the Medici more trouble than all the city put together. But there were traitors in the bosom of the city; the gates were opened to the besiegers, and Michael Angelo concealed himself from their vengeance by leaving the territory of Florence.

Alexander di Medici, gonfalonier, ordered that no means should be spared to find out where Buonarotti had concealed himself, and his retreat was soon discovered. He was arrested, and taken to Florence. Michael Angelo appeared before the duke, and with head erect, fearlessly acknowledged the part he had taken in the resistance of the city, and quietly awaited the judgment which should be pronounced upon him.

But, to his great surprise, and that of all the assembly, Alexander advanced towards the artist, gave him his hand, conducted him to the throne which he had just left, and forced him to be seated.

"I have punished the rebel" said he, "in causing the engineer of the fortifications of Florence to be brought here under escort; and now, behold, how I recompense the talent of the greatest artist that ever existed."

The Duke Alexander had been inspired to this conduct, worthy of a sovereign, by Pope Clement VII., his brother. Michael Angelo showed his gratitude to both, by erecting the tombs of Julian and of Laurent di Medici, in the Church of San Lorenzo.

The statue of Julian di Medici expresses strength and energy, that of Laurent meditation, therefore it has been called *Il Penseroso*. If all the works of Michael Angelo were not *chefs-d'œuvre*, before which every one must bow, *Il Penseroso* would be marvellous. Two figures, couched at the feet of the portraits of Julian and Laurent, complete these monuments. One of these statues, the Night, inspired a certain unknown poet to write the following stanza, which was found upon the tomb: —

> "La Notte, che tu vedi in sì dolci atti
> Dormire, fu da un angel scolpita
> In questo sasso; e, perchè dorme, ha vita:
> Destala, se nol credi, e parleratti."

"The Night, which you see sleeping so sweetly, was sculptured in this marble by an angel, and because she sleeps, she lives. Awake her, if you do not believe it, and she will speak to you."

This is the answer of Michael Angelo: —

> "Grato m'è il sonno, e più l'esser di sasso,
> Mentre che il danno e la vergogna dura.
> Non veder, non sentir m'è gran ventura.
> Però, non mi destar, deh! parla basso!"

"It is pleasant to me to sleep, and still more to be in marble, in this time of misery and shame. To see nothing, to hear nothing, is happiness to me. Pray speak softly, then, not to awaken me!"

When these two magnificent monuments were completed, Michael Angelo departed for Rome, where he was called by Clement VII. There he had to sustain a process against the Duke d'Urbin, on account of the tomb of Julius II., which the great sculptor had been obliged to leave against his will. This tomb, which, according to the first idea of Michael Angelo, was to have been a gigantic edifice, was reduced very much in size. Notwithstanding the offers of the Pope, who wished to free him from the successors of Julius II., the celebrated sculptor declared himself ready to continue the Mausoleum, and finished the colossal figure of Moses, designed for this monument.

This statue, which nothing can equal, either as an inspiration or as a work of art, is the admiration and despair of artists; grand, proud, and terrible, as the genius which created it, it gives an idea of what the tomb of Julius II. would have been, if Michael Angelo could have carried out his plan.

It was while he was working on his Moses, that Clement VII. urged him to paint the two extremities of the Sistine Chapel, of which Julius II. had forced him to decorate the vault. Michael Angelo, who had always preferred sculpture to painting, excused himself as long as he could, but he was again obliged to yield, and, as soon as he commenced the work, he applied himself with great ardor to his frescoes. The Pope desired that the Fallen Angels should be represented on one side of the chapel, and the Last Judgment on the other.

Clement VII. died about the time the cartoons for the Last Judgment were made, and Paul III., his successor, fearing that he might not see this sublime work, persuaded the Duke d'Urbin to allow other sculptors to finish the tomb of Julius II., the statue of Moses sufficing, according to his judgment, for the ornamentation of the Mausoleum.

The Duke d'Urbin complied with the wishes of the new pontiff, and Michael Angelo undertook the Last Judgment.

This fresco cost the artist eight years of assiduous labor: but what a picture! Michael Angelo was, perhaps, the only one among all the painters who have inscribed their names on the pageantry of art, in letters of gold, who was capable of rendering the grand and sublime spectacle of generations of human beings coming out of their tombs, to appear before the Supreme Judge of the living and the dead.

A profound and sublime thinker, an inspired poet, Michael Angelo knew how to give all imaginable attitudes to this crowd of figures; how to portray all the passions, regrets, and movements of the soul upon their features. There is not a sentiment, noble and good, or base and wicked, which cannot be found in this immense work: the entire history of humanity is there. And as the great day of justice has come, vice, which has been so long triumphant, is confounded, while humble and persecuted virtue finally receives its recompense.

Ten groups, of angels, saints, martyrs, of the dead shaking off their winding-sheets, of demons, and of the condemned, placed under an eleventh group, representing the Supreme Judge, surrounded by the Virgin, St. Peter, and Adam, compose this picture; in which there is so much grandeur and truth, that one cannot contemplate it without an emotion of terror.

In this fresco, Michael Angelo has put his own portrait, in the costume of a monk, who points out Christ descending upon the clouds. This work, unique in its kind, produced an inexpressible sensation; it had most ardent admirers, and severe critics; but criticism is destroyed by time: admiration still lives. The Pope, however, was not particularly pleased with this composition; and the grand master of ceremonies took the liberty to say, in the presence of Michael Angelo, that the picture would look better in a tavern than in the church. He was punished for his inconsiderate speech;

for the next morning he figured in hell, under the features of Minos. He ran to the Pope to complain; his holiness answered, smiling, —

"All power has been given me in heaven, and upon earth, but not in hell. If you are there, so much the worse for you; I am not able to take you out."

When the first moment of surprise had passed, Paul III. rendered justice to the genius of his painter, and required new works of art. The architect, San Gallo, had built the chapel Pauline, by the order of the Pope; and Michael Angelo decorated it with two large pictures: the Conversion of St. Paul and the Martyrdom of St. Peter. These two frescoes are not as well preserved as that of the Last Judgment.

Old age came upon Michael Angelo without impairing his faculties. After having finished the paintings which the Pope desired, he resumed his favorite art, sculpture; and produced a new *Descent from the Cross*, a magnificent group of four figures, cut from one block of marble.

The great artist hoped to finish his days peaceably in his studio; but it was not to be. The church of St. Peter, founded by Constantine, in the year 324, had fallen into ruins. Nicholas V. intended to rebuild it; but death had not allowed him time. Julius II. undertook it, and committed the plan of the edifice to Bramante and San Gallo. But notwithstanding the enormous sums of money which they expended, the work did not advance, and Paul III., seeing the impossibility of pursuing this enterprise without a man of genius to take direction of it, begged Michael Angelo, who had distinguished himself as an architect at the construction of the Library of San Lorenzo, in Florence, to accept the title of architect of St. Peter's.

Michael Angelo, who was then seventy-two years of age, knowing the responsibility and care of such an undertaking, would gladly have avoided it; but Paul III. was so persistent, and so ably demonstrated the glory which the completion of the Basilica would give to religion, that Michael Angelo consented to all that he asked.

Michael Angelo found it was impossible to execute the plan of Bramante, modified by San Gallo. He proved this to the Pope, and traced a new plan, which reduced the edifice to the form of a Greek cross. He suppressed a number of details, which he thought injurious to the majesty of the whole, and Paul III. gave his entire consent to the simple and grand proportions of his plan.

Michael Angelo, fearing that death might overtake him before he had proceeded so far with the Basilica that it would be impossible to change anything, commenced his work the day after his appointment. On assuming this charge, he made an express condition that he would accept no recompense; and this generous conduct placing him at his ease, he took the immediate direction of all the work in hand; thus ruining the covetous hopes of a great number who speculated upon the disorder introduced into this great undertaking.

It is useless to say that these people were enemies to Michael Angelo. But the great man had learned from his youth to despise the wicked and envious; so that, despite cabals and vexations of all sorts, he kept on firmly towards the end which he had proposed to himself. It was in vain that the Grand Duke of Tuscany, wishing to take advantage of the last sparks of this rare genius, urged him to come to his court; Michael Angelo refused to leave his Church, saying to himself, to leave it would be a great loss, a great shame, and a great sin.

Michael Angelo consecrated seventeen years to this work; and if he had not the pleasure of seeing it completed, he had, at least, the certainty that it would be finished with a religious respect for the plans he had traced.

He did not abandon his ordinary occupations, even while a prey to a slow fever, which he felt would carry him to his grave; on the contrary, he seemed to hasten all the more as death approached. He finished his laborious career on the 17th of February, 1563. He died as he had lived, an honest man, and a good Christian.

His will was calmly dictated to his nephew, Leonardo Buonarotti, in these terms: "I leave my soul to God, my body to the earth, my property to my nearest relatives."

Michael Angelo had never married: his affection was devoted to his art, and prevented his thinking of the cares of a family. Arrived at that age when one begins to feel the need of a friend and a support, he found all he desired in the devotion of his servant Urbino, whose death cast a gloom over his declining years. He was so much attached to this servant, that he took care of him during his last illness, and passed whole nights at his bedside, although then in the eighty-second year of his age.

"Life was dear to me," he said to one of his friends, "while I had my Urbino; dying, he has taught me how to die, and I now await death without fear, but with longing and with joy. He was mine for twenty-six years; I found him faithful and true; and now that I had made him rich, I hoped that he would be the comfort of my old age: but I have lost him! No other hope remains but that of meeting him in Paradise."

These regrets show us the kindness of Michael Angelo's heart; a kindness not the less real because it was concealed under a somewhat rough exterior. Exposed to the malice of the envious from his youth, the great artist had become somewhat misanthropic; he loved solitude, and found his greatest pleasure in labor. An enemy to nonsense, falsehood, and meanness, he would never condescend to flatter any one, therefore he owed nothing to intrigue. Besides, his wants were so limited, that he could easily dispense with the favors of the great. In his extreme sobriety he was satisfied with a piece of bread and a glass of water, and the luxury of his dress did not exceed that of his table. When he became rich, his habits of austere simplicity were very little changed; but he procured for himself the sweetest of all pleasures, that of making others happy. His relations, his servants, and young artists striving to advance, received the greater part of the fruits of his labor. He loved to make presents, but feared to accept them, because he considered them as inconvenient ties, difficult to be broken, and he loved his liberty too well to risk compromising it.

Besides being a sculptor, architect, and painter, Michael Angelo was also a poet. He delighted in Dante and Petrarch, to whom he devoted his few hours of leisure. He composed quite a number of sonnets, replete with the nobleness and generosity of his soul, but tinged by a bitter melancholy, caused by the injustice of others.

The reading which he preferred to all the Italian poets, was that of the Holy Scriptures, from which he drew those great inspirations, which he reproduced with his pencil or his chisel, and he learned to attribute all his success in those labors to Him to whom he owed his genius.

We should be astonished to see how many great works a life of eighty-nine years sufficed to produce, did we not know that this illustrious artist was endowed with an untiring assiduity, great energy, abundance of thought, and an extreme facility for labor. He not only consecrated his days, but a great part of his nights, to work.

His admirable genius was appreciated, as it ought to be, not only by the Popes, but by all Europe. The Sultan Soliman, the Emperor Charles V., the Seigniory of Venice, and Francis I., endeavored to induce him to leave his country by most advantageous offers; but he loved Florence and Rome, the seat of the fine arts. Although sensibly affected by the testimonies of admiration which were bestowed upon him, he refused the fortune and honors which awaited him among foreign princes.

Francis I., who knew so well how to appreciate an artist, ardently desired to have this famous genius at his court, and Michael Angelo would, without doubt, have given him the preference; but the king was obliged to content himself with casts of the beautiful statues of the Florentine sculptor, after having asked permission in a letter delivered to Michael Angelo, by Primaticcio.

"Sir Michael Angelo.

"Being very desirous of possessing some of your works, I have charged the bearer, the Abbé of St. Martin de Troys, whom I send from beyond the mountains, to beg you, if you have some excellent statues ready made on his arrival, that you will allow him to take casts from them; and also from the Christ of the Minerva, and the statue Notre Dame de la Febbre; that I may adorn one of my chapels with them, as I am assured that they are among the exquisite and excellent in your art. I have authorized the Abbé to pay you well for said favor.

"May God bless and keep you, Sir Michael Angelo.

"Written from Saint Germain en Laye, the sixteenth day of February, 1546.

"Francis."

We terminate the history of Michael Angelo, by saying, that if there is anything more glorious than having excelled in three different arts, it is that one cannot find a single act in his long life, which could prevent his being considered as the most loyal and most irreproachable man of his century.

BENVENUTO CELLINI.

Benvenuto Cellini, a painter, sculptor, and engraver, was born in Florence in 1500. His father, who was one of the musicians employed by the Grand Duke, had long wished for a son, so that his birth was joyfully welcomed, and he received the name of Benvenuto, or Welcome. As soon as he was old enough to study, Cellini, whose ambition was to make a virtuoso of his son, put a music-book into his hands; but Benvenuto manifested the greatest repugnance for the notes he was to decipher, and drew upon himself frequent reprimands and punishments. He was very intelligent, and had a good memory: he was capable of learning all that was taught him: but when the will was wanting, was unconquerably obstinate.

He became disgusted with music, and declared to his father that he never would be a musician. Master Cellini, having undertaken to overcome his repugnance, he ran away from the paternal home, and took refuge in Florence. There he offered himself to a silversmith, who, prepossessed by his good appearance, took him as an apprentice. Benvenuto applied himself arduously to his lessons, and soon became very skilful in the art of chiselling gold and silver. His master confided to him the most difficult and delicate works, and he acquitted himself admirably. Perceiving that he must understand drawing to become a good silversmith, as he desired, he devoted himself to it, and even learned painting.

Having executed works of great beauty, he returned to his native city, where he soon gained a high reputation. The Grand Duke wished to retain him there; but Benvenuto was not long contented in one place, and had for some years desired to see Rome. He went there unknown; and notwithstanding the many celebrities of all kinds who were in the city, he soon acquired a reputation, by producing some of his marvellous gold and silver work, such as vases, cups, and ewers, so richly engraven, and wrought with so much patience and taste, that, however precious the material might be, it was nothing in comparison. The Pope, recognizing the talent of this artist, appointed him Director of the Mint, and gave him the execution of a great number of medallions.

Benvenuto occupied all his leisure in sculpture. He knew how to model, and had cast statuettes and little figures in gold and silver; he soon undertook larger works, in which he gained a brilliant renown. Proud of his success, he fancied himself beyond the law, and submitted to no other rule than that of his own violent, impetuous, and capricious temper. Generous at heart, he would not have sought a quarrel; but he could never forgive a declared enemy, and was ever ready to obtain justice for their calumnies with sword or poniard. Space fails us, to recount the numerous adventures related in his Memoirs; for Benvenuto was also a writer, and related his deeds with the pride of a man who knew how to show himself superior to the vulgar.

When he committed some crime, as, for instance, killing an adversary in a duel, or infringing upon the orders of the Pope, he would hide himself among his friends, and not re-appear until the Pope, regretting the loss of so much talent, showed signs of indulgence. Once it happened that he had no time to flee; but instead of giving himself up to the force which surrounded his house, he distributed arms to some of his apprentices, and sustained a siege, in which he came off conqueror.

There was as much of the soldier as the artist in this extraordinary man: the agitated life of the camp would have been agreeable to him, and he would have acquired glory in such a sphere. The Constable of Bourbon having come to besiege Rome in 1527, Pope Clement VII. intrusted Benvenuto with the defence of St. Angelo, and the event proved that he was not mistaken in his estimate of the courage and ability of the sculptor. Cellini displayed as much prudence as bravery: with only a handful of brave men, he sustained the attacks of a large army, and caused much loss to the enemy. The city fell into the power of the Constable, but the Castle of St. Angelo, in which the Pope had taken refuge, was not captured.

Benvenuto travelled through all Italy, leaving at Naples, Venice, and Florence, vases and arms of infinite value. He afterwards went to Paris, where he was received with great honor by Francis I. This prince, who was a passionate lover of the arts, tried to retain Benvenuto at his court; but the latter, who was very sensitive, having had some bickerings with envious people, on whom he could not take vengeance, as he had been accustomed to do in Italy, did not yield to the solicitations of Francis I., and returned to Rome.

He was not happy in that city. Pope Clement VII. was dead, and his successor, Paul III., had less indulgence for Benvenuto. After having threatened him several times with the vengeance of the laws, if he did not behave as an obedient and faithful subject, he put him in prison. Cellini was in despair: he had thought that his genius protected him from such a fate. His health became impaired: he feared he must succumb to the chagrin of seeing himself unacknowledged, and deprived of his dear liberty. Perhaps he could not have survived, had not the recollection that many prisoners had succeeded in baffling the watchfulness of their keepers, and made their escape, animated his courage. He made many attempts, which his imagination approved, but which succeeded only in causing him to be more closely guarded, and he began to despair of success; when Francis I., having heard of his captivity, ordered his ambassador to recommend this artist, whom he greatly loved, to the clemency of the Pontiff.

Paul III. complied with the request of his Most Christian Majesty, and set the prisoner at liberty. Cellini went immediately to his protector to thank him, and devote the talent he so much admired to his service. Francis received him as an old friend, gave him the castle of Nesle as a residence, and ordered everything which was necessary for the execution of the works he should undertake, to be placed at his disposal. Benvenuto, happy to find himself free, set to work with good will, and showed himself worthy of the kindness of the king. Admirable arms, and vases of rare richness, were produced; and while chiselling these objects of marvellous beauty, and making jewels, such as never before had been seen, for the ladies of the court, he meditated a statue of Jupiter, which should be his *chef-d'œuvre*.

Benvenuto had a countryman at the court of Francis I.—Primaticcio. He was a sculptor, painter, and architect, and had been sent by the Duke of Mantua to the King of France; who, wishing to create marvels for the palace of Fontainebleau, had need of a great artist. The Italian had fulfilled all the requirements, and Francis had recompensed him by loading him with riches and honor, and above all, by according to him his friendship. Primaticcio was one of the chief personages of the court; artists solicited his protection, and his position as commissary general of the king's buildings, gave him power to dispose of the paintings and sculpture destined to embellish the royal residences. Cellini, sure of his genius, had no fear of rivalry, particularly as he had been called to France by the king himself: he did not think he owed Primaticcio more than the simple compliments exchanged between equals. The painter of Francis I., thinking his superiority was threatened by the new comer, and fearing to divide with him the favor of the monarch, to whom the adventurous and bold character of the Florentine was not displeasing, saw in him a rival, and treated him as an enemy.

At that time there was a person in France who possessed more power than the king,— it was the Duchess d'Etampes. Charles V. knew this so well, that, having obtained from Francis I. permission to traverse his states in order to punish the Gantois revolt, he did not feel sure of going out of them safe and sound until he had made an alliance with the Duchess. How he succeeded is well known. Francis I. having received the Emperor at his palace of Fontainebleau, where the court was, just as they were about sitting at table, two ladies of the suite of the Duchess approached Charles V., and having a ewer and a gold basin, they offered him to wash. Madame d'Etampes stood behind them, holding a napkin. At the moment she presented it to the Emperor, he designedly slipped from his finger a ring of great value. The Duchess picked it up, and offered it to him.

"Your hands are too beautiful to give it up," said Charles V., adding flattery to the worth of the present; "keep it, I pray you, for my sake."

We cannot say how much blood might have been spared Europe if this ring had not been offered to Madame d'Etampes.

But to return to Benvenuto: what we have just related was intended only to show the power of the Duchess. Primaticcio, who knew how to gain the favor of the Duchess, calumniated and prejudiced her against Cellini, who soon perceived that the favor of the king was nothing in comparison to hers. Obstacles were placed in his way, his genius was questioned, and when he submitted the project of casting a statue of Jupiter for Francis I., Primaticcio obtained permission to purchase antique marbles in Italy, and to cast such statues and groups as he could not buy. Benvenuto understood that his adversary, by suggesting comparison, had taken the best way to underrate the merit of the work he intended to do: but he did not shrink from it.

He worked on his *Jupiter* during the absence of Primaticcio, and finished it before he returned; but the Duchess d'Etampes prevailed upon the king not to allow the statue to be set up until Primaticcio returned with his. The antique marbles were much admired, as also were the statues cast from the most celebrated which Italy possessed; but, after having contemplated all these *chefs-d'œuvre*, they could not refuse the most flattering praises to the work of Benvenuto. Cellini owed this triumph more to his address than to his talent. The groups brought from Italy were arranged in the gallery through which the king had to pass, and the *Jupiter* was placed in a bad light. Cellini knew how to remedy this evil, by putting little rollers under his statue, by means of which he was enabled to advance the master of the gods towards the King of France at the desired moment.

Benvenuto remained some time longer with Francis I.; then, tired of seeing himself exposed to the jealousy of Primaticcio, and feeling that he was not liked by the nobles, to whom his haughty manners were disagreeable, he took leave of his noble protector, and returned to Florence. He cast the statue of Perseus, which is considered his *chef-d'œuvre*, in bronze, for Duke Cosmo di Medici, who desired it.

In Italy he found the envy which he was seeking to avoid. The middling class of artists, whom he did not treat courteously, were his enemies. He nearly killed Baccio Bandinelli, by whom he had been calumniated; but when he saw him pale and trembling, he pitied and pardoned him. The continual conflict with his rivals soured his temper, and made him misanthropic; his work failed to afford him distraction of mind. He grew old in the midst of persecutions, exposed to base intrigues, and, disgusted with humanity, saw the approach of death with joy. He was a zealous admirer of the genius of Michael Angelo, whom he survived six years. Having, like him, suffered all the sadness of isolation, he expired in 1590, at the age of seventy years.

Benvenuto Cellini has never been equalled as a silversmith; and if he is not immortalized in this art, he still holds a high rank among the painters and sculptors of Italy. He is also noted as a writer, and his *Memoirs*, if we excuse the vanity which seems to have dictated them, are distinguished by a naive and charming style.

CANOVA.

Antonio Canova was born in 1747, at Passagno, a small Venetian city. At a very early age he became the protégé of Signor Falieri, one of the first personages in Passagno. While a young child, Antonio took great pleasure in making small figures with crumbs of bread, or bits of clay: these were much admired by his mother and his school companions. As he grew up, he employed all the time not occupied in learning to read and write, in modelling all sorts of animals. One day he made a lion of butter, which was served at the table of Signor Falieri; and he, charmed with the propensity of Canova for sculpture, provided him with a teacher.

Antonio profited so well by his instruction, that in a few years he was advised to go to Venice, to study with Torreti, who was considered a very able sculptor, the age of the great masters having passed, and the arts fallen into complete decay. In a short time Canova equalled his teacher, and many prizes being awarded to him by the Academy of Fine Arts, he hired a small shop, in which he established himself. At seventeen years of age, he executed a group of *Orpheus and Eurydice*, which gave him celebrity; and his works beginning to be sought after, he quitted his shop for a more convenient atelier.

The greatest eulogiums were bestowed upon his second group, of *Dedalus and Icarus*, which appeared soon after. For a long time Venice had not had a sculptor worthy of the name; so that the works of Canova, however imperfect they might be, had enthusiastic admirers, and several patricians ordered statues from the young artist. The group of *Dedalus and Icarus* was sold for one hundred sequins; and Canova, on receiving this sum, joyfully cried out, "At last I shall go to Rome!"

He felt that he could never reach the perfection to which he aspired without a master, and wished to find models and advice in the city of the fine arts. Gavino Hamilton, an English painter, having seen the *Dedalus* in plaster, thought that a young man, endowed with so rare a genius, ought to be encouraged, and by his advice the Senate of Venice granted three hundred ducats to Canova, and the ambassador of the republic to the Pope called him to Rome, where he went in 1779.

There he found an excellent adviser in Gavino Hamilton, whose love for the antique had made him a connoisseur in art. The study of the great works of Michael Angelo enlarged his ideas, improved his taste, and made him feel the need of learning everything possible in his art that was unknown to him. Until then he had obeyed his instinct only while working, without having any exact ideas of the rules he ought to observe, or of that ideal which gives so great a charm to the works of painters and sculptors. This instruction he never had, and he was indebted for it to the Chevalier Hamilton and to Lagrenée, director of the school founded at Rome by Louis XIV.

The ambassador of Venice placed a block of marble at the disposition of Canova, and he made of it an *Apollo crowning himself.* Although this statue was superior to the two groups of which we have spoken, it was not irreproachable. The Apollo was deficient in that grandeur and beauty which imagination lends to the gods: it was a well-chosen model, but did not attain the ideal desired by the young artist. However, Canova had improved too much to feel discouragement. He continued to study with fresh ardor, and went to Venice to finish some works which he had previously begun in that city. While working, he planned a new group, for which he wished to seek and slowly mature a subject.

Canova returned to Rome in 1792, and made a *Theseus Conqueror of the Minotaur.* This group showed the intelligent study which the young man had made of the antique models, and astonished the amateurs by an execution which seemed to reveal a well-formed talent. The taste for the antique had been out of fashion for some time; so that the appearance of the group of *Theseus* signalized a revolution in the arts. M. Quatremère de Quincy, afterwards the friend and historian of Canova, having heard that a young Venetian had just composed a very remarkable group, wishing to judge of the justice of the praises given to it, went to the studio of the sculptor. Canova was absent, and the amateur had a good opportunity to examine the work of which he had heard so much, quite at his ease. He recognized that it merited all the praise which had been bestowed upon it; and, foreseeing the brilliant career which awaited the young artist, offered him his friendship and his counsel. Canova thankfully accepted the precious offers, and found a second brother in his new friend.

The sculptor had chosen to represent Theseus at the moment when, conqueror of the monster, he seated himself triumphantly on the body of his enemy. Thanks to this idea, Theseus, who, in the efforts of a contest, could have appeared only as a man, showed, in the calmness of victory, the majesty of a demigod. This work, though one of the first by which the artist made himself known, is still mentioned with honor.

Canova has left many famous works, among which we shall enumerate the principal which deserve the admiration of posterity. He was intrusted with erecting the tomb of Pope Clement XIV. in the Church of the Holy Apostles at Rome, and placed the statue of this Pope standing upon the Mausoleum, with his hands extended, as if to bless the people. The head of the statue is exceedingly beautiful, and, as it were, radiant with that divine charity, that inexpressible kindness, which was the peculiar characteristic of Clement XIV. The tomb of Clement XIII., which he erected, and which is still admired in the *Basilica* of St. Peter's, surpasses in purity of taste that of Clement XIV.

The Mausoleum of Maria Christina, Arch-duchess of Austria, is a vast composition of an original idea, but the effect is complicated; nine statues of life size, of which each passed for a *chef-d'œuvre*, ornament this monument.

The Countess d'Albani, whose friendship for the celebrated poet Alfieri has never been denied, called Canova to Florence, to erect a monument to him in the Church of Santa Croce, which is one of the most beautiful works of the sculptor. Many statues, among which is a *Psyche as a Child*, and a *Washington*, date from this period. *Psyche*, holding a butterfly by the wings, is a little wonder of taste and delicacy; *Washington*, a white marble statue, in Roman drapery, was made for the senate chamber of South Carolina, in the United States: it is marked by a grandeur and simplicity worthy of the antique.

In 1798 Canova left Italy, and travelled through a part of Prussia and Germany, with Prince Rezzonico. On his return from this journey, which lasted two years, he was appointed inspector general of the fine arts, by Pius VII., and received the title of Roman Knight. His reputation had spread through Europe, and he was invited to Paris, by Bonaparte, in 1802. The artist accepted, with the Pope's consent, and was received with all the distinction due to his rare merit. He was shown all that France possessed of fine sculpture, both ancient and modern, and the Institution of Fine Arts admitted him to the rank of foreign membership.

Canova went to Florence again in 1815. Through the conquests of Napoleon, the Museum of the Louvre was enriched by the most remarkable *chefs-d'œuvre* of painting and sculpture possessed by foreign museums. The allied powers, after having overcome the great man who had conquered them so many times, did not forget to reclaim the artistic treasures of which he had despoiled them, and it was agreed that all these monuments should be returned to their former owners.

The pontifical government, to which a large proportion of these monuments belonged, sent Canova to Paris, with the title of Ambassador, and power to bring back the statues carried from Rome, and attend to their transportation.

Having executed this commission to the satisfaction of the Pope, Canova was rewarded with a diploma, which testified that his name was written in the golden book of the Capitol, with the title of Marquis d'Ischia. To this title was added a gift of three thousand crowns, Roman money. Canova, enriched by his labor, and simple in his tastes, consecrated his new fortune to the prosperity of the arts. He was a zealous and benevolent protector of talented youth, to whom he opened his purse, and freely gave his advice.

The last years of his life were occupied in constructing a church in his native town, Passagno, where he intended to place a colossal statue of Religion, which could not be admitted into the Basilica of St. Peter's. This building is a Rotunda, in stone, in imitation of the Parthenon at Athens, which is of marble.

Canova died at Venice, the twenty-second of October, 1822, without seeing the completion of his church. He was buried with great pomp, and there were magnificent funeral services in honor of him in all the Italian cities. For many years this classic country had not produced a genius comparable to Canova, and during his long and glorious career, he enriched it with a great number of *chefs-d'œuvre.* It was just that all Italy should render him this last tribute of respect.

PAINTERS.

THE FIRST PAINTERS.

Very little is known of the history of painting among the Greeks until the ninetieth Olympiad, that is to say, four hundred and twenty years before the Christian era. However, it is certain that the origin of this art is much more remote, since they painted at the time of the siege of Troy: historians tell us that Helena drew, on tapestry, the many battles caused by her abduction.

The first Greek painters made use of one color only. Eumaris used two, one for the skin, the other for the clothing. Cimon, his pupil, used still more. Heretofore painters had represented only two figures, and these standing side by side, presenting a front view. Cimon gave them various attitudes, and conceived the idea of putting folds in his draperies.

Bularchos, who lived about seven hundred years before Christ, painted the *Battle of Magnesia*, and, according to Pliny, Candaulus, king of Lydia, paid for this picture its weight in gold.

Without doubt Bularchos had pupils and successors; however, there is no mention of any painter between him and Panœnus, brother of the famous sculptor Phidias. Panœnus painted the *Battle of Marathon.* It would be difficult to give an idea of the enthusiasm which the sight of this picture excited; its chief personages were portraits of striking resemblance.

The celebrated Polygnote appeared about the same time, that is, four hundred and fifty years before the Christian era. This painter was born at Thasos, an island in the Ægean Sea. He studied under the best masters, but dissatisfied with their teachings, declined following them, and devoted himself entirely to the study of nature. He ornamented the porticoes of Athens with paintings of subjects from episodes of the siege of Troy.

For this beautiful work the Athenians offered him considerable sums, which he generously refused, saying, that since he had been so happy as to obtain the applause of an enlightened people like those of Athens, he had nothing more to desire.

This answer was carried to the tribunal of the Amphictyons, and the tribunal ordered, by a decree which was solemnly promulgated, that Polygnote should be lodged in the State Palace, nourished at the public expense, exempted from taxes during his whole life, and that every city in Greece, where he should choose to go, should receive him with honor, and entertain him magnificently. "The Chiefs of the State," said this decree, "reign by force, but the artist reigns by his talent; then it is just to render more homage to him who owes everything to his own merit, than to those elevated to power by force of circumstances."

Polygnote, so worthily recompensed, worked with new ardor, and perfected himself daily. At that time they painted in encaustic, or wax, upon ivory and wood. The colors for this kind of painting were laid on while warm, and lasted, without alteration, for many centuries. If we may believe the historian, the beauty of the picture of the *Sacking of Troy*, by Polygnote, would have been preserved during nine hundred years; and it would have braved the outrages of time still longer, if it had not been destroyed at Constantinople.

Apollodorus, who was celebrated at Athens some time after Polygnote, gave a great impetus to painting: he was the first who joined the understanding of color and the science of foreshortening to correct drawing. His paintings were true to nature, and he gave the appearance of movement and life to the scenes which he represented. He studied the distribution of light and shade with extreme care, and left the works of all his predecessors far behind him. In the time of Pliny, there were two pictures by Apollodorus, at Pergamos: an *Ajax destroyed by Minerva*, and a *Priest at prayer;* both these pictures are regarded as *chefs-d'œuvre*.

Apollodorus had many disciples, the most illustrious of whom was Zeuxis, who was to surpass his master.

He was not slow in discovering the wonderful ability of his pupil, and the success of the young man embittered his last days. Excited by blind jealousy, Apollodorus laid down his pencil for the pen, and published a satire against Zeuxis, in which he accused him of having stolen his talent from him: this satire served only to enhance the reputation of the artist to whom Apollodorus rendered such brilliant homage.

ZEUXIS. — ARISTIDES.

Zeuxis was born at Heraclius: he was naturally gifted with a taste for the arts, particularly for painting. A pupil of Apollodorus, he soon equalled his master, and discovering new processes, his works were sought in preference to those of Apollodorus. An artist seldom sees the pupil whom he has taught surpass him, and diminish the splendor of his name, without bitterness of feeling. Apollodorus used his poetical talent in decrying Zeuxis, who did not trouble himself to reply to the railleries and injuries of his master.

"If I were not the most able," said he, "I should be less hated; his hatred is the most sincere homage which my talent could desire."

The satire of Apollodorus served only to draw the attention of all Greece to the masterpieces of Zeuxis, and happy was he who possessed one of them. Connoisseurs admired the purity of design, the truthfulness of coloring, and the grace of posture to which no other painter had attained, and purchased his pictures, actually covering them with gold. In a few years Zeuxis possessed an immense fortune, and was surrounded with the luxuries of a prince. He dressed in purple, and was followed by a retinue of servants when he went out. At the Olympic games, his slaves were conspicuous by the magnificence of their attire, upon which the name of the great artist, to whom they had the honor of belonging, was embroidered in letters of gold.

Zeuxis now declared that he would sell no more of his pictures; that no one was rich enough to pay the value of them. However, it is said that when he made a present of a picture to a friend, he first put it on exhibition in his studio, and required payment from those who came to admire it.

Zeuxis worked slowly; he would never allow any picture to be criticised which he did not think worthy of his high reputation. Some one having expressed astonishment at the length of time he required, while ordinary artists painted so rapidly, Zeuxis replied, —

"It is because I work for immortality."

He did not deceive himself, for his glory has come down to our times.

The great artists were generally conscious of their talents; and if modesty has enhanced the merits of many of them, it is not in pagan antiquity that their names are to be found. Zeuxis did not believe that any painter could compete with him, and he wrote below one of his pictures, which represented an athlete, "It will be easier to criticise than to imitate this."

Yet he was not the only artist of which Greece was proud: Timanthes shone in Sicyon, Aristides in Thebes, Parrhasius in Ephesus, and Pamphylis in Macedonia.

Parrhasius enjoyed an immense reputation, and was considered a king among painters. Zeuxis, on his part, claimed the same title, and it was agreed that each of them should submit the work which he considered as his best, to the examination of judges chosen from both sides, and that a jury should decide.

Zeuxis excelled in the imitation of nature, and painted flowers and fruits exquisitely. He offered a picture for examination, which represented a child carrying upon its head a basket of grapes. This work was no sooner exposed on the place where the judges were assembled, than the birds came to peck at the finely painted fruit. The multitude burst into loud acclamations of applause, and Zeuxis, sure of the victory, received the felicitations of his friends. Parrhasius admired the talent of his adversary; but he did not despair of success, and stood silent near his picture. A curtain of a light and silky stuff covered his work, and every one was impatient to see it drawn aside.

Zeuxis, a little annoyed by the calmness of Parrhasius, tore himself away from the compliments of his party, and went towards him, saying, —

"Why do you delay letting us see your *chef-d'œuvre?* Draw the curtain."

"This curtain is my picture;" replied Parrhasius.

Zeuxis did not believe him, and stretched forth his hand to draw the light curtain aside.

"I am conquered!" cried he, recognizing his error. "I have deceived only birds; but Parrhasius has deceived me."

Zeuxis never forgot this defeat; and when his friends wished to console him, by saying that one must be a great artist to deceive the instinct of the birds, he replied,—

"If my picture had been as good as you pretend, the sight of the child who carries the basket of grapes would have frightened away the greedy birds."

This reflection appeared as just to his friends as to himself. But the victory of Parrhasius did not detract from the general admiration of the paintings of Zeuxis.

The city of Agrigentum sent a deputation to him, begging him to paint a portrait of Helen. Zeuxis consented, on condition that they should select a model for him from among the most beautiful girls in Agrigentum. The Agrigentines found it very difficult to choose, and therefore conducted to Athens all those who appeared to have a right to the preference. Zeuxis retained five of them, and taking whatever was most perfect from each, composed a magnificent picture, which was considered his *chef-d'œuvre.*

Zeuxis, as we have said, imitated nature marvellously; but he was less successful in rendering the sentiments and the passions of the soul,— a talent absolutely necessary to the painter who desires to please and to touch the feelings.

Aristides of Thebes, inferior to Zeuxis in regard to the elegance and finish of his pictures, excelled him very much in expression. Zeuxis spoke to the eyes, Aristides to the soul. If Aristides painted a sick person, the beholder was moved to pity his sufferings; a beggar, he was tempted to offer him alms; in short, he animated his subjects. Pliny speaks of a picture in which the artist represented the pillaging of a city. In the foreground a woman, struck in the breast by a poniard, lay in the agonies of death. A little child, fallen at her side, was groping towards her to seek its ordinary nourishment. The poor woman seemed to look at it with pity and affright, for it was not her milk, but her blood, that he was about to suck. The engrossment of her mind, her maternal anguish in the face of death, whose merciless grasp she felt, the heart-rending farewell look she cast upon the infant, all these impressions were so truthfully rendered, that those who stopped to look at the picture were moved to tears, or to curse the war which brought such grief in its train.

If Aristides had been more careful in coloring, if his pencillings had been softer, or not so austere, few painters could have equalled him. These faults did not prevent his having a glorious career, and his pictures were so highly valued, that he was paid ninety thousand francs for his *Combat against the Persians*.

There were many of his paintings in the city of Corinth, when it was taken by the Romans. At this period the masters of the world were very ignorant in matters of art: Attalus, king of Pergamos, having offered a considerable sum for one of these pictures, the consul Mummius imagined that there must be some magic virtue in the picture, and refused to let him have it. The soldiers, knowing no more of the value of paintings than the consul, broke the *chefs-d'œuvre* without remorse, or used them for tables on which to play with dice.

But to return to Zeuxis, whom we have for an instant forgotten. This painter worked many years, and always with good success. If we can believe Verrius Flaccus, it was his talent which cost him his life. Looking at the portrait, or rather the caricature of an old woman which he had painted, he burst into such an immoderate fit of laughter as to cause his death.

PARRHASIUS. — TIMANTHES.

Parrhasius, son of the painter Evenor, was for a short time the pupil of his father; but, when finding that he could learn nothing more of him, he consulted only his own genius, and made rapid progress in drawing: he studied proportions carefully, and exceeded his predecessors in correctness of features. Under Socrates he learned the expressions which ordinarily characterize profound affections, or lively sentiments of the soul, and was intent upon rendering them truthfully. His figures were elegant; his touches wise and sprightly; his pencil easy and graceful.

The fortune of Parrhasius soon equalled his celebrity, and his opulence exceeded that of Zeuxis. He had so great an opinion of his own talent, that he never spoke of himself without the greatest eulogiums, never went out unless dressed in purple and crowned with gold, and thought that no one in the world could pretend to equal him.

His victory over Zeuxis only increased his pride, and an assembly of painters meeting at Samos, he presented himself, sure of excelling all his rivals. The subject given was the indignation of Ajax at seeing the arms of Achilles awarded to Ulysses.

The picture of Parrhasius was magnificent; but that of Timanthes of Sicyon bore off the palm. Parrhasius would not acknowledge himself vanquished, as Zeuxis had done a few years previous.

"I pity Ajax," said he, to one of his friends; "see him conquered a second time by an adversary unworthy of him."

Parrhasius was wrong in denying the merit of his rival, for Timanthes was one of the most illustrious painters of antiquity. He was gifted with great genius, to which all historians have rendered justice, and all have considered his picture of Iphigenia as a masterpiece.

In this composition, Timanthes represented Iphigenia adorned with all the graces of youth, all the nobleness of a brave and generous soul, and that aureole of sublime devotion on the brow, together with all the melancholy charm which the approach of a cruel death could shed upon the physiognomy of a young girl. Calchas, calm and majestic in his grief, stood near the altar, ready to accomplish the sacrifice required by the gods. Profound sadness was imprinted upon the countenances of Ajax and the other personages present at the scene; but nothing could compare with the heart-rending desolation of Menelaus, uncle of the princess. Thus far the artist had a right to be proud of his work; he had succeeded marvellously; but he had yet to paint the despair of Agamemnon. Understanding that he could not succeed in expressing the tortures of the father about to sacrifice that which he loved most in the world, the beautiful and delicate Iphigenia, his pride, his hope, his only joy, for the salvation of the army, Timanthes had the ingenuity to cover the face of the unhappy prince with a veil, and leave the affected spectator to imagine this immense and terrible grief.

This is a proof of genius, because the artist leaves infinitely more to imagination than it would have been possible to express. Succeeding artists have taken advantage of this idea, and the great French painter Poussin did not fear to make use of it in his picture of *Germanicus*.

We cannot help thinking that the judgment of Parrhasius, in regard to the picture of his adversary, was governed by a spitefulness which rendered him unjust. However, new successes speedily consoled him for this defeat. He painted an allegorical picture for the Athenians which gained him universal applause. It is well known that no people were so unstable as the Athenians, now proud and haughty, then timid and humble; to-day full of humanity and clemency, to-morrow savage, vindictive, and cruel. The talent by which Parrhasius succeeded in representing this fickleness in its various phases, set a seal upon his reputation.

The greatest reproach that can be made to this artist is, that he was inordinately proud of his talent. It is true that he has been accused of cruelly torturing to death a slave, whom he bought at the taking of Olynthus, by Philip, king of Macedon, that he might have a truthful representation from which to paint the agonies of Prometheus while a vulture was gnawing his vitals. But we should remember that proofs are needed for such a story; and as there are none, we prefer to believe that Parrhasius was indebted to his talent for the skill with which he rendered the sufferings of Prometheus, rather than to the sight of tortures inflicted upon his slave.

Similar acts of cruelty have been imputed to modern

artists, among them Michael Angelo; but as their entire life discredits such deeds, why may we not suppose that Parrhasius has likewise been unjustly accused.

Some time after the death of Parrhasius and Timanthes, the Greek school was divided into two factions; the school of Athens and that of Sicyon, which Apelles has imortalized.

APELLES.

Apelles, the most illustrious of the painters of antiquity, was born in the island of Cos, three hundred and thirty two years before the Christian era. Pithius, his father, finding that he had great taste for the arts, sent him to Ephesus to learn painting of Ephorus, who had a considerable number of pupils.

Apelles made such rapid progress as to astonish his teacher. Not only did he possess great facility for learning, but he was also extremely industrious. He would have considered a day lost in which he had not made marked progress. Such a disposition would suffice to enable a young man of medium ability to make himself superior; and it is no wonder that Apelles, so gifted by nature, should soon be obliged to seek a higher school than that of Ephorus.

At that time Pamphilus, of Amphipolis, directed the most celebrated school of Greece. He was learned in the sciences, in literature and the arts; but painting was his specialty. It was considered a great honor to be admitted among his pupils; and although he required an engagement of ten years, and the payment of one talent, that is, five thousand and four hundred francs, French money, the number of young people who presented themselves was so great that Pamphilus was obliged to refuse money.

Painting was most esteemed among the liberal arts, and every family was anxious that some of their children should learn it. The right to learn painting was regulated by a decree of the state, which permitted those of the highest rank, then those young people of families in easy circumstances; but formally interdicted the privilege to slaves.

Apelles presented himself at the school of Pamphilus, who, satisfied with his examination, gladly received him upon his accepting the condition of remaining ten years. Correct and elegant drawing, a noble and bold touch, and above all, an inimitable grace, made the productions of Apelles so many *chefs-d'œuvre.*

The young painter had acquired a great reputation before he left the school of Pamphilus for that of Sicyon, which was thought to excel all others in the truly beautiful. Apelles perfected himself there, and his name was celebrated throughout Greece.

So faithful were his delineations of nature, that she seemed to guide his pencil. He seized her slightest expressions, her faintest shades, and reproduced them with an inexpressible charm. He was endowed with an inventive genius, arranged his personages with taste, and knew how to spread the charm of poetry over all his compositions.

Although he used but four colors, they were true, vivid, and brilliant. The composition of the varnish which he used has never been known: Pliny says that its essential properties were to render the colors smoother and softer, to improve the appearance of the painting, and to preserve it from dust. The secret of making this varnish, of which Apelles was the inventor, died with him, and was only replaced, centuries after, by the discovery which John Van Eyck made of painting in oil.

Apelles was not unconscious of his own rare merit: but, wiser than Parrhasius, he admitted that of others without jealousy, and, persuaded that man has always something to learn, he was grateful to the visitors of his studio for their advice and suggestions. Finding these suggestions occasionally useful, he placed each picture on exhibition, as it was finished, that the public might freely praise or criticise. Concealed behind a curtain, he listened to what they said, enjoying the disinterested praises accorded to him, and improving by such criticisms as he found to be just.

One day, a shoemaker, who, like others, stopped before a picture thus exposed, observed that something was wanting in the sandal of one of the personages, and spoke of it; Apelles, knowing that the shoemaker was a better judge than he, corrected the fault. The next day, the same picture being on exhibition, the shoemaker, very proud at seeing that his criticism was accepted, thought himself a man of talent, and began to criticise the leg to which the sandal belonged. But Apelles, coming forward, and striking him on the shoulder, said to him, "Ne sutor ultra crepidam." (The shoemaker must not go beyond his last.) These words have been rendered proverbial by the fables of Phædrus.

Apelles, desirous of seeing celebrated painters, went to Rhodes, where Protogenes lived. This illustrious artist was absent when Apelles called at his studio. Apelles amused himself by sketching upon canvas where a picture was already commenced. Protogenes, who did not expect a visit from Apelles, exclaimed, when he saw the drawing, "Apelles has been here!" So true it is that a single line betrays a great master. Protogenes added lines still more perfect to the sketch; but when the illustrious visitor came again, he surpassed his previous work. Protogenes, filled with admiration, proclaimed him the greatest painter in the world, and swore eternal friendship with him.

From this time these two great men professed the highest esteem and most disinterested affection for each other. The friendship which unites two artists of eminent talent, and excites a noble emulation between them, defies hatred and envy. This friendship is as beautiful as it is rare; unfortunately, men of genius, who seem so well constituted to understand each other, often allow pride and the immoderate desire of glory to take possession of their hearts; unwilling that another should share in this glory, they sacrifice every noble and generous feeling, and their rival becomes almost their enemy.

Alexander the Great, having seen the beautiful works of Apelles, chose him for his painter, and forbade any other to take his likeness. The first portrait which the artist made of this prince was an *Alexander the Thunderer*, which was proclaimed a *chef-d'œuvre, par excellence*. The hand which held the thunderbolt was particularly admired it was so finely painted that it seemed to come out from the clouds by which it was surrounded. Alexander was in ecstasy; he loaded the painter with riches, and honored him with his friendship. He took pleasure in going to see him paint, and in conversing with him upon the secrets of his art.

The picture of *Alexander the Thunderer* having been placed in the temple of Diana, at Ephesus, the conqueror wished to have another portrait, and begged Apelles to paint him mounted upon Bucephalus; to which the artist consented. When the picture was finished, Alexander was not so well satisfied as with the first, and complained that his beautiful battle-horse was not well represented. Apelles, who was quite satisfied with the horse, was about to try to prove to the king that he was mistaken, when a mare, passing near where the picture stood, stopped before the horse, and began to neigh. The painter turned to Alexander, and said,—

"Shall this animal be a better judge of painting than the King of Macedon?"

Alexander, smiling, gave his hand to the artist: after such a proof, Bucephalus could not fail of being perfect.

While the conqueror lived, Apelles enjoyed his affection and kindness. Great princes have always honored artists, and the glory which they have received from them has often been more durable than that of their conquests.

After the death of Alexander, Apelles went to Egypt, and lived for a time at the court of Ptolemy. This prince did not accord him the friendly protection which Alexander had done. Envy, which creeps about thrones to prevent the approach of talent and merit, was frightened at the reception of the Greek painter by Ptolemy. He must be sent away, cost what it would, for they had as much to fear from his uprightness as from his great genius. They accused him of having entered into a conspiracy to murder the king. It was in vain that Apelles defended himself, setting forth the guarantee of a pure life, wholly consecrated to the culture of art; his opponents had too much interest at stake to allow his voice to be heard, and he was about to be condemned, when the real conspirators were discovered.

Apelles hastened from this inhospitable court, and went to Ephesus, where, under the influence of a soul filled with indignation at the mean and cruel conduct of his enemies, he painted the best known of his works — the picture of *Calumny*.

He died soon after, never having seen his sublime talent grow dim, nor having met a rival who could be preferred to him.

Apelles left three treatises relative to art, which existed in the time of Pliny, and in which he gives details upon the study of the passions and sentiments expressed in the human face; upon the science of position; upon the manner of seizing resemblances; and finally, upon the profile. It is said that he was the first who made use of profile. According to Pliny, he invented it to conceal the deformity of Antigonus, who had but one eye, and who requested him to paint his portrait.

The portrait of *Antigonus on Horseback*, *Venus Anadyomenes*, — that is to say, coming out of the water, — and *Diana in the Midst of a Choir of Virgins*, are the most highly esteemed of the great master's works, after the *Calumny*.

The ancients have given the following description of this picture: —

A man with long ears, similar to those of Midas, is seated on the right hand of the composition; he extends his hand to Accusation, who is approaching from a distance; near him are two females, one of whom appears to be Ignorance, the other Suspicion. Accusation comes forward under the form of a perfectly beautiful woman; her face is red, and she appears to be violently agitated and excited with anger: in one hand she holds a burning torch; with the other she drags a young man by the hair of his head, while he lifts his hands to heaven. A pale and disfigured man acts as her conductor; his sombre and fixed appearance and his extreme leanness make him resemble those sick persons who are attenuated by long abstinence: he is easily recognized as Envy. Two other women accompany Accusation, encouraging her, arranging her vesture and caring for her ornaments: one is Deceit, the other Perfidy: these are followed in the distance by a woman, whose sadness and black and torn garments announce Repentance; she turns her head, sheds tears, and is confused at seeing tardy Truth advancing.

PROTOGENES.

Protogenes was born about the year 350 before the Christian era, at Caune, a city situated upon the southerly side of the Island of Rhodes. Nothing is known of his infancy or youth, except that he passed them in poverty: we do not even know the name of the master who taught him painting. Without doubt it was some obscure painter, whose lessons, without the aid of the genius with which nature had endowed Protogenes, would have failed to produce fruits.

Passionately fond of labor, but never willing to leave a work which he thought he could improve, the young artist remained many years unknown. At the age of fifty years, Protogenes was employed, in subordination to another, in the decoration of the magnificent vessels which the Greeks enriched with painting and sculpture: the work was admired, and he was better paid than he had hitherto been, besides having leisure to paint subjects of his own choice.

He painted some charming little pictures, and portraits of striking resemblance and fine finish. These pictures and portraits were the commencement of his fortune and his reputation; but Protogenes saw only one point in this fortune and reputation; namely, liberty to study art without the distraction of material preoccupation.

Aristotle, who was very fond of this artist, and appreciated his talent, advised him to leave the simple things which he was in the habit of painting, and undertake some great composition. The philosopher wished Alexander, his august pupil, to choose Protogenes to represent the victories which have rendered him immortal; but Protogenes, who knew the danger of forcing genius, would not suffer himself to be seduced by the brilliant hopes with which Aristotle tried to inspire him, and preferred to obey his own inspirations: however, Aristotle continued to urge him, until he at length consented to undertake a battle-piece.

Protogenes joined much delicacy and energy to correct drawing. His picture representing the *Hunter Jalysus* is considered his best piece. He worked upon it seven years, living only upon vegetables and water, fearing that the use of meats and wine would weaken his mind and make his hand unsteady. At the end of seven years, he considered the principal figure only as finished; the others appeared to him very imperfect; but that which chiefly occupied him was the dog of Jalysus. In vain those who saw the picture expatiated upon the beauty of the dog; Protogenes was not satisfied with it. He wished to represent it as panting, the mouth foaming, and he had not succeeded. The more praise he received, the more he wished to make it as perfect as possible. He set himself to work with renewed ardor, and passed several days in trying to make the dog as he wished it; but, notwithstanding his talent and patience, his efforts were unsatisfactory. Despairing of success, he effaced, for the hundredth time, perhaps, the foam, which he could not imitate, and in a fit of vexation, threw his sponge, wet with the color he had just removed, at the dog's mouth. What did he care if he spoiled the picture, since he could not make it what he desired?

But O, joy! chance had done for him what art had failed to do: now it was like real foam coming from the jaws of Jalysus' brave companion, and difficult as Protogenes had been to be satisfied, he now asked no more.

When Apelles saw this picture, he cried out, "The

genius of man has never produced anything more wonderful!" He was extremely surprised to learn that these beautiful works received but little admiration, and that the Rhodians could not appreciate them. He then offered to buy all the pictures which Protogenes should make, since his fellow-countrymen did not care to keep the works of an artist who was an honor to his country. However, it was not necessary to accept this generous offer; for the Rhodians, having heard what Apelles said of the talent of Protogenes, opened their eyes, and proclaimed him truly illustrious: they bought his pictures to prevent their ornamenting the palaces of foreign princes. They paid a great price for the *Hunter Jalysus*, the hunter passing for the grandson of the Sun, and the founder of Rhodes.

Protogenes was unwilling to deliver this picture without retouching it, and it was not completed when he heard that Demetrius Poliorcetes was about to besiege Rhodes. This news caused him to redouble his zeal, so that if anything should happen to him, his picture might be completed. The painter lived in a suburban town, which was soon invaded by the enemy's troops; but neither the noise of arms, nor the interruption of the soldiers, who came into his studio, could disturb him for a moment.

Demetrius, hearing that a Rhodian continued to paint as if all was quiet about him in the midst of the perplexities of the siege, thought that the Rhodian must be Protogenes, and wished to see him.

Demetrius called him by name, and after having paid a just tribute of admiration to his works, asked him how he could be sufficiently composed to paint, surrounded as he was by danger.

"I knew," said the painter, "that you wage war against the Rhodians, and not against the fine arts."

The prince, pleased with this answer, assured him of his friendship. Guards were stationed at the door of the studio, that the artist might be undisturbed; and a few days after, Démétrius, perceiving that the only means by which he could get possession of the city would be to burn the place on which the studio stood, preferred to raise the siege rather than expose the works of Protogenes to almost certain destruction.

Thus Rhodes owed its safety to the talent of Protogenes; and we can well imagine that they rendered him the most flattering homage.

Zeuxis, Aristides, Parrhasius, Timanthes, Apelles, and Protogenes were the most celebrated painters that Greece can boast of. It was not long before the art which they had carried to so high a degree of perfection began to decline, and the wars of which Greece was the theatre hastened their decay. It is said, however, that Asclepiodorus, Nicomachus, and Pausias, all contemporaries of Apelles, preserved the traditions of the great masters. Asclepiodorus drew so correctly as to meet the approbation of Apelles. Nicomachus painted with great facility: it is said that he made pictures as Homer made verses; and Pausias decorated the ceiling and walls of the palace of paintings in encaustic, and represented flowers most truthfully. He succeeded equally well in other styles, and a picture in which he painted Drunkenness, so that the face was seen illumined through the enormous glass from which he was drinking, has been much praised.

Then came Euphranor, Nicias, Timonachus of Byzantium, who all made laudable efforts for the glory of painting; Pyreicus, also, painted common subjects, as markets, inns, barbers' and shoemakers' shops, and caricatures of all sorts, which were very much liked.

Art never recovered her dignity after Pyreicus, and Greece, conquered by the Romans, had no more celebrated painters.

TITIAN — GIORGIONE.

Tiziano Vecelli was born at Cadore, on the borders of Friuli, about the year 1477, and at first received a learned education. He lived in habits of intimacy with philosophers and poets of his time, with Ariosto at Ferrara, Pietro Aretino at Venice, &c. His family was one of the oldest of the republic of Venice, and Saint Titian, Bishop of Odezza, his patron, belonged to the family.

His father put him under the care of the teacher of

the village nearest his castle, until he was old enough to be sent to some college of note. Here he learned to read and write, and appeared to have no desire to go farther in his studies, at least in the sciences which his professor taught. He had no greater pleasure than to escape the vigilance of this teacher, and run through the fields gathering flowers, whose brilliant colors he admired, and making bouquets. Returning to his class, he would destroy the beautiful flowers, and use their juice in painting other flowers upon his copy-books.

At first, the young Titian was severely reprimanded, because he not only did not know his lessons, but he distracted the attention of his schoolmates, who were curious to examine his pictures. When the teacher became convinced that his pupil had a decided taste for the arts, he informed Signor Vecelli, and advised him not to thwart him in this vocation.

His advice was accepted, and Titian was taken to Venice, and at the age of twelve years placed in the studio of Gentile Bellini. Gentile and Jean Bellini were then in great reputation, and although united by the strictest friendship, they worked with extreme ardor, and endeavored to surpass each other. Gentile immediately recognized the gift of the young Vecelli, who made rapid progress in a short time, but who, once initiated into the principles of painting, no longer adhered to the rules of the master. Gentile tried in vain to guide him, and finally, indignant at what he supposed to be obstinacy, predicted that he would never be anything but a dauber.

Gentile was chosen by the republic of Venice to go to the Sultan Mahomet II., who was desirous of employing a skilful artist, and Titian passed into Jean's studio. The method of Jean was nearly the same as that of Gentile, but his style was bolder than that of his brother: the attempts of Titian, remarkable for softness, grace, and a peculiar charm, pleased him.

The first known works of Jean Bellini are some portraits, an *Angel holding the young Tobias by the Hand*, a *Nativity*, and a picture representing the *Virgin, St. Roch*, and *St. Sebastian* — a picture which he painted for the church of his native village.

About this time Giorgio Barbarelli, of Castel Franco, entered the school of Jean Bellini. This new pupil, about the age of Titian, was of humble origin; but his manners were so elegant, his mind so distinguished, that no young Venetian gentleman could surpass him. A fine voice, a rare talent for music, joined to an agreeable exterior, had opened the most aristocratic halls to him, and Jean Bellini knew that he was an artist of great hope, when he consented to admit him into his studio.

Very soon Giorgio was the king of it. His bold, proud, and lively character conciliated the affection of all his fellow-students, while his aptness gained for him the esteem of his master. Giorgio, bestowing the same ardor upon painting which he did upon other things, and being endowed with an exquisite feeling for the beautiful in art, soon learned all that Bellini could teach. The study of the works of Leonardo da Vinci opened to him a new field, into which he boldly rushed.

Jean Bellini, too much a slave to routine, blamed the impetuosity of his pupil, and tried to lead him back to the sobriety of colors, and austerity of the types which he had himself adopted; but the genius of Giorgio spoke louder than the precepts of Bellini, and although the master predicted what would happen, he could not help admiring this young talent, and showing particular affection and indulgence to Barbarelli.

Titian became the intimate friend of Giorgio, and his ardent admirer. He found in his pictures what he had so long regretted as wanting in those of Bellini — life, color, and grace. Therefore he took more pains to imitate his fellow-student than his master, and succeeded so well, that it was almost impossible to distinguish his work from that of his friend.

Giorgio, who was very tall, strong, and handsome, exercised great influence in the studio, and they gave him the surname of Giorgione. It is well known that the Italian language admits of augmentatives and diminutives. Giorgione signifies great George, George the strong, as Giorgino would signify little George, George the slender. Barbarelli has retained the surname given him by his companions.

Giorgione, although a fellow-pupil of Titian, was his

only teacher for some years; it was his style, and not that of Bellini, which the celebrated Titian imitated. They both remained in Bellini's studio, occupied in painting church pictures. It must be acknowledged that this kind of painting was not very pleasing to Titian, who, at that time, did not understand how much poetry there is in the scenes borrowed from Holy Writ. Bellini was frequently obliged to repress the wanderings of this ardent imagination of Titian, who felt more at his ease when representing divinities of fable than monks and martyrs. Giorgione was of the same opinion as Titian, but the difficulty of getting employment elsewhere obliged them to be patient.

One day, when Giorgione had gained a wager, our two hair-brained youths, having some money in their pockets, excused themselves from going to the studio, and were absent until they had spent their last cent. Then they began to think how they could appear before Master Bellini, who, they knew, would not countenance such pranks.

"Let us risk it," said Titian; "we deserve a reprimand; we will submit, and that will be the end of it."

"I think you are mistaken in judging of Master Jean's clemency," replied Giorgione; "believe me, it is better that we should not go back to him."

"Bah! we will acknowledge our fault, and he must pardon us."

"Let us go, then," said Giorgione, whose resolute character at length gave way.

It was in vain that the two apprentices knocked at Jean Bellini's door; it was never more to be opened to them. Giorgione had not been deceived; the master, fearing the influence of their example in this conduct upon the other pupils, had resolved not to receive them again.

Giorgione and Titian were much embarrassed: they were without work, and without money; but, at their age, one has so much confidence in the future that courage soon revives.

"Work never fails those who seek it in earnest," said Giorgione; "and as we both have talent, we shall have as much work as we can do, as soon as we shall be known."

"Yes, but until then?"

"O, well! until then we will paint portraits; and if we ask a reasonable price, we shall earn our living."

At first they earned very little; and having moderate desires, the two friends lived very happily. Painting, at this time, was much in vogue in Italy, and especially in Venice. Giorgione and Titian began by painting portraits of friends, and soon became too well known to be anxious for the morrow. But this did not satisfy their ambition: they longed for fame and fortune.

One day, when Giorgione awoke, he said to his friend, who shared his bed, —

"I have thought of something which cannot fail to give us honor and riches, and which only needs your consent."

"What is it?" said Titian, who had the most entire confidence in his friend.

"It is simply the question of painting the façade of our house in fresco."

"The façade of our house?" repeated Titian.

"Of the house we inhabit, if you mean that it does not belong to us. Be quiet; we shall do better than that, and in a year or two there will not be a palace too beautiful for us. How you look at me! One would think that you did not understand what I'say."

"I declare that you would do me a favor by explaining."

"Child! who cannot imagine that at the sight of our beautiful frescoes, — for they would be magnificent, — every person who passes will ask who did them, I will answer for it."

"That is true, and we shall be known much sooner than in limiting ourselves to painting portraits."

"Doubtless; but that is not all. Seeing how our paintings improve this house, which looks so homely and sad, every noble Venetian, and every rich merchant, will take a fancy to embellish his with similar ornaments. And to whom will they apply? To the two young painters, of course, who first had the idea of decorating in this manner."

"You are right," cried Titian; "let us go quickly to work."

All happened as Giorgione had foretold. Very soon

his name and that of Titian were known throughout the city, and they had much more work than they could do. The brothers Bellini had long been the kings of painting in Venice; but without disputing their merit, there was found in the pencils of the two young artists something sweet, soft, and living, which gained for them the preference.

The Doge Loredano wished to have his portrait from the hand of Giorgione; and he was so much pleased with it, that to recompense the artist, he engaged him to paint the façade of an immense building, which served as a warehouse for merchandise brought from Germany.

Everything being in common with the two friends, Giorgione took two thirds of the work, and confided one to Titian, and each chose the subject which best suited him. The bold, proud, and learned composition of Giorgione was much admired; but that of Titian, sweet, graceful, and charming, was received with universal enthusiasm. Both were attributed to Giorgione, because he had contracted for the work. Habituated as Giorgione was to consider himself more able than his companion, he felt a certain displeasure at the sight of Titian's works, whose beauty he could not deny, and this displeasure soon became jealousy.

The friends of Giorgione, not knowing how the work had been distributed between the two comrades, warmly felicitated him, whom they supposed to be the author of it: it was their opinion that not even the greatest masters could disavow the minutest details of these beautiful frescoes; but they signalized some of Titian's figures, particularly that of *Judith about to cut off the Head of Holofernes*, as pencillings of marvellous beauty. It had been difficult for Giorgione to bear the idea of Titian's being his equal; what, then, could be his feelings on seeing himself surpassed? Jealousy stifled all friendship for him whom he called his brother. With a heart overflowing with bitterness, he shut himself in a room, refusing admission to Titian.

It was in vain that the young man insisted upon knowing the cause of such cruel treatment; in vain he supplicated Giorgione to receive him, assuring him that some misunderstanding had caused his displeasure. Giorgione, who would not for the world have acknowleged the sentiments which had taken possession of him, declared that he would not listen to any justification which he could make, and that he would have nothing more to do with him.

Titian could not believe this, and tried to meet him in his walks, or in some of the public places which they had been accustomed to visit together; he could not be persuaded that the sweet ties which had united them, and thanks to which they had so happily supported their ill luck, were forever broken. Giorgione avoided seeing him, and Titian, losing all hope of a reconciliation with the friend of his youth, resolved to quit Venice, which had become irksome to him, since he must enjoy the benefit of the reputation which his young and rare talent began to create alone. He remained only long enough to finish a picture destined for the church of the Frari. His very large figures, full of life and strength, at first little pleased the Venetian amateurs, accustomed to the rather dry paintings of the Bellini; yet when, after the first surprise, they rendered ample justice to this *chef-d'œuvre*, Titian was cited as the first painter in Venice, and people were happy to obtain one of his paintings.

But Titian wished to travel: he left for Vicenza, promising to return. In Vicenza he decorated the audience hall of the Palace of Justice, choosing the *Judgment of Solomon* for his subject. The sight of this picture drew forth a cry of admiration from the public, who wished to retain the artist in their city; but their entreaties were of no avail.

He went to Padua, where he painted the history of St. Antonio, patron of that city, in three beautiful frescoes, which have been carefully preserved by the school of St. Antonio, of Padua, and copied by many celebrated painters at different epochs. The inhabitants of Padua had never seen anything comparable with these frescoes; and they were so urgent to have more of Titian's pictures, that he prolonged his stay in that hospitable city until 1511.

Giorgione, who remained in Venice after the departure of Titian, painted, among other works, a *Christ bearing his Cross* — a magnificent picture.

The reputation of Giorgione had suffered no diminution. If the superiority of Titian was no longer doubtful to a certain number of amateurs, the merit of his old friend was not the less indisputable, and he continually received orders from all parts of the country. But what did he care for wealth? What for glory? He had lost that which made the charm of his life — the certainty of excelling every rival, and the friendship of Titian. His good humor, his unchangeable gayety, abandoned him; the world became odious to him, and he confined himself to the most absolute solitude. This sudden change ruined his health, and after languishing for some time, he died at the age of thirty-two years.

Sebastian del Piombo was his first pupil, if we except his schoolmate and friend, Titian, whose master he really was.

Few painters have put so much strength and fire into their pictures as Giorgione. The portraits by this artist are living pictures; his landscapes touched with exquisite tact; his taste delicate, his complexions true, and his *chiaro-scuro* irreproachable. The brothers Bellini had cultivated painting, conscientiously, as they found it; but Giorgione added much to the dominion of art, and created, as it were, the new school which Titian was to make illustrious.

After the death of his unhappy friend, Titian returned to Venice, and finished several works commenced by Jean Bellini and by Giorgione. Among them was a large fresco destined to ornament the Council Hall, and representing the Emperor Frederick Barbarossa at the feet of Pope Alexander III. Instead of confining himself to the original drawing, Titian changed the arrangement, and introduced the portraits of the most celebrated personages of his time, from the army, the magistracy, the church, and the arts, all in costumes suitable to the age which the scene represented.

This fresco was properly appreciated, and Titian received a title which was reserved for the best Venetian painters. This title gave the right to a small pension and the privilege of painting the portrait of each new doge, in consideration, however, of paying eight crowns per portrait.

The renown of Titian soon spread through all Italy, and the Duke of Ferrara, Alphonso d'Este, whose palace was open to all great artists, invited the Venetian painter to honor it with his presence. Titian accepted the invitation of the duke, and displayed all the richness of his pencil in three subjects borrowed from mythology. Two of these pictures represent Bacchus and his court, and the third, an infinite number of little Loves, which great painters are pleased to copy. Augustino Carracci considered these two pictures the most beautiful in the world, and Domenichino, who studied them with care, wept bitterly when he saw them packed for Spain.

Titian made the acquaintance of Ariosto at Ferrara. Friendship soon united these two men of genius, who immortalized each other, the painter by the portrait of the poet, and the poet by consecrating his verses to the painter.

After the three mythological scenes in which Titian allowed his pencil to follow the flight of his fancy, he returned to religious subjects. The encomiums passed upon the mystic pictures of Albert Durer at the court of Ferrara, inspired him with the idea of a magnificent Christ, which he painted upon the door of a wardrobe, with so much patience and love, that an enthusiastic admiration saluted its appearance.

No sooner was Titian reëstablished in Venice, in 1515, than he received an invitation from Pope Leo X. to visit Rome. Nothing could have been more agreeable to him than to visit the country of the fine arts, and to add something of his own composition to the immortal *chefs-d'œuvre* of Michael Angelo and Raphael; but his numerous friends retained him in Venice, and forced him to thank the Pope for his kind intentions.

Titian made a great number of portraits. The doge, the first captains, and all the lords of the republic, sought the honor of having their portraits taken by this able artist. He painted two *Battle-pieces* for the senate of Venice, — which were afterwards destroyed by fire, — an *Assumption of the Holy Virgin*, a *St. Nicholas*, *St. Francis*, *St. Catherine*, and *St. Sebastian*.

The *St. Sebastian* was the object of a very singular criticism. Vasari, author of the Lives of Italian painters, says, that "Titian was not much troubled about representing this martyr; that he made a real man of him, and one could not help shuddering at sight of his wounds." What greater praise than such a criticism!

About this time Titian also painted *Christ at Table between St. Luke and Cleophas*; and this picture was found so beautiful, that the gentleman who had ordered it made it a present to the republic, saying that such a treasure should not be hidden in a private gallery. Afterwards appeared the *Martyrdom of St. Peter*, in which Titian displayed all the magical vigor of his pencil, and which passed not only for the *chef-d'œuvre* of this illustrious master, but which, with the *Transfiguration* by Raphael, and the *Communion of St. Jerome* by Domenichino, is considered the most beautiful which has been produced in painting.

Titian's glory increased faster than his fortune; for the magnificent pictures which at the present time are almost covered with gold, were far from being well paid. He was living very modestly, when his friend Aretino introduced him to the Cardinal Hyppolite di Medici.

Charles V. having come to Bologna to be anointed, the cardinal spoke to him of Titian. The emperor immediately sent for him, and desired his portrait. Titian painted the emperor on horseback, covered with armor, and so majestic that Charles V. was enchanted, and paid Titian one thousand crowns in gold for the portrait, and assured him of his protection.

The generous and illustrious persons who accompanied the emperor had their portraits taken also, and recompensed him largely. Among them, those of Antonio Leva and Don Alphonso d'Avolas are the most celebrated.

Titian, enriched by the liberalities of Charles V. and the nobles, returned to Venice, where he continued to work until 1543, when he went to Ferrara, to paint the portrait of Paul III. It would be impossible to speak of all that he did at that time; the mere mention of his pictures would fill pages.

The Pope was so delighted with his portrait that he tried to induce Titian to go to Rome with him, but he had promised to accompany Urbino to the Duke Francis of Rovera. Two years after, however, he complied with the request of Cardinal Farnese, and accepted the royal hospitality which he offered him at Rome.

Titian was received with all the honors due to his talent. Paul III. placed the apartments of the Belvidere at his disposition, and treated him as if he were a prince. The Venetian artist painted an *Ecce Homo* with an admirable expression, and then a second portrait.

It is said that Titian having placed this portrait of the Pope upon a terrace to dry the varnish, the passers by, thinking it was the Pope taking an airing upon the terrace, made their obeisance to it. This mistake was very flattering, both to the Pope and the artist.

Titian remained in Rome only one year, but he left a beautiful *Danaë* for the Duke Octavio Farnese, a perfect *chef-d'œuvre* in life and coloring.

Paul III. offered lucrative positions to Titian and his son, if he would remain in the capital of the Christian world; but a permanent residence in Rome did not please the illustrious artist: he returned to Venice, his home, where he seemed to renew the vigor of youth. He was welcomed by excellent friends, and lived happily, passing his time in labor and pleasant conversation, until Charles V., who had not forgotten his painter, called him to his court at Innspruck, where wealth and honor awaited him. It seemed as if the emperor could not be happy without his favorite artist; he wished that Titian should accompany him in all his journeys, granted him admission to his apartments at all times without being announced, created him count and knight, and ennobled his family forever.

Titian was seventy-six years old when Charles V. wished him to paint his portrait for the third time. Charles was arrayed in the insignia of imperial majesty; Titian stood by his easel, sketching the noble features, veiled already with that shade of sombre melancholy which afterwards inspired him with the singular resolution of burying himself alive in the monastery of St. Just. The emperor and the painter were conversing together; suddenly the pencil slipped from the painter's hand, and fell to the floor. Before any one made a motion, Charles stooped, picked it up, and handed it to Titian, who, stupefied and confounded, received it with tears in his eyes, saying, —

"Ah! sire, you confound me!"

"How then! Is not Titian worthy to be served by Cæsar?"

This great emperor, who considered himself as above all others, thought he never could show sufficient deference to his painter. In public, he placed him on his right hand and showed him so much attention that the princes of royal blood were jealous of him. They ventured to make some observations on the subject to the emperor, who replied, —

"I know a great number of princes and kings, but I believe that there are not two Titians in the whole world."

At Innspruck, the Venetian artist painted the portrait of Philip II.; of Ferdinand, king of the Romans, of Maria, his wife, and of their seven daughters, whom he grouped together in a charming picture. He also painted other illustrious personages; but the work from which he received the greatest honor was an *Apotheosis of Charles V.;* a composition in which the Trinity, escorted by a troop of Cherubims, of exquisite beauty, receives the homage of the Virgin and the Saints. This picture, inundated with light, makes him who contemplates it realize the eternal joys of the blessed.

After an absence of five years, Titian returned to

Venice, and was admitted to the Senate, to give an account of his travels; such an honor was only accorded to ambassadors. The doge, surprised at the recital which he made of his sojourn at the court of Charles V., said, —

"After all the honors that kings and emperors have conferred upon you, Sir Titian, it will not be in our power to recompense your talent worthily."

"May it please your grace," replied Titian, "there is a recompense which it is in your power to grant me."

"Speak, Sir Painter, and what you ask shall be granted."

"Permit me, then, your excellency, to finish the Council Chamber at my own expense."

This proposition was received with due gratitude; and Titian, who found that, on account of his age, he should not be able to accomplish the great work he had undertaken, engaged the services of several painters of talent, — Tintoretto, Paul Veronese, and Horatio Vecelli, his second son, who had embraced the same career as himself, and whose teacher he was.

Besides this work, Titian was constantly assailed with orders from Charles V., to whom he was too much indebted not to strive to satisfy him. He therefore sent him a *St. Sebastian*, a *Mater Dolorosa*, painted upon stone, and a large picture, representing *Religion pursued by Heresy*. For these pictures he received new honors and new pensions.

Charles V. died, and Philip II., who had already chosen Titian for his painter, continued to attach a great value to the works of this eminent artist. Among the pictures painted for him were *Diana and Actæon*, *Andromeda and Perseus*, *Medea and Jason*, the *Martyrdom of St. Lorenzo*, the *Flagellation of Christ*, and a *Magdalen*.

It is said that Titian gave the *Magdalen* such an expression, that the king said he had never seen anything more striking; and, complimenting the painter, he asked "why his Magdalen wept thus." The artist answered, that she was begging, with tears in her eyes, that his majesty would pay Titian the pension which Charles V. had wished to leave him. Philip, severe as he was, could not help laughing at the hint, and ordered the Viceroy of Naples to pay the great painter without delay.

But the most important work, for the King of Spain, was *The Last Supper*, an immense picture, which cost Titian seven years' labor, and is regarded as a masterpiece in coloring.

Titian worked, with undiminished power, to an advanced age. A *Transfiguration*, and an *Annunciation of the Virgin*, and some others of inestimable value, belong to the last years of his life. All the illustrious visitors of Italy made it a duty to pay their respects to the noble old man, whom they always found in his studio, in the midst of favorite pupils and fervent admirers.

Henry III., King of Poland, having made a voyage

to Venice, before the death of Charles IX. called him to the throne of France, paid a visit to Titian, in company with the Dukes of Ferrara and Mantua. He conversed with the great painter, admired, as a true artist, the paintings which his studio contained, and the king chose several, begging Titian to name the price of them; but the illustrious old man forced him to accept them, as a testimony of his gratitude for the royal visit.

No artist ever enjoyed more honor and wealth than Titian: however, he was not exempt from domestic troubles. Pomponio, his eldest son, who had entered the ecclesiastical state, conducted himself very badly; and the scandal of his conduct nearly broke the heart of Titian, who found no consolation, except in labor. While in this state of feeling, he chose the Passion of Christ, and the Martyrdom of Saints, in preference to other subjects.

This great man arrived at the age of ninety-one years without having given up his pencil. His youthful and ardent spirit continued to inspire him; his hand scarcely trembled, but his eyes were somewhat weakened, which caused him to think that his coloring was never strong enough. He imagined that his old pictures had the same fault, and resolved to rectify it; and many of his best works would have been lost to posterity, if his pupils had not thought of a method to prevent it, without afflicting the noble old man, whom they loved and respected as a father. They mixed his colors with olive oil, which would not dry, so that they could at night wipe off the colors which Titian had put on in the day.

It was hoped that he would live to be a hundred; but he fell a victim to an epidemic which decimated Venice in 1576. The news of his death cast a gloom over the whole city; for a moment every one forgot his own troubles in the loss of this man of genius.

When the Senate heard of the death of Titian, they made an exception to the ordinance requiring the destruction of the bodies of those who died with plague, and immediately decreed that the remains of the great artist should be carried into the church Dei Frari, with all the pomp displayed at the funeral of the doges. All Venice followed the hearse of Titian, appearing to forget the raging contagion which threatened them.

Titian was one of the most admirable geniuses who ever lived. All his works have a seal of grandeur and poetry which astonishes and charms. "The beings which he creates seem to have the high consciousness and enjoyment of existence, the bliss of satisfaction, so like, yet so different, from the marble idealizations of Grecian antiquity. The air of an harmonious, unruffled existence seems to characterize them all. Hence they produce so grateful an impression on the mind of the spectator, hence they impart so refined and exalted a feeling, although generally but a transcript of familiar and well-known objects, — representations of beautiful forms, without reference to spiritual or unearthly conceptions. It is life in its fullest power; the glorious freedom of earthly existence; the liberation of art from the bonds of ecclesiastical dogmas. Italy, Germany, England, and Spain possess a great number of his paintings, and there are twenty-two in the Museum of the Louvre, in Paris. Titian's church-pictures are as fine as his portraits, his pen-drawings are excellent, and his landscapes can be compared only to those of Salvator Rosa and Poussin. No one could give more truth and life to his works than Titian, who excelled other painters in *chiaro-scuro*. However, it is to be regretted that he had not combined more correctness of drawing with the magic of his coloring and the elevation of his style."

Such was the opinion of Michael Angelo, — an opinion which posterity has confirmed. In a visit which he paid Titian, — introduced by Vasari, — Buonarotti, severe, but just, could not repress the expressions of admiration at the works of the Venetian. However, a slight frown showed Vasari that he did not express all his thoughts; and when they left the studio, he pressed him for an explanation.

"I never saw anything more perfect than those pictures, in regard to composition and color," he said; "and if Titian had only learned drawing in his youth, he would have been the greatest painter in the world."

The moral qualities of Titian were not inferior to his talents. He loved simplicity and work so much, that

he remained as little as possible at the courts of kings, and was never willing to be long absent from his native country. He loved to visit the places in which he passed his childhood, — the old castle where he was born, and the village school where he learned to read. The days he spent in them were his festive days. How sweet and dear are the remembrances which recall the caresses of a mother or the innocent pleasures of youth!

Some historians accuse Titian of avarice; but there is nothing to justify such an accusation. His house was kept royally; all his servants boasted of his generosity. When he received princes, or royal strangers, he treated them with great magnificence: for example, one day two Spanish cardinals came unexpectedly to dine with him. Titian received them with his accustomed cordiality, and invited them into his studio. While they were expatiating on the beauty of his works, he went to a window, and, throwing a purse filled with gold to a domestic, he said, "I have company to dine."

The dinner was served in princely style.

He received enormous sums of money, and left his children in easy circumstances; but, if he had been avaricious, his fortune would have been immense. Horatio Vecelli died of the pest a few weeks after Titian; and the inheritance of the illustrious painter passed into the hands of his unworthy son, Pomponio, who dissipated the whole of it in a few years, and died in indigence.

Titian, like Michael Angelo, had illustrious friends. Versed in science and letters, he often gave Ariosto good advice, which was received with gratitude. He was also connected with Aretino, who was then called the divine poet, or the scourge of kings, — a man of rare talent, but of perverse mind, and licentious manners.

Titian never yielded to the pernicious influence of Aretino's conversation, and during his long life had the happiness of being guided by the principles of honor and virtue.

RAPHAEL SANZIO.

Raphael Sanzio was born on Good Friday, March 28, 1483, at Urbino, a small town situated between Perouse and Pesaro, in the States of the Church. His father, Giovanni Sanzio, an ordinary painter, destined him for the career which he had himself embraced, and was his first instructor. But God had put a ray of the sacred fire which we call genius into the soul of this child, and Giovanni, surprised at his astonishing progress, immediately recognized that it was not in his power to teach him.

A Madonna, in fresco, which Raphael painted upon the wall of his maternal house, set Jean Sanzio to thinking.

"This child," said he, "will never be a poor artist,

like myself: if he receives some good instruction, he will not fail to do me honor."

Jean reasoned wisely, and did better still in taking his son to Perouse, where Pietro Vanucci, better known as Perugino, was flourishing. Sanzio's address prepossessed the master in his favor; he was a charming child, sweet, amiable, and frank, with a thoughtful and spiritual face, and very gentle manners.

"What can you do?" asked Perugino.

"Almost nothing, Master Perugino," answered Raphael, timidly; "but if you will teach me, I shall soon be able to give a different answer, for you are a good painter, and I shall be a docile pupil."

This answer pleased Perugino; he put a pencil into Raphael's hand, who immediately sketched the Madonna, which he had painted some days before from recollection. The master, astonished by the boldness and correctness of this sketch, said to Jean Sanzio, "You can leave your boy here; and it is for *me* to thank *you*."

The father and son separated, a little sad at their first parting, but delighted with the success of their undertaking; for Perugino was very difficult in the choice of pupils. This master well merited his reputation. Painting had made some progress under Giotto; but it was reserved for Perugino to create those beautiful types of the Virgin, noble heads of old men, and those lovely figures of angels, which were to make the glory of the Roman school, and to become the ideal of beauty, under the magic pencil of Raphael.

The young Sanzio felt all that was sweet and poetic in the manner of his new master, and promptly assimilated himself to it. Never was a more beautiful genius developed by more assiduous labor. Raphael had promised to be a docile pupil: he kept his word. His attention in listening to his master's advice, and putting it in practice, his aptness, and his charming character, soon made him more dear to Perugino than all his other pupils.

For two years he worked under the direction of his master; then he undertook the unimportant parts of Perugino's pictures, and acquitted himself so well, that able connoisseurs found it difficult to distinguish between the work of the master and that of the pupil. Perugino knew that Raphael would not be satisfied to equal, he would surpass him; but he loved him too much to allow jealous fear to disturb him.

Sanzio was seventeen years old when he painted his first picture. Taking advantage of the absence of Perugino, who was in Florence, he went to Citta di Castello for a vacation. No sooner had the people of the town heard that he was a pupil of the great master of Perouse, than they came to beg him to paint a picture of St. Nicholas for their church. This was an excellent opportunity for the young artist to try his skill; and he did not refuse. It was a perfect success, entirely in Perugino's style; it was found worthy to figure among his best works. Afterwards Raphael was desired to paint a *Christ on the Cross,* then a *Holy Family;* and in proportion as he grew bolder, and followed Perugino less, his pictures assumed a greater charm.

The following year he painted the *Marriage of the Virgin,* otherwise called the *Sposalizio,* — a picture which was said to be only a copy of the same subject by Perugino, but in which the genius which was to make Raphael the king of painters shone forth.

About this time Pinturicchio, fellow-pupil of Raphael, but much older, was called to Vienna, to decorate the library of the cathedral: finding this too great a task for him, he proposed to Raphael to take part. The young man accepted; and Pinturicchio, acknowledging his superiority, begged him to take charge of the cartoons for the frescoes; this he also did very willingly, regarding Pinturicchio as his superior. These two painters created quite a sensation; and all amateurs agreed in saying that it was the most beautiful work ever done.

Despite his modesty, Raphael began to understand that he was making very slight progress under the direction of Perugino, and that the study of the works of other renowned artists would be useful to him; he therefore refused to accept some advantageous offers which were made to him, and went to Florence. Leonardo da Vinci and Michael Angelo were about finishing their cartoons for the frescoes of the Council Chamber; and these magnificent cartoons, as we have already stated, were on exhibition for the instruction of young artists, until Florence, freed from the troubles which oppressed her, should demand the execution of the paintings, of which these sketches had excited so much admiration.

Raphael was astonished by the rapid stride in the way of progress made by Leonardo da Vinci; but the style of Michael Angelo, which, youthful and full of fire, left far behind him all that had been seen up to that time, pleased less than it astonished him.

Obliged to go to Urbin, he made only a short stay in Florence. At the end of a year he returned, with a letter of recommendation to the gonfaloniere from the Duchess d'Urbin. Through this recommendation he was graciously received by the chief magistrates of Florence, and an occasion to display his talent soon offered itself. Two portraits, a *Holy Family*, and some other pictures, soon placed him in the first rank of artists of the city, among whom was Fra Bartolomeo della Porta.

Raphael and this painter, already celebrated, soon became firm friends, and the two profited by the connection. The manner of Perugino — a manner which Raphael had followed — was correct, but rather dry; Bartolomeo's contours were somewhat fuller, softer, his coloring richer and more truthful, but his types were not so pure, and he was ignorant of the art of perspective. The two friends improved each other's deficiencies; and this exchange of good advice formed an imperishable bond between them.

It is thought that Raphael formed the acquaintance of Francia in Florence; and it is delightful to see this rare genius arrive at the apogee of glory without forgetting the respect due to Perugino, his master, nor the friendship which he had made, while young, with fellow-artists.

In the pictures which he painted at Florence, Raphael endeavored to correct the faults which we mentioned, and to raise himself to the highest point of progress which art had made, and at the same time to remain faithful to the instructions of Perugino. This is what is called the first manner of Raphael.

While at Florence, he thought of undertaking some great work, which could place him at the side of Leonardo da Vinci and Michael Angelo, and the protectors which the Duchess d'Urbin had given him were disposed to furnish him with necessary means, when a great calamity came upon him: he was sent for to take the last farewell of a dying father.

He hastened to Urbin, hoping still to preserve the object of his tenderness, but he arrived only in time to see him draw his last breath. The dream of glory which Raphael had cherished lost half its prestige, for henceforth alone in the world, he would have neither father nor mother to be proud of his success. To arouse him from the depression caused by this terrible blow, the Duke d'Urbin urged him to paint some pictures; and, with his soul filled with grief, Raphael painted a

Christ on the Mount of Olives, — a Christ the type of sadness and resignation. Two *Virgins* followed, then a *St. George*, and a *St. Michael*, now in the Museum of the Louvre.

His friends advised him to travel, in order to dissipate the melancholy, which was only increased by dwelling in his native village. He went to Perugia, hoping to find some of the young people with whom he had studied; but Perugino was at Rome, and his pupils had dispersed. However, it was pleasant for Sanzio to be again in Perouse; and he complied with the earnest wishes of friends in leaving some traces of his passage there. Two or three pictures, and a fresco representing Christ in his glory, surrounded by angels and saints, increased his reputation very much, and on his return to Florence he received numerous orders.

The *Virgin*, known as *La Belle Jardinière*, still to be seen in the Museum of the Louvre, is considered as one of the best of Raphael's first method. He left the care of finishing the drapery of the *Assumption* which he had commenced, and which was wanted immediately, to Ghirlandaio, one of his friends. While he was at work upon it, a letter from his uncle Bramante, architect of Julius II., called him to Rome.

The Pope had had palaces and temples built, and he wished to have them decorated. Bramante, having heard of the talent of the young Sanzio, seized this opportunity of making his fortune. Raphael joyfully accepted the invitation; and as soon as Bramante remarks, Bra- *[text obscured]* the that fame had not exaggerated the talent of his relation, he presented him to the Pope.

Julius was charmed with the sweetness, modesty, and good manners of the young artist, and allowed him to make trial of his pencil upon one of the halls of the Vatican. Raphael was transported with this unexpected good fortune, and set himself to work with a certainty of success. His first painting at Rome was the homage of gratitude to his master, Perugino: he chose for his subject the School of Athens, and painted the portrait of him, whom he regarded as his second father, as one of the Greek philosophers, whose pupils, among whom was Raphael himself, were listening attentively to his instruction.

Julius was so much charmed by the sight of this beautiful fresco, that, carried away by his impetuosity, he declared that there was nothing beautiful in his palace, and ordered all the frescoes which decorated it to be scraped off. Among these paintings were many of Perugino's; and Raphael, feeling the sadness which such treatment would cause his old master, obtained permission to have the hall of Charlemagne spared, because it was there that Perugino had labored the most.

Raphael continued his work, happy in meriting the approbation of the Pope. He painted four frescoes for *La Camera della Segnatura;* the subjects comprehended Theology, Poetry, Philosophy, and Jurisprudence; i. e., the representation of those high pursuits which belong

Christ of more elevated tendencies of human nature. The *School of Athens* represented Philosophy; and the young artist had given so true an expression to each of the philosophers, that it was easy for those who knew the doctrine of these sages to give a name to each.

"Theology (erroneously called *La Disputa del Sacramento*) is divided into two parts: the upper half represents the glory of heaven, in the solemn manner of the early painters. In the centre is the Savior, with outstretched arms, throned on the clouds; on his right, the Virgin, sweet and affectionate in expression and mien, bows before her divine Son in heartfelt adoration; on the left, St. John the Baptist. Over the Savior appears a half figure of the Almighty, and below him hovers the Dove of the Holy Spirit. Around this group, in a half circle, sit the patriarchs, apostles, and saints — sublime, dignified figures, with the noblest solemnity and repose in their appearance. Over them hover on each side three angel youths; below these, as if supporting the clouds, are a multitude of angel heads, and four boy-angels hold the books of the Evangelists beside the Dove. In the lower half of the picture we see an assembly of the most celebrated theologians of the Church. All these figures, especially as regards the expression of the heads, are completed with most striking and characteristic individuality, and are enlivened by a conscientious study of detail." These pictures caused Raphael to be considered the first painter of his time.

While Sanzio was creating these sublime works, Bramante, who for a long time had been jealous of the affection of Julius II. for Michael Angelo, persuaded the pontiff to desire his sculptor to paint frescoes rather than make statues; he thought that his nephew would certainly carry off the palm, and humiliate the severe Buonarotti. But nothing was impossible to the genius of Michael Angelo, as we have already seen; and the paintings of the vaulted ceiling of the Sistine Chapel placed him in the same rank as Raphael, although of a different style. However, Raphael had nothing to do with this wish of the Pope, which caused so much disappointment and trouble to the sculptor. The young man, contented with his lot, which certainly was a very happy one, never thought of disputing the favor of the Pope with Michael Angelo; and it is much to be regretted that the intrigues of ordinary men made rivals, if not enemies, of these two immortal geniuses.

Young men from all parts of the country came to Raphael, desirous to study under his direction; and he was much beloved by his pupils, whose growing talents contributed not a little to his glory, by enabling him to undertake a much larger number of works than his own strength would have permitted him to accomplish. It seems as if this incomparable painter, having a presentiment of his premature death, wished to hasten the completion of labors which were to transmit his name to posterity.

Augustino Chizi, a rich merchant of Sienna, having built a palace on the borders of the Tiber, Sanzio undertook to decorate it, and painted such marvellous heads of prophets and sybils that all Rome wished to admire them. Two pictures, a *Galatea* and a *Psyche*, appeared almost at the same time; which, however, did not prevent the rapid advancement of the decoration of the halls of the Vatican: the *Miracola di Bolsena*, the *Deliverance of St. Peter*, and the *Punishment of Heliodorus*, display the genius of Raphael in all its brilliancy.

The death of Julius II. deprived our artist of an enlightened and benevolent protector; but Leo X., who succeeded this pontiff, ordered Raphael to continue his works upon the Vatican. No less zealous for the arts than his predecessor, he feared this young artist might go elsewhere to paint. Raphael showed himself worthy of the distinction. His picture of *Attila marching upon Rome*, and that in which St. Leon stops the conqueror at the foot of Mount Valerio, were not inferior to his preceding pictures.

At Bramante's death, Leo X. chose Raphael for his architect, and the court of the Vatican was continued upon the model given by this artist, who wished to ornament its porticoes in the antique manner found in the Baths of Titus, and studied by him with extreme care. Raphael made the designs of these porticoes to the *Loggie*, with the assistance of Jean d'Udine, one of his best pupils. The Loggie are open galleries built round three sides of the court of St. Damascus (the older portion of the Vatican palace). They consist of three stories, the two lower formed of vaulted arcades, the upper by an elegant colonnade. The first arcade of the middle story was decorated with paintings and stuccoes under Raphael's direction; it leads to the Stanze, so that one master's work here succeeds to another. It was Jean d'Udine who painted the instruments of a magnificent *St. Cecilia*, destined for the chapel of St. Giovanni in Monte, at Bologna.

The case which contained this picture was addressed to Francia, the old friend of Raphael, with a request that he would attend to the unpacking, and repair whatever injury the voyage should have caused to the picture. Francia felt very much flattered by the trust committed to him; but the *St. Cecilia* had no need of his pencil.

Vasari, in his History of Painters, mentions the sending of this picture to Francia, and adds, that this artist was enchanted to see a work of Raphael, of whom he had heard so much praise since they left the studio of Perugino. The arrival of the picture was announced to him by a very affectionate letter from his friend Sanzio, and accompanied by a design of the *Nativity*, from the hand of Raphael. "But," added Vasari, 'Francia was stupefied at the sight of this admirable *St. Cecilia*, and, feeling that he was deceived in considering himself a master, became melancholy, and soon died.

There is reason to believe that Vasari was mistaken

on this point; for, according to other writers of the time, Francia lived nineteen years after seeing Raphael's work, and he was then tolerably advanced. We prefer this version to the other, for Francia's soul was too loyal and generous to be accessible to envy.

The reputation of Raphael had become European. The celebrated German painter, Albert Durer, sent him his portrait, painted in water colors. Raphael returned the compliment by begging Albert Durer to accept some drawings, so highly finished that they could be considered real pictures. As to sending his own portrait, he had no time to paint it, as he had told Francia, when he received a present of his portrait.

Albert Durer was not only a painter of great talent, but he was likewise a very skilful engraver. When Raphael understood the method by which this master transmitted his works to posterity, he encouraged Marc Antonio Raimondi to study this improved engraving; and the young man succeeding beyond his hopes, he employed him to engrave a great number of designs, which were soon scattered through Germany, France, and Holland, and were everywhere admired.

Having finished the second hall of the Vatican, Raphael gave the drawings for the third hall to his pupils, and contented himself with overseeing and correcting their work. The subjects of these frescoes are the Victory of St. Leon over the Saracens, the Justification of Pope Leo III., and the Coronation of Charlemagne.

Julio Romano, Francesco Penni, Jean d'Udine, Polidore da Caravaggio, and many other young artists, distinguished themselves in this work.

The fourth hall was also commenced, and Raphael, in the fresco which represents the naval battle in the port of Ostia, gained over the Saracens, and in which the burning of Borgo Vecchio is stopped by the benediction of Pope Leo IV., exceeded his previous works.

By the boldness of expression which Raphael gave to this picture, he made it terrific; his sweet and graceful manner was so much changed, that Michael Angelo, seeing it, cried out, —

"He has seen my paintings!"

And so he had, for in spite of the precautions which Buonarotti had taken (when forced by Leo X. to finish the decoration of the Sistine chapel) that no one should see his work before it was finished, the architect Bramante introduced Raphael secretly, in Michael Angelo's absence, so that he had leisure to study the energetic and sublime paintings of this old sculptor.

However it might be, Raphael's triumph was complete; and Leo X., not knowing how he could recompense such a genius, offered him a cardinal's hat, and at the same time Cardinal di St. Bibiane offered him the hand of his niece, one of the richest and handsomest women of Rome. Raphael, not knowing which of the offers to accept, refused neither, and asked time to decide.

It is certain that with the creation of some new piece

almost daily, the illustrious artist had no time to determine promptly upon so weighty a matter. He received orders from all quarters; princes and kings demanded his pictures, or even less than that, a drawing only, if he could not send pictures.

The Pope had appointed him architect, then director-in-chief of antiquities, and these two places increased his labors. He not only directed the excavations in Rome, but, knowing that the Roman art was derived from the Greek, he sent artists into Southern Italy and Greece, to collect and send to him all the designs, or precious fragments, they could find. He had to correspond with all these young people, to classify all that he received from them; and if we think of the decoration of the Vatican halls, and the court of the Loggie, with which he was busily occupied, and besides that he must now and then paint a picture for a church, a convent, or a palace, we find it difficult to understand how he could have done it all, notwithstanding the coöperation of zealous and devoted pupils.

These pupils were numerous; and when Raphael went with them to the Vatican or the Loggie, many of his admirers joined them, making a very imposing train of attendants. One day, Michael Angelo, who always went alone, seeing Raphael surrounded by this brilliant suite, murmured with some bitterness, —

"Accompanied like a king!"

"Alone, like a hangman!" replied Raphael.

This meeting furnished the subject for a large picture, by one of the best French artists, M. H. Vernet: it is in the Luxembourg Museum.

The nuns of St. Marie di Palermo begged Raphael to paint a *Christ bearing his Cross,* for their convent; and he produced a Man-God, whose sufferings, resignation, and charity were expressed with so much truth, that those who saw it cried out, "It is a miracle!" The enthusiasm was so great, that Raphael hastened to pack it, fearing it would not be sent to its destination.

The vessel which carried this *chef-d'œuvre* was beaten by a tempest, and cast upon the rocks, where it broke. The crew all perished; the merchandise was lost, excepting one case, which the waves carried to the coast of Genoa. Some fishermen, seeing it, put a boat to sea, and took the case into port, where it was opened. There they found Raphael's picture intact: the winds and waves had respected it!

The Genoese, thinking they could retain this strayed picture, were much delighted; but the good nuns of Palermo, uneasy at not having their picture, finally learned that, by a marvellous chance, it had arrived safe and sound at Genoa. They immediately claimed it, and were refused; they then complained to the Pope, who had some difficulty in causing it to be restored to the right owners.

It was a day of great rejoicing for the convent of Notre Dame when the *Christ bearing his Cross* was placed in their church; nothing as beautiful had ever been seen in Palermo, and the monastery was visited by all the artists and amateurs of Sicily.

This picture, *della Spasimo*, as they called it, was ranked among the things which every stranger passing through Palermo was expected to see. The good sisters were very proud of it, but they soon found that obscurity is the surest guardian to happiness.

Philip IV., travelling through Sicily, saw their treasure, and, though a king, was jealous of it. As a king has many means of gratifying his covetousness, one day, or rather one night, *Lo Spasimo* was carried from the chapel and taken to Spain. What surprise and grief the next morning! The nuns complained bitterly of the theft, and again had recourse to the Pope; but Philip, rejoicing in his trick, had no idea of giving up his prize. However, he acknowledged that the convent was right in complaining, and resolved to indemnify it for the loss. He offered an annuity of a thousand piastres, which was accepted, and thus the picture became his legitimate property.

This picture was sent to Paris by Napoleon's generals, during the war with Spain, and remained there six years; but in 1816 it was given back, and placed in the royal gallery of Madrid, of which it is still the finest ornament.

Raphael painted the victories of Constantine, in the great hall of the Vatican. This was his first attempt in the grandiose manner, which is called his third style. In this he succeeded equally as well as in the other two styles, and it would be impossible to describe the enthusiasm which these paintings excited.

Pope Leo X. desired Raphael to draw designs for the tapestries which he intended to have made in Flanders, for the Sistine chapel. Sanzio drew and colored magnificent cartoons, which he delivered to two of his best pupils, Van Orlay of Brussels, and Coxis of Malines, giving them orders to superintend these rich tapestries. These cartoons are now to be seen in the palace of Hampton Court, in England.

After this, Sanzio painted his famous picture of the *Transfiguration of Christ.* The picture is regarded as the best of all his masterpieces. One can never weary of admiring its beautiful figures; those heads, of such varied expression, of style so noble and elevated, as if enlightened by a ray of divine glory: but the head of Christ exceeds all that art has produced in majesty and beauty.

This most sublime creation of Raphael was his last. The *Transfiguration* was unfinished when he died.

According to an old document, found in Rome, the cause of his premature death was as follows: One day, when Raphael, who was indisposed, was working in the palace Farnese, he received an order to go to the Pope. Fearing that his holiness might be waiting for him, he ran as quickly as possible, and arrived at the Vatican covered with perspiration, and out of breath. He remained for some time, discussing the plan of St. Peter's, which then preoccupied Leo X. He became chilly, perspiration was checked, and he returned home, seized with a violent fever, which conducted him to the tomb in a few days.

Raphael was very delicate; one might say that he was all spirit and genius, and it is difficult to understand how, working as much as he did, he could attain the age of thirty-seven years. Too great a love of pleasure also contributed to hasten his end, which he saw approaching, if not without regret, at least without a murmur. He told his pupils that he had but a few moments to pass with them; he consoled them in their profound affection, addressed words of encouragement to each of them, predicted their success, took leave of them, and asked the succor of religion. His calmness never left him, and those who saw him so smiling could not believe that he was so soon to finish his brilliant career. Finally, on the 7th of April, on Holy Friday of 1520, he gave up his soul to Him who had so richly endowed it.

The Pope, being informed that his beloved painter was no more, fell into profound dejection, from which he rallied only by shedding abundant tears: he declared that he had lost the most beautiful jewel of his tiara. All Rome was in mourning; every one wept as if he had lost a relation, or a friend. Raphael was laid out in his studio, and the wonderful picture of the *Transfiguration* was placed at his head. The number of visitors, which was immense, could not restrain the testimony of their admiration of the picture, or their tears at the sight of the beautiful young man, sleeping in death, who, if God had permitted him to attain the ordinary limits of human life, would have done so much for art.

Leo X. ordered that the body of the artist should be deposited in the Pantheon, as he had desired, and Cardinal Bembo was charged with writing his epitaph.

According to Raphael's will, his fortune, which was great, was divided between Francesco Penni, surnamed *il Frattore*, because he had had the direction of all the affairs of the great artist, and Giulio Pippi, better known as Julio Romano, one who was dearest to his heart. Both were Raphael's pupils, and had the charge of finishing the works which he left incomplete; they acquitted themselves of the duty with religious respect.

One of the clauses of this will appropriated a considerable sum to the restoration of one of the chapels of the church of Santa Maria della Rotunda; and one of the houses which Raphael owned in Rome bears an inscription, stating that this real estate guarantees the payment of the annual rent due to this chapel.

For a long time the academicians of St. Luke thought they possessed the cranium of Raphael, but Doctor Gall, to whom the cranium was submitted when in Rome, declared that it was impossible that it should have belonged to a man of genius. Differences having arisen between the Academy of St. Luke and another learned society, which claimed this head as that of its founder, the Pope ordered that the mortal remains of the illustrious painter should be exhumed.

Then it was seen that the skeleton of Raphael had not been mutilated. His precious bones were exposed some days to public view, then put into a marble case presented by the Pope, and, with great pomp and ceremony, placed where, according to his wish, he had been at first interred; that is to say, in that same chapel of Santa Maria della Rotunda, called the chapel *della Madonna del Sasso*, which the great painter had ornamented with magnificent works. Never was an artist more esteemed, or more generally beloved, than Raphael, nor was there ever a person more deserving of admiration and love. He remained simple in the midst of grandeur, modest at the height of glory, faithful to gratitude and friendship. By his rare qualities he enhanced the brilliancy of his incomparable genius.

CORREGGIO.

Antonio Allegri owed his surname of Correggio to the village of Correggio, where he was born in 1494, of an honest, but poor family. He passed his infancy and youth in obscurity, but he had received of God that creative genius which, without a teacher, without models, with no borrowed assistance, knows how to produce admirable works. Correggio found within himself the talent which he developed by labor and the study of nature.

Which his first works are, is not known, but all the compositions which he has left are masterpieces. He consecrated the fruit of his first productions to the sustenance of his parents: when married, and the father of a numerous family, he redoubled his ardor, that no one under his humble roof should suffer for the necessaries of life. Gentle, modest, and excessively timid, Antonio never thought a picture sufficiently well finished, and was satisfied with whatever recompense he received for his work. Without doubt he had heard of those happy painters, whose pictures were covered with gold by amateurs, and whom princes loaded with presents and honors. To think of such success for himself was out of the question: he wished but for one thing, to be able to make his wife and children comfortable. Yet he was conscious of his own merit, for one day, after having admired a picture of Raphael's, he cried out, on comparing it with his own work, —

"I, also, am a painter!"

Correggio's principal works are at Parma. He painted some magnificent frescoes in the grand tribune of the cathedral of that city, for which he received in payment a few sacks of corn, some wood, and a little money. Afterwards he painted the cupola of St. John, and that of the dome of the cathedral. The *Ascension of Jesus Christ*, and the *Assumption of the Virgin*, represented there, are two admirable compositions, in which, besides the majesty and grace which characterize all his works, he had displayed a wonderful knowledge of foreshortening, inasmuch as he never had any instruction, and had never studied the *chefs-d'œuvre* of Rome and Venice.

Having deducted from his modest salary the sum rigorously necessary for the subsistence of his family, Correggio used the remainder in the purchase of the canvas and colors which he needed for new pictures, and continued his work with exemplary courage. His wife sustained him in the hope of better days; she recognized and admired the genius which was unappreciated until after his death.

In this way Antonio painted many pictures, the most celebrated of which are, the *Nativity of our Savior*, *St. Jerome*, the *Magdalen*, a *Holy Family*, the *Marriage of St. Catherine*, now in the Museum of the Louvre; a *Christ on the Mount of Olives*, which the unfortunate artist was obliged to give up for a debt of four crowns; some mythological scenes, and the *Night*, in the Gallery of Dresden, which, except to Raphael's *Virgin*, is considered as the most precious jewel in that rich casket.

But all the assiduity of Correggio was insufficient to drive misery from his humble dwelling. The children were growing, and bread was becoming necessary for those for whom the milk of the mother had for a time sufficed. Sickness also came upon the family, and there was no bread in the house. The provisions were almost exhausted, and Antonio, fearing to hear his children say those cruel words, which, several times, had almost broken his heart, "I am hungry," set out to procure some assistance.

There were sixty crowns due to him in Parma: this seemed an enormous sum to people reduced to misery. Correggio had several times asked payment, but the subaltern employers, with whom he dealt, always deferred a settlement. Disagreeable as it was to ask so often for his due, he armed himself with courage, and, taking his cane, went to Parma, where, after much trouble and disputing, he finally obtained a settlement. They paid him the sixty crowns in copper money; and the poor artist, happy in the thought of the joy which he should carry to his wife and children, gayly took the heavy load upon his shoulders and set out.

The heat was excessive, and Correggio, enfeebled by fatigues and privations of all sorts, was soon obliged to slacken his pace. He thought of waiting till the morrow, but the idea that his children were crying for bread caused him to press forward: he arrived at his house before sunset, panting for breath, bathed in sweat, and nearly exhausted. Being very thirsty, and having nothing but water, he drank a large quantity: that night he was seized with a violent fever, which caused the death of this great man, who was not yet forty years old.

Nature has reproduced herself in all the works of this eminent artist, and none of the geniuses spoken of in this history, not even the divine Raphael, has succeeded in giving to his compositions the grace which characterizes those of Correggio. Without having learned the secrets of his art from any master, without having studied antiquity, without having left his own country, Antonio Allegri raised himself by his genius to the rank of one of the first painters in the world. If he can be reproached with slight incorrectness, and sometimes a certain singularity in the air of the head, the attitudes and contrasts, he overbalances these defects by such great qualities, that they seem only as shadows destined to throw out the light. The rich arrangement of his compositions, an elevated taste, delicate and tender pencilling, a large and powerful manner, an enchanting color, and something vague, sweet, and soft, which the Italians call *morbidezza*, and which can hardly be expressed in English, gave an inimitable charm to his pictures.

Contemplating the beautiful works of Correggio in the Paris museums, one understands all that there was unutterable and bitter at the same time in the words of Antonio, the poor countryman, who hardly earned as much as the mercenary laborer of the soil: "I, also, am a painter!" And one is seized with profound pity for this man, so grand, so simple, so good, whose crown of genius was a crown of thorns. It is not rare to see artists expiate glory by grief, and he will not be the only one whose fate will excite the sympathy of our readers.

Correggio has left only a small number of drawings, and his only pupil was Francesco Mazzuoli, who became celebrated under the name of Parmesan. After the death of this incomparable man many painters studied his works, and were inspired by his genius.

PAUL VERONESE.

Paul Cagliari was born at Verona, in 1532. His father, who was a sculptor, desiring that his son might pursue the same calling, taught him the principles of drawing. Paul manifested a great inclination for this study, but he could not succeed in working clay and wax, and showed very little taste for this essential part of the art. His ill success did not trouble him: he wished to be a painter, and so often deserted the studio of his father for that of his uncle, Antonio Badile, that he was finally permitted to leave it entirely.

Antonio, though not a first class painter, was not wanting in talent, and the young Cagliari had so great a desire to learn, and so much natural facility, that his progress astonished, not only his family, but the amateurs of painting who frequented the house of Master Badile. Every one predicted brilliant success, and Antonio, one day, said to him, —

"Despite your youth, you are more skilful than I, my dear nephew; but it will not be sufficient that you are the first artist of Verona: there are in the world many great works to be studied, many masters to be consulted, and as I depend more upon your talent than mine to bring my name into honor, I advise you to visit Venice, Florence, and Rome. One has never done well enough, when one can do better; one never knows enough, when he can learn more."

This advice was quite to Paul's mind, for he had long desired to travel. But his father's ideas were different; he was growing old, and, preferring the solid to the brilliant, he would have liked that the young man should establish himself near him, and by his labor create and assure a fixed, though modest, position. Antonio Badile was obliged repeatedly to point out the great destiny in reserve for his son, and to urge him to decide upon his departure.

At length Paul left Verona, promising himself not to return until he should have visited all Italy, and become a great artist. The Cardinal di Gonzaga, who had seen some of his works, called him to Mantua, and the young painter, happy to commence his career under the patronage of so powerful and enlightened a man, accepted this invitation with gratitude. The cardinal treated him, not as a beginner who gave great hopes, but as an artist already celebrated; and this reception inspired Cagliari with an ardent desire to show himself worthy of such distinguished benevolence, and he immediately began to work.

The *Temptation of St. Anthony*, which he made for the church of Mantua, excited public admiration, and the cardinal made him brilliant offers to remain with him. Cagliari would have accepted, for he loved his protector, and he could hardly expect more flattering applause or more perfect kindness; but he remembered his uncle's advice, and begged the cardinal to permit him to follow it. The cardinal made no great opposition; and the young artist, laden with presents, departed, filled with gratitude for the noble hospitality which had been accorded him at Mantua.

At that time there were many great painters at Venice — Titian, Giorgione, and Tintoretto: Paul went to Venice, where he soon gained a good reputation. Tintoretto, who, by patience and perseverance, had acquired a remarkable talent, and who had had much difficulty in overcoming the obstacles which rivals opposed to him, was then occupied in paintings ordered by the Senate. When the Senate saw Veronese's pictures, in which they observed as much boldness as grace, as much force as ease, and a faithful rendering of nature, they associated him with Tintoretto.

Tintoretto was not jealous at seeing himself associated with a strange artist; Cagliari, on his part, professing the highest esteem for Tintoretto, who was self-taught, did not fear to manifest it; and as Tintoretto worked for the love of work, Paul Veronese for the love of glory, and neither of the two demeaned themselves to vile calculations of interest, their rivalry was only a noble emulation, in which was no mean sentiment.

Among the works which Cagliari produced at this time is a fresco, representing Queen Esther before Ahasuerus. This magnificent composition excited great enthusiasm in Venice, and the republic engaged the author of it to decorate the Library of St. Mark. Paul, who had followed the manner of Titian, of Giorgione, and of Tintoretto, his rival, now began to form a manner of his own, in which he could give himself up entirely to the inspirations of his genius.

Thenceforward Veronese was considered one of the most able painters in the world. But he did not allow himself to be blinded by success; he left Venice, and went to Rome, not doubting that the studies of the *chefs-d'œuvre* of Michael Angelo and of Raphael might be profitable to him. He admired the sublime compositions of those illustrious masters, and spent considerable time in Rome, occupied in the contemplation of these wonders. He might, perhaps, have forgotten himself for years, had he not promised to return to Venice. The Senate reminded him of his engagement through the ambassador Girolamo Grimani, in whose company he had made the journey.

On his return to Venice, Paul painted the *Apotheosis of Venice,* with his enthusiasm exalted by the remembrance of the beautiful paintings he had seen: this picture received unanimous applause. Antonio Badile was not deceived in predicting that his nephew would be a great artist, and Veronese had done well in following the advice of this worthy relation: "One is never sufficiently learned when there is more to be learned."

Other works, still more remarkable, succeeded the *Apotheosis of Venice*. Paul Veronese excelled in grand compositions. His vivacious, elevated, and fruitful imagination, his delicate, sure, and easy pencil, his talent to decorate the background of his paintings, his taste for rich and varied ornament, were better adapted to immense than to more restrained pictures. The *Banquets* of this artist are all that can be desired in this style.

The most celebrated of these pictures is the *Marriage of Cana*, which he painted for the refectory of San Georgio Maggiore at Venice, now in the Louvre. It is thirty feet wide by twenty feet high. The scene is a brilliant hall, surrounded by majestic pillars. The tables at which the guests are seated form three sides of a parallelogram; the guests, about one hundred and thirty in number, are supposed to be almost entirely contemporary portraits, of admirable execution. The most remarkable feature is a group of musicians in the centre, in front, around a table, also portraits. Paul Veronese himself is playing the violoncello; Tintoretto a smaller instrument; the gray-haired Titian, in a red damask robe, the contra-bass.

Another not less remarkable composition is the *Feast of the Levite*, in the Academy at Venice (formerly in the refectory of San Giovanni e Paolo). Louis XIV., having heard of the beauty of this picture, offered the reverend fathers a large sum for it, which was refused. They could not think of giving up this splendid picture, the admiration of all the visitors to the convent. The king, without complaining, let them see how much he regretted their refusal. Louis XIV. was then in the fulness of his power; and as the displeasure of these fathers was of little consequence to the republic, provided that it could satisfy the King of France, the picture was taken from the convent in the night, and sent to Paris.

Almost all the capitals of Europe are proud to show some picture of this great painter, and engravings have rendered them popular. He would have left many more, if death had not cut him off in the plenitude of his talent, and while the friends of art were counting upon years of success. When, on Easter Sunday, 1588, it was announced that Paul Veronese, who had been sick for a few days, was dying, the joy with which the people of Venice were celebrating the day was changed to mourning. In him they regretted not only the eminent artist, but the *good* man, in the full meaning of the word. If the higher class recognized him as one of them, boasting of his talent, his high-mindedness, and the aristocracy of his language and manners, the lower class also boasted that he never disdained them; they spoke of the goodness of his heart, of his affability, and related traits of benevolence and generosity which were unknown during his life.

How admirable is the alliance of genius with virtue! Posterity will ever delight in rendering homage to those whose foreheads are irradiated with this double crown.

No painter could display all the richness of his art better than Paul Veronese; his compositions are marvellously imagined, and not less marvellously executed; his positions are true, noble, and graceful; his types are of varied and rare beauty, his color extensive, and his draperies of a taste and magnificence which belong only to him. However, it is to be regretted that the painter, carried away by his genius, should have failed in historical fitness, by giving to his personages the faces and costumes of the celebrities of his own times, forgetting the singular anachronisms which result therefrom. Sometimes he painted for practice only; and for this reason, all his pictures are not equally beautiful.

Paul Veronese has left a great number of drawings, which amateurs consider as very precious, and never tire of admiring their fine arrangement and numerous details. He has also left some crayon studies.

The painter honored his art by the noble and disinterested manner in which he exercised it: the matter of money-making never entered into any of his plans, and he never thought of what his pictures would bring, excepting when he wished to aid some unfortunate person, or some artist without resources.

It is said, that, being much pleased by the manner in which he was received in a country-house in the suburbs of Venice, he testified his gratitude by a present of one of his pictures. During his sojourn in that villa, he secretly painted a picture representing the family of Darius at the feet of Alexander, and left it in the chamber when he departed. In this picture, twenty figures, of life-size, were painted in a very short time, and by snatches; but it is none the less a *chef-d'œuvre*.

Paul Veronese died at the age of fifty-eight years. He left two sons, Charles and Gabriel, who both followed the art of painting. Charles had much natural taste, and might have equalled his father, had not too severe application abridged his life. Gabriel painted only as an amateur; however, with the assistance of his uncle, Benoit Cagliari, he completed many unfinished pictures left by Paul Veronese. Benoit, Paul's brother, had often worked with the great artist; yet, modest as industrious, he little thought of the reputation he could acquire by claiming some of the works which they had done in common.

Alexander Veronese was not of the same family. The surname of Veronese was given to him, as to Paul, from the city of Verona, his birthplace. Vigorous coloring, correct drawing, and graceful pencilling distinguish the pictures of this artist; but they cannot be compared to those of the painter whose history we have given.

GUIDO.

Guido Reni was born at Bologna, in 1575. Daniel Reni, his father, was a flute-player, and destined him, when quite young, to music. He applied himself to it to satisfy his parents; but he had much more taste for painting: when he knew that no one saw him, he left his piano to draw figures on the walls, which he rubbed out as soon as he heard the least noise. With all his care, he was detected; and his father, understanding that he would never make anything but an ordinary musician, and hoping to make a great painter of him, placed him in Denis Calvart's studio.

He never repented this step: the young Reni's uncommon powers, added to great application, soon made him one of the best pupils of the Dutch painter. Denis was not without talent; but he had neither the boldness of touch nor the facility of execution which Guido possessed, and in a few years saw himself surpassed by his pupil. About this time, Louis Carracci, aided by his cousins, Augustine and Hannibal, founded a new school of painting at Bologna, which was to compete with that of Master Calvart, and profess entirely different principles.

The manner of the Carracci, approved by some connoisseurs, greatly displeased Denis, who declared himself their enemy, and threatened to send away, in disgrace, any of his pupils who should dare to imitate any of these new masters. Meanwhile Guido had been struck by the peculiar character which went out of this school. Denis Calvart was attached to the manner of Caravaggio, who had substituted the servile imitation of nature for the study of the beauties of antiquity, and the admirable compositions of Raphael, of Michael Angelo, and of Titian. The Carracci had risen against this pretended reform; they wished to lead back painting to the state from whence Caravaggio had made it depart, to restore the purity of drawing, the pleasant and flattering brilliancy to color, and to replace the freaks of imagination by learned and graceful compositions.

Guido, enlightened by his own genius, understood that the efforts of the Carracci would be crowned with success, and became the secret partisan of their method. It was difficult for him to endure the bitter criticisms which Calvart made of their works; however, his mild and timid disposition, and the respect which he had for his master, prevented his making any manifestation. The jealousy of Denis grew bitter in proportion as the reputation of the Carracci increased; and, seeing that his pupils did not sympathize with him as he wished, he burst into passionate reproaches and ill usage.

After one of these scenes, which took place almost daily, Guido left Denis Calvart, in company with Albano, his protégé, Guercino, and some other young persons, and went to the school of Carracci, where they were admitted without difficulty.

Louis and Hannibal were not slow in appreciating the talent of Guido; and, foreseeing that he would do honor to themselves, they taught him with the utmost care and attention. Guido improved wonderfully: if he had made progress under the direction of Calvart, he could not fail to astonish his new masters, whose method appeared to him as simple as excellent.

Soon after adopting it, he painted the picture of *Orpheus and Eurydice*, a noble work, with a vivid and true coloring, great skill in *chiaro-scuro*, and an easy, yet bold touch. Young as Guido was, he was considered a good artist, and the Carracci put his picture in competition with that of Caravaggio.

Michael Angelo Caravaggio was not a man to bear what he considered an insult patiently, and war broke out between these two schools. Guido, the object of the teasing and vexatious annoyance of the partisans of this artist, learned that it is no easy matter to be a renowned painter before being a man; but he showed much wisdom and moderation in many encounters, and answered the vindictiveness of his enemies by saying,—

"I prefer the manner of the Carracci to that of Caravaggio, because I like the light of day better than the darkness of night. I have no objection to his following his taste, only let him permit me to follow mine."

Finally, the justice of his remarks quieted his enemies,

and they allowed him to work in peace. The felicitations which Guido received encouraged him to deserve them. He did not, like many young people, imagine that, because he had been successful, he had nothing to learn; on the contrary, he redoubled his exertions, and, not content with merely studying the works of great masters, he wished to imitate them. He copied the beautiful picture of *St. Cecilia*, which Raphael sent to Bologna, and presented it to Cardinal Facchinetti, his protector. People expatiated upon the beauty of this picture, and the facility with which the young artist had imitated the incomparable Raphael; and Guido, having sent two other pictures to Rome about the same time, was invited to go thither.

Guido, who had long dreamed of Rome, the beloved city of artists, was overjoyed. His friend Albano, already there, had mentioned him to several celebrated painters. Albano had not forgotten all the kindnesses he had received from Guido while they were with Denis Calvart.

Josépin gave Guido Reni, in whom he saw not only the friend of Albano, but the adversary of Caravaggio, a very favorable reception. He presented him to several illustrious personages, who knew of him through his works. The fine appearance of the young artist, his elegant manners, intelligence, and charming conversation, completed what the sight of his pictures had commenced, and he was not long in becoming the painter *à-la-mode.* All drawing-rooms were open to him, and people vied with each other who should first order pictures from him.

Josépin had never pardoned Caravaggio the victory gained in a competition between them; and, believing Guido Reni more capable than himself to revenge this defeat, he intrigued with Cardinal Borghese, so that a *Crucifixion of St. Peter* was taken from Caravaggio, and given to Guido.

No sooner had Caravaggio, who was absent from Rome, heard what had happened, than he challenged Josépin to a duel. Josépin refused, saying his title as gentleman would not permit him to fight with a plebeian. Caravaggio, whose temper was violent and impetuous, was excited beyond measure at such an answer. He resolved to go to Malta, and get the order of knighthood, so as to deprive his enemy of all pretext for refusing his challenge. But, before leaving, he wished to see Guido, whom he hated, and permitted himself to insult him. Reni answered in the same tone, and Caravaggio, whose fury deprived him of reason, seized a sword, and wounded him badly in the face.

After this exploit he fled from Rome, and, not giving up the desire of being revenged on Josépin, he went to Malta, where he obtained the title of knight, as he desired. His violent temper led him into many tragic adventures, which ended in a miserable death.

Guido recommenced work as soon as he was cured of

his wounds. Paul V. selected him to decorate his private chapel, at the palace of Monte-Cavallo. A *View of Paradise*, which he painted upon the arched ceiling, and an *Annunciation*, behind the grand altar, charmed the Pope, who never wearied of admiring the facility with which his painter worked, and the freedom of his mind in sustaining conversation, while his pencil was never still for a moment. Paul V. went to see his chapel every day, and took great pleasure in conversing with Guido, as Julius II. had with Michael Angelo, and Leo X. with Raphael.

The favor which Guido Reni enjoyed excited the jealousy of some of his rivals. They calumniated him at the pontifical court; and, having succeeded in influencing the Pope's treasurer, they caused the artist much trouble. Guido, humiliated at being obliged to demand a price for his work, and to barter with a man whose ill will was but too evident, left Rome without saying a word to any one, and returned to Bologna.

His fellow-citizens received him with the greatest cordiality, thanked him for returning to them, and gave him orders for pictures. He then painted the *Apotheosis of St. Dominico*, and the *Massacre of the Innocents*. These two pictures were not finished when Guido received a visit from the Legate of Bologna, who was sent by the Pope to beg him to go back to Rome.

Paul V. had heard of the departure of his favorite artist with as much pain as surprise; and, not knowing the route he had taken, he sent couriers in all directions, with orders to bring him back, after having promised reparation for all the injuries and annoyances which he had sustained. But Reni was too far in advance of the couriers to be overtaken, and continued his route peaceably to Bologna; meanwhile, the Pope threatened disgrace to those who had offended his painter, and thus deprived Rome of eminent talent. As soon as he received the news of Guido's arrival in his native town, he wrote to his legate, ordering him to send Guido back immediately. But Guido was not disposed to yield to the wishes of the legate, and it was not until after long negotiations that he at length consented to return to Rome.

When the cardinals were informed of his arrival, they sent their carriages before him, using the ceremonies observed at the entrance of ambassadors and great persons, and Paul received him with testimonials of the most sincere affection. He granted him a large pension, gave him a magnificent equipage, and made the enemies of the painter understand that they would not be safe in attempting anything against him in future.

Having finished the entire decorations of Monte-Cavallo, Guido undertook that of Santa Maria Maggiore, and surpassed himself in this admirable work. His reputation increased so much, that, to obtain a picture, it was necessary to pay very dearly for the smallest, and even before it was commenced. Princes and kings disputed for his works, and, although he painted rapidly, he could not satisfy them all. We can judge of the rapidity with which he painted, by the fact that the Duke John Charles of Tuscany, having asked him to paint a head of Hercules, he did it in the presence of the prince, in less than two hours. For this head he received sixty pistoles, a gold chain, and the medallion of the duke.

Out of his studio, Guido was modest, affable, and full of indulgence and kindness; but as a painter, he was proud, ostentatious, and haughty. While working, he was magnificently dressed; and his pupils, ranged on either side, listened to his instructions in profound silence, saw him paint, prepared his pallet, and cleaned his brushes. He never set a price upon his pictures: he received a recompense, and not a salary. He would have lived in opulence, if he had not been led away by the passion for gambling, to which he sacrificed enormous sums.

New contrarieties, caused by the jealousies of others, induced Guido to leave Rome a second time, and repair to Bologna, where he painted the *Labors of Hercules*, some mythological scenes, a *Madonna*, and an *Annunciation*, which are thought to be remarkable composisitions. Each of these pictures had been ordered by a king or a sovereign prince. No artist ever enjoyed a higher reputation. He was invited to Naples, where important works were confided to him; but Ribera and other Neapolitan painters threatening to kill him if he did not leave the city, Guido, who knew that everything was to be feared from the envious, preferred to leave rather than be the object of their persecutions. It was at about this time that he began to give himself up to his unbridled passion for gambling. The fortune which he had so nobly acquired was swallowed up in a short time; he had recourse to usurers, and when this resource failed, he recommenced painting. It required vast sums of gold to feed the insatiable passion for gambling; and Guido, losing the respect he had hitherto had for his talent, careless of his glory, delivered pictures, which once he would have blushed to sign, to any who would buy them.

When fortune failed him, which was often the case, when he had played and lost some considerable sum upon his word, he hastened to acquit himself; and, under similar circumstances, he has been seen to paint three pictures in one day. While he was young and strong, he found in his inexhaustible fecundity the means of satisfying the emotions which soon become the life of the gambler; but when age and its emotions had weakened him, he had recourse to his friends, and made debts which he found it impossible to pay. Repeated demands wearied those friends who had at first offered their purses to him, and the artist, who might have been the happiest of all Italy, died of chagrin and misery in 1642.

The compositions of Guido are distinguished by richness and majesty. His pencilling was easy, light, and flowing, his touch vivid, graceful, and full of spirit, his drawing correct, his draperies are superb, his heads full of expression and nobleness, and his complexions fresh and life-like.

The most perfect works which he left are at Rome and Bologna. There are also fine ones at Geneva, Modena, and Ravenna, — indeed, in almost all European museums. There are many in the Louvre, among which is an *Annunciation*, painted for Queen Marie de Medicis.

Guido was also a sculptor, musician, and engraver. He engraved many religious subjects, painted by Hannibal, Carracci, Parmesan, and other artists, and many have engraved after him. His drawings are much esteemed for their boldness and delicacy of touch, the beauty of the heads, and the great taste displayed in the draperies.

DOMENICHINO.

Domenico Zampieri, surnamed Domenichino, was born at Bologna, October 21, 1581. His father was a shoemaker, who, thanks to his assiduous labor, had acquired a comfortable independence, with which he was enabled to educate his son as well as the young people of the best Bolognese families were educated. Domenico profited well by the instructions which he received, and was much beloved by his teachers for his docility and exemplary mildness. Zampieri possessed a good heart, just principles, a modesty which sometimes degenerated almost into timidity. His parents thought him best fitted for the ecclesiastical state, if he showed no dislike to the calling.

Very soon another vocation revealed itself to him. Pictures of the best artists, which he contemplated with indescribable pleasure, inspired him with a taste for drawing, for which all other studies were neglected. He gradually gave up reading, and renounced the amusements natural to his age, to employ the time in copying, at times badly, the engravings and drawings bought with the limited sums destined for pocket-money.

For a while he said nothing of the taste, which he considered a passing fancy; but when he was sure that nothing would please him so much as painting, he confided it to his father, who loved him too much to raise objections to his wishes. He was taken from college, and placed under the charge of Denis Calvart, the Dutch painter, then in repute at Bologna, as the father of Domenico preferred to confide his son to him, rather than to the Caravacci, whose attempts at reform in their school had found little favor with him.

Two of Calvart's best pupils, Guido and Albano, had recently left him to go over to the Carracci, and the jealousy of the foreigner against his rivals had much increased. Unjust, as an envious person always is, he defamed the Carracci unmercifully, criticised their manner, and denied their talent. According to him, Louis, Augustine, and Hannibal were ignorant, ambitious people; and the revolution in painting, which they were trying to bring about, would end in the complete ruin of the art.

At first the young Zampieri supposed his master was right, and he labored zealously to follow his instructions. But when he had made sufficient progress to judge for himself of the merits of a picture, he studied those of the new school, and found that Denis treated the works of the Carracci very severely. For himself he observed that the drawing was very correct, the coloring good, the attitudes noble and truthful, and that they excelled in that in which his master was deficient, a faithful imitation of nature.

Zampieri secretly procured some models of the Carracci, which he copied as secretly. Denis had expressly forbidden that any of these models should be brought into his studio. It was only in the absence of the master that Domenico substituted Carracci's pictures for those which had been given him to copy. One day, while busily occupied, Calvart unexpectedly entered, before he had time to put away the prohibited model.

The master, in a fury, seized the picture, tore it in pieces, and trampled it under his feet. He abused Domenico, who dared not undertake to justify himself, and determined to allow the storm to pass over. But Denis was not the man to forgive such an offence; from that day Zampieri became the object of his hatred; he had no words of kindness or encouragement for him, treating him with harshness and despite, and predicting that he would never be anything but a dauber.

With all his mildness and patience, Domenico became tired of continual reproaches and vexations; he much regretted that he had not gone to the Carracci rather than to this violent man, who would not listen to reason; but he dared not go away, and did not tell his father all that he had to suffer. One day, however, Denis, more irritated than usual against his adversaries, perhaps because he could not deny their merit, criticised them with the greatest bitterness, and as usual, after having vented his rage upon the Carracci, he turned upon Zampieri.

"Pardon me," said the timid pupil, calmly, "I had no wish to offend you: I thought, to become an artist, it is good to study the works of many masters, to imitate what is good in each."

The answer was just; and precisely because it was so, Calvart became furious, and, lacking better arguments to oppose to his pupil, he seized an easel and struck him. That was more than Domenico could bear: he left the studio with tears in his eyes, and returned to his father, from whom he could no longer conceal his troubles. Zampieri, indignant, gently reproached him for not having complained before: he then went to Louis Carracci, to beg him to take care of his son.

Domenico presented himself the next morning, and was received with all the affection which his suffering for the cause of his new masters induced. Louis was particularly friendly to him on account of his timidity and sweetness, and his feeble and slender appearance: he gave him the name of Domenichino, little Domenico, a name which he always afterwards bore.

The Carracci were zealous and kind in their teachings; under their instruction Domenichino made rapid progress. However, he was not one of those artists who possess an intuitive knowledge, and need almost no instruction; his genius was colder, more reflective; it needed study and labor to make it fruitful. Louis Carracci was just the master for such a pupil, for he had himself been accused of incapacity in his youth. He made it a point to encourage Domenichino, and inspire him with a certain confidence in his own powers.

At first he did not succeed; and prizes having been offered to those who should paint best, in the studio, Domenichino refused to compete with the other pupils, but he painted the picture required. On the day fixed for the distribution of prizes, the work of each was carefully examined by the three Carracci: Louis, to whose care Zampieri was specially confided, told him that it was a pity he had not tried his skill. Domenichino blushed, went away for a moment, and returned bringing a picture, which he showed the professor with a trembling hand.

No sooner had Louis cast his eyes upon it than he judged it worthy of being presented to Augustin, Annibal, and the amateurs who always united with them in deciding the merits of the competitors. Again they examined all the works, and compared them with that of Domenichino, to which the preference was unanimously accorded. This triumph filled the young artist with joy, without enfeebling his modesty.

Albano was among the number of Louis Carracci's pupils. He was charmed with the good qualities of Domenichino, and became his intimate friend; from that time nothing was wanting to the happiness of Zampieri, until Albano, who was some years the elder, left the school of Carracci, and went to Rome, with an ardent desire to study the works of the great masters. Annibal Carracci was there, and took pains to get him some orders, and to introduce him. But Albano did not forget his friend, and after a sojourn of one year, he sent him several drawings which he had made after Raphael.

Domenichino was surprised at the progress which Albano had made, and determined to go to the city which possessed so many admirable masterpieces. Without informing Albano of his intention, he unexpectedly presented himself, and was joyfully received by his friend, who presented him to Annibal, and he, in consequence of the length of time he had been with Louis, allowed him to share his labors. Zampieri appreciated the service rendered by his friend, and acknowledged it with the most heartfelt gratitude; for without this succor, his timidity would have prevented his finding a protector in Rome, where he was unknown.

Annibal Carracci was painting the frescoes of the Gallery Farnese, — magnificent pictures, for which the artist had the grief of being troubled concerning payment when they were finished. Domenichino was happy to work with, and receive the advice of such a master. All the time which he did not occupy in the Palace Farnese, he spent at the Vatican, before the sublime compositions of Raphael and Michael Angelo; this was his only amusement.

Domenichino's love of labor was rewarded by great success, and a picture of the *Death of Adonis*, confided to the pencil of the young man by Annibal, produced great sensation in the world of artists and connoisseurs. This work places Domenichino at once in the rank of painters then at Rome. He was not allowed to enjoy his good fortune in peace: envy created numerous enemies, who persecuted and troubled him greatly. Albano remained faithful, consoled and encouraged him, or tried to make him despise the injustice of those whom his growing reputation overshadowed. Domenichino's moderation was admirable, but his feelings were cruelly wounded at seeing those whom he considered almost friends turn against him.

Augustin Carracci, jealous, like the rest, of this new rising star, ranged himself with the enemies of Domenichino. The reflection, the slowness with which the young man worked, gave Augustin the idea of naming him the Ox; which name he used in speaking either of or to him. Annibal rarely agreed with his brother Augustin, though he loved him very much: he defended Domenichino, whose future greatness he foresaw, and one day he said to Augustin, who was using the gross appellation of Ox, —

"If God permits you and me to live a few years longer, my brother, we shall see the field of painting fertilized by this ox, which ploughs so steadily and laboriously."

When the *Death of Adonis* appeared, Bolognese Agucchi recommended the young Zampieri to the cardinal, his brother, who promised to protect him: but discussions upon the merits of the picture were caused by the jealous painters, which cooled off their good dispositions, and the cardinal postponed the fulfilment of his promise. A new work brought forth the talent of Domenichino into full light: the *Deliverance of St. Peter* was much admired, and Cardinal Agucchi confided *the decoration of the Chapel of St. Onuphre* to the *modest artist.*

Domenichino acquitted himself wonderfully of this work, and showed himself from day to day more worthy of the protection accorded to him. *Susanna and the Elders, St. Paul caught up to Heaven,* a *St. Francis,* and a *St. Jerome* were successively produced.

The charge for erecting a monument to Annibal Carracci, who died about this time, was given to Domenichino: he made a plan for it, and did some of the sculpturing himself; he also painted the portrait of him, who had been his teacher and friend, above the monument.

The reputation of the young artist continually increased. Cardinal Aldobrandini selected him to decorate the Palace Belvidere; and some time after Cardinal Odoardo wished him to paint some scenes from the life of *St. Bartholomew,* for the Abbey of Grotta Ferrata. While occupied with the last work, he chanced to see a young girl whose candor and modesty pleased him, and he determined to ask her in marriage. Fearing to make the proposition, he waited until his position was sure, so that he should not be refused; yet, desirous to give this girl, whom he had approved in his heart, a proof of his sentiments, he painted her, in one of his pictures, in the costume of a page. The resemblance was so striking, that the name of the young girl was circulated from mouth to mouth, and her parents, instead of feeling flattered, as Domenichino supposed they would, were indignant; and using their influence, and that of their friends, with Cardinal Odoardo, they succeeded in having the artist dismissed.

It was fortunate for Domenichino that Albano remained in Rome, to sympathize with, and console him, in this new affliction. This friend procured for him a part of the painting to be executed in the Castle of

Bassano, where he displayed so much talent, that the direction of the frescoes for the Chapel of St. Andrew were confided to him.

There he came in competition with Guido, whom he had before seen in the school of the Carracci. Domenichino painted a *St. Andrew beaten with Rods*, and Guido a *St. Andrew at Prayer*. The work of Guido was judged superior to that of Domenichino, and he received four hundred crowns for it, while Zampieri received only one hundred and fifty crowns. Domenichino felt this severely; he had flattered himself that he painted, at least, equal to Guido. He determined to leave a city where his talent was so little appreciated, and to return to Bologna. He was on the point of leaving, when he received an order for the *Communion of St. Jerome*, for the great altar of San Girolamo. He returned to his pencil, and animated by the desire of a brilliant revenge for the injustice which pursued him, he produced a work which deserved a place near those of the great masters. Every one wished to see the *Communion of St. Jerome*, and all unprejudiced connoisseurs declared that this excellent picture could be compared with the *Transfiguration* by Raphael.

In presence of such success, envy, crushed by the impossibility of contesting the beauty of this sublime composition, was silenced; but, growing bold, she soon began to murmur that it was nothing but a copy; that if Domenichino had succeeded in the painting, the idea was not his own, and that he had borrowed it from Auguistino Carracci, one of his old enemies. It was true that Augustino had touched this subject, but Domenichino had much surpassed him, and there existed between the two painters only the analogy, which is so often found between those of different masters who have retraced the same scenes; for example, the *Holy Family* or the *Adoration of the Magi*.

Domenichino's *St. Jerome* was engraved, and spread throughout Europe; and the reputation of the painter threatening to obscure that of his persecutors, Lanfranc, who, notwithstanding his incontestable talent, had taken sides with the persecutors of Zampieri, caused Augustino Carracci's picture to be engraved, hoping to diminish the glory of Domenichino by the comparison.

Deeply afflicted with such proceedings, and the hatred which they proved, our artist, who never injured any one, and who wished to love his enemies, was upon the point of leaving the field free to their calumnies, and going to live alone in some secluded retreat; but, though working hard and living simply, he had not the means to pay his travelling expenses. He saw the pictures of other artists covered with gold, and he received but a trifling sum for his. The *Communion of St. Jerome*, which is still considered a masterpiece of painting, brought him only fifty crowns. He was at that time obliged to contend with the discouragement which took possession of his soul, and find his only comfort in assiduous labor.

He was charged to paint the frescoes in the Chapel of St. Cecilia, in the Church St. Louis des Français, where his work was so satisfactory, that they begged him to decorate the Cathedral of Fano. Domenichino desired so much to leave Rome, that he joyfully acceded to the propositions which they made him, and departed, happy to escape, at least for a time, the numerous vexations which made life a torment.

The family Nolfi, at Fano, received him with all the distinction due to his merit, and he set to work with a serenity of feeling which he had not enjoyed for many years. He learned to inspire his works with his own feelings; the frescoes representing the history of the Virgin, with which he ornamented the Cathedral of Fano, breathed celestial happiness. The years which he devoted to this work were the happiest of his life, and he never forgot them. The calmness he then enjoyed brought back the remembrance of his childhood, and he wished to see his native city again. He hoped that his fellow-citizens would receive him as an artist of whom they could be proud. He was doomed to be disappointed. Bologna reserved all her sympathy for another of her children, for Guido, who returned to her, surrounded by princely splendor, while Domenichino came back as poor as he left.

His hopes blasted, he returned to Rome, but was immediately recalled by a noble Bolognese family to take charge of a large picture destined for the Church of San Giovanni in Monte. This picture was to represent the Virgin with a Rosary. While at work there, the Lords of Ratta, his new protectors, presented him to the parents of a young girl, named Marsabilia Barbetti. Domenichino, attracted by the good qualities and uncommon beauty of Marsabilia, offered her his hand. The young girl, flattered on her part by the talent of Zampieri, and affected by his trials, consented to undertake to make him forget them.

The parents promised a considerable dowry, but when it was necessary to pay, difficulties arose, and Domenichino, forced to sustain a lawsuit against his wife's family, received only the wreck of the fortune she was to possess. However, he was easily consoled, for Marsabilia was a good and devoted companion, filled with tenderness and respect for the artist; she roused his courage, by predicting future good fortune, and knew how to make her humble home so pleasant and happy, that if he desired wealth and reputation, it was only to lay them at her feet.

Two children cheered the heart of Zampieri, who, remembering the long years of suffering and isolation, thanked God for having taken pity on him. These two children, his pride and joy, were taken from him by death. It was a terrible stroke for the poor father, and Marsabilia silenced her own grief that she might console him. She tried to lead the thoughts of the artist to the glory which he had commenced to forget in his domestic felicity; she persuaded him to return to Rome.

Gregory XV., who loved Domenichino very much, and who, before ascending the pontifical throne, had been godfather to one of his children, received him most graciously. Cardinal Montalte, who was about building the Church of St. Andrea della Valle, chose Zampieri, upon the recommendation of the Pope, to decorate it. The artist needing distraction, gave himself entirely to this work, and produced frescoes which excited enthusiastic admiration. Nothing so perfect had been seen since Raphael's death. The *Four Evangelists*, and a picture of the *Martyrdom of St. Agnes*, were eminently beautiful. The Pope wished to felicitate Domenichino himself, and all the illustrious people of Rome imitated Gregory XV.

Zampieri, sensibly affected by these proofs of interest, desired to show that he was worthy of them, by producing something still better. He pondered upon a composition for the Cupola of San Andrea which should surpass anything he had yet done; and he thought of it night and day. When his thoughts were matured, flattering himself with the idea of success, he heard that Lanfranc had begged, and obtained from the cardinal, the painting of the dome. More saddened than surprised by this new cross, Domenichino did not try to revenge himself; he had suffered so much that resignation began to be easier to him. The Pope, hearing what had been done, wished to indemnify him for the injustice, and gave him the superintendence of the palace and papal buildings. During the life of Gregory XV. he distinguished himself in this position, for he was a good architect as well as a good painter. After the Pope's death, Domenichino, who had many enemies in Rome, impatiently awaited important orders from some other city, which would enable him to leave Rome.

One day he entered his house joyfully, and told his wife to prepare to go.

"Have you, then, received good news?" asked she.

"Excellent. They have written to me to come to Naples to decorate the Dome of St. Gennaio."

"To Naples!" exclaimed the young woman, turning pale.

"Yes, to Naples: and think of my joy, the Cupola of San Gennaio, much larger than that of San Andrea, will admit of my giving full expression to the ideas which I have already conceived, and to prove to those who preferred Lanfranc how much they erred. But what is the matter with you? Why do you not sympathize with my feelings?"

"You forget," replied Marsabilia, mildly, "that at Naples, more than elsewhere, you will have to contend with the jealousy which has ever pursued you."

"No, I forget nothing. I know that the Neapolitan painters have sworn not to allow any stranger to dispute the palm with them; but because I am requested to go, they can have no reason to reproach me. Besides, here I have enemies, as you well know. Why then should the fear of meeting others in Naples, prevent me from undertaking a work worthy of myself?"

"You know how ardently I desire your glory," replied Marsabilia, "yet, I know not why, but I feel that it is not good for you to go there. Give it up, I beg of you, if not for your own safety, at least for that of your wife and your child."

Marsabilia's prayers being of no avail, she resolved to accompany him to Naples. Her presentiments were but too just. The Neapolitan painters, headed by Ribera, hearing that Domenichino was about to undertake the painting of the Dome of San Gennaio, resolved to throw so many impediments in the way of the new comer, and to humiliate him to such a degree, that he would gladly abandon the work. But Domenichino bore it all patiently; he closed his eyes to the persecutions of which he was the object, and not wishing to demean himself by contending against their malice, he only occupied himself with his work. Every day they threatened him anew, but he disregarded them, until, having escaped the dagger of an assassin hired to kill him, he left Naples. His wife and children were to join him after a brief delay, but they were hindered by those who wished to have the cupola finished by Domenichino. When he heard that, he returned to the dear objects of his affection, from whom he could not be long separated.

He resumed his pencil, resolving not to lay it aside until the cupola was finished, in despite of hinderances.

His resolution astonished his enemies, without disconcerting them: they intrigued with the workman who had the charge of preparing the mortar upon which Domenichino was painting, and through money and promises induced him to mix cinders with the lime and sand.

What was the despair of Domenichino when he perceived that numberless cracks marred his painting! All his labor was lost, and he was forced to recommence. He was at a loss to understand the cause of the trouble, until he recognized the work of his enemies, and began to fear that they would find other means to injure him. Assured of the treason of the workman whom he employed, he forbade the approach of any assistant: he made his mortars, and applied them himself; he ground his colors. Alone, shut up in the church, he repaired his damaged work as well as he could; but his health, enfeebled by all that he had suffered, gave way under this new chagrin and excess of labor which he was imposing upon himself.

He was not yet reëstablished, when he was secretly informed that his enemies were resolved to poison him, and he felt obliged to prepare his own food. His life, which had been only a succession of troubles, availed him little: he cared to preserve it, only that he might finish his work. But notwithstanding all his precautions, all the trouble he took to withdraw himself from the bad designs formed against him, tradition assures us that he was poisoned by a mercenary hand. If it were not so, it is easy to imagine that his end was hastened by cares and chagrins, and his enemies are not the less responsible for his death.

Even his death did not satisfy their hatred; they unjustly criticised the works which he had commenced, and Lanfranc, who was empowered to finish them, intrigued until he was permitted to scrape off all that his predecessor had painted. Not content with this outrage to the memory of Domenichino, the Neapolitan artists advised the Spanish viceroy to require the restitution of the sums which the unhappy painter had used; and, shameful to relate, this advice was followed.

Few artists have had so much to contend with, and suffered so much from the envious as Domenichino. If it is true that envy attaches itself to great talents, the number of those who can pretend to surpass him is very small. His merit, so long contested, has been recognized, and posterity, at least, renders him justice. Poussin, a great admirer of his numerous works, has named him the painter par excellence.

It is impossible to find more accurate compositions than those of Domenichino. In them the passions are expressed with perfect truth, the designs are pure, the attitudes well chosen, the bearings of the heads are simple, and of an astonishing variety, the draperies thrown on with exquisite taste, the colors fresh and soft. His frescoes are more esteemed than his oil-paintings; everything about them is studied with the most extreme care, harmony reigns throughout, and nothing betrays fatigue, because Domenichino, always the master of his subject, solved all the difficulties which he should be likely to meet beforehand. He had no love for society where his simple exterior and lack of accomplishments prevented his succeeding; he tried to be sufficient unto himself. After long hours of work, his recreation was a long walk into the country; and while he exercised his body, he occupied his mind with the subjects of his choice. So great was his desire to render his pictures truthful, that he studied himself for a model, giving himself up to gayety or sadness, according to the sentiments he desired to portray.

His character was good, humane, and generous; neither hatred nor the desire of vengeance ever caused an unkind thought: he used to say that he preferred being the victim rather than the executioner.

He died at the age of sixty years.

RIBERA.

Joseph Ribera, born at Xativa, near Valencia, in 1588, was at first destined to the military career, which his father had followed, and was sent, when quite young, to

Valencia, for his education. Endowed with great intelligence, he made rapid progress, and his teachers foretold a brilliant career for him, when suddenly he showed a disgust for study, and occupied himself with drawing and painting.

His father, who regretted to see him take this fancy, tried to turn his attention; but Ribera declared that he could never be other than a poor doctor or a bad soldier if he followed a constrained vocation, while if left to follow the bent of his inclination, he was sure of becoming a famous painter. Despite his youth, he said this with so much conviction, with so much confidence in himself, that his father permitted him to leave the university for the studio of Francisco Ribalta.

Joseph, who really had great taste for the arts, was not slow to distinguish himself under the direction of this able master, and Ribalta allowed him to partake of his labors. This should have satisfied the ambition of Ribera; but, in proportion as he improved, his desire to see the *chefs-d'œuvre* of Italy, of which he had heard so much, increased. Just when Ribalta felicitated himself upon having found a successor in his pupil, Joseph announced his intention to depart. His eldest brother, who was going to take the command of a company of cavalry in the kingdom of Naples, had much difficulty in persuading him to wait until they could go together.

At first all went on merrily, and the voyage appeared charming to the two young people; but the officer having been made a prisoner in the first encounter, Joseph alone, without support, without any resources whatever, in a foreign country, regretted Spain, which he had so joyously left. His regrets soon passed away; for Ribera had the heart of a man in his youthful body: he determined not to return home. He had come to Italy to see the wonders of Rome; he would see Rome. He set out on foot, begging along the route when too cruelly pressed by hunger, and sleeping under the beautiful sky. He arrived at Rome, exhausted by fatigue, and hardly covered by miserable rags. To present himself to an artist in such a predicament was to expose himself to an inevitable affront, and Ribera was too proud to risk it. He lived in Rome as he had lived in getting there; he needed very little; a crust of bread, a few vegetables which he could find in a corner, were sufficient.

He passed the days in studying the works of the masters in the churches, or in drawing, in the streets, whatever seemed to merit his attention.

Cardinal Borgia, going one day to the Vatican, in his carriage, perceived him occupied in copying the fresco which ornamented the façade of a palace. He ordered his people to bring the little mendicant to him.

Ribera advanced to the carriage of his eminence.

"What were you doing there?" asked the cardinal.

"I was drawing, your grace," replied Joseph.

"Then you are an artist?"

"No, your eminence; but I shall be. For that purpose, I left my country and my home."

"Really, you are a foreigner?"

"I am a Spaniard, my lord."

"And you have neither friend or protector in Rome?"

"Your lordship can see that but too well," replied the young man, casting an ironical and pitiful look upon his vesture.

"Will you show me your sketch?"

"Here it is."

"It is very well done!" cried the cardinal, after having examined the rough drawing. "You have too much talent to be abandoned; I will give you a place in my house."

The coach drove on, and a footman, approaching Ribera, offered to take him to the Borgia palace. He accepted with as much pride as joy, for he knew that artists were well recognized and hospitably entertained by such personages.

Ribera forgot only one thing; that was, as he had himself said to the prelate, if he reckoned upon becoming a celebrated artist, he was not one at the time. He hoped to be respected; he was only kindly treated: he imagined that he should have a place in the drawing-room, and at the table of the cardinal: he was only admitted to the antechamber and the pantry. His pride, which had been much raised, was cruelly wounded; yet he had suffered too much from actual want to renounce the unexpected good fortune which he met. The cardinal advised him to continue his studies, and left him the free disposition of his time. Nothing could have been better for the young man than to take advantage of his peaceful position by studying for his future career. It was what he wished to do; but he deferred taking his pencil for some days, then weeks passed, and finally months, without his going to work in earnest.

Ribera was more reflective than people generally are; he felt that he must contend with misery to sustain his energy, and that his brilliant hopes would come to an end if he slept in his borrowed opulence any longer.

"It shall not be said of me that I left my country to be only a valet here!" cried he, after thinking of what he was going to do. "I will put on my old clothes, and resume my former life: rags are preferable to a livery. Hurrah for my joyous misery! I was sometimes hungry, but always free."

His plan made, Ribera hastened to put it into execution. Leaving the palace Borgia, he resumed his vagabond life; but he no longer begged. He had learned to know the city, and the resources it offered. A dealer in second-hand wares bought a copy-book of his drawings for a few small pieces of money, which sufficed for Ribera's wants until he could gain a new supply. It often happened that he disposed of his sketches without the necessity of applying to the trader, who treated him badly: some rich child, seeing them spread out, was pleased, and bought of him, paying generously.

Fortune having favored him in this way several times,

Ribera bought pencils and colors. He began to make himself known, at least to the young people whose position was not far above his own. Not knowing his name, they called him *Lo Spagnoletto*, the little Spaniard, — by which name he is well known at the present time.

By patience, labor, and economy Joseph was enabled to dress himself decently, so that he could present himself at the studio of some master. The beautiful works of Michael Angelo and of Raphael excited his enthusiasm; but these great geniuses had passed away, and among the painters then in repute, Caravaggio pleased him best, by his bold and somewhat extravagant manner. He went to Caravaggio, and showing what he had done, with no other teacher than Nature, begged him to receive him as a pupil. Caravaggio recognized excellent qualities in Ribera's works. The young man, filled with confidence by this benevolent reception, related his history: the character of the little Spaniard pleased the painter, who was himself fond of adventures. Ribera became his pupil, and was not the least enthusiastic of his partisans; he understood the manner of the painter at once, and imitated it so well that, when Caravaggio died, it was impossible to distinguish the pictures of the master from those of the little Spaniard.

Ribera was not twenty years old at that time: the desire to see, and to study, which had brought him to Rome was not in the least diminished, and he went to

Parma, where Correggio had left magnificent works. The style of Correggio, of which the distinctive character is inimitable grace, deeply impressed Ribera, habituated to the wild, savage energy of his deceased professor. Seized with enthusiasm at the sight of these immortal pictures, he was not content to admire them only, but he copied them with such patient attention, that he succeeded in reproducing their gentle beauty. He recognized what was false and extravagant in the style which Caravaggio had made fashionable; he retained this master's powerful touch, his vigorous coloring, and much of his fire and boldness; but he tempered these qualities, which with Caravaggio had degenerated into faults, by something sweet, melancholy, and graceful, borrowed from an intelligent and deep study of the works of Correggio.

Happy in his success, he returned to Rome, not doubting that his talent, which was bursting forth in a new light, would procure him an honest fortune, if not a brilliant reputation. He was deceived: his friends, and the traders with whom he dealt before his departure, were more surprised than satisfied with the progress which he had made, and advised him to go back to Caravaggio's method, which would be more useful to him.

To be rid of their importunate solicitations, and, perhaps, also forced by necessity, he went to Naples, still rich in illusions, but so poor in fact, that, not having money to pay for his lodgings, he was obliged to leave his cloak in pawn. The poverty, which he had escaped for a while, was all the more difficult to bear when it returned to assail him, because he was conscious of his own power, and had the will to display it, if occasion only offered. He went through the city, asking for work: finally he met a picture-dealer, who, touched with pity as much as others had been with fear, by the sight of his destitution, furnished him with materials for painting, and promised to give him work, if he really had talent.

This was all that Ribera asked. He commenced by a portrait; and the honest trader, perceiving that the artist had not boasted falsely, paid him well, procured him work, became his protector, and soon after gave him his daughter in marriage.

The position of the Spaniard, so long poor and unknown, finally changed. His father-in-law's fortune and relations afforded the means of spreading his works, which he carried to as high a degree of perfection as possible. He was beginning to enjoy some reputation, when a singular circumstance brought him to distinction. Italian painters were in the habit of exhibiting the pictures which they had finished: this custom had a twofold advantage; it gave renown to the artist, and permitted him to improve by the criticisms of the multitude. Ribera was too eager for glory to miss showing his works. One day, when he placed a *Martyrdom of St. Bar-*

tholomew upon the balcony, the crowd became so compact, that the viceroy, seeing the assembly from the terrace of his palace, thought it was a riot, and ordered his officers to go immediately and reëstablish order.

On learning that what he supposed to be cries of sedition were only the enthusiastic acclamations of the people, at the sight of a *chef-d'œuvre* his surprise was very great. He wished to see the picture and its painter immediately. Ribera presented himself at the palace, where he received the warmest felicitations. The viceroy partook of the emotion which had excited the crowd. Recognizing a fellow-countryman in Ribera (the vice-royalty of Naples depended on Spain at that time), he cordially extended his hand to him in presence of the court, named him his painter, assured him of a good pension, and required him to come and establish himself in the palace.

The fortune of Ribera was made; he received orders from all parts: churches, convents, public buildings, palaces, were all to be enriched by his productions. A *Descent from the Cross*, and a *Virgin*, known as *La Madonna Bianca*, sealed his reputation. The king of Spain, Philip IV., to whom the Viceroy sent some of Ribera's pictures, loaded him with presents and honors. Success did not weaken Ribera's love for work; on the contrary, he redoubled his zeal, in order to be equal to his rapidly increasing fame. His ardor was so great, that several times he passed a whole day at his easel, without eating or drinking. This assiduity affecting his health, the viceroy made him promise to have a servant always near him, whose business it should be to tell him how many hours he had worked.

There was not a house in Naples more elegantly fitted up than Ribera's: fortune had come to him with all honors. It would have been difficult to recognize the poor Spagnoletto, obliged to sell his sketches for a bit of bread or a portion of macaroni, in the elegant lord seen promenading with the viceroy, or conversing with princes and dukes. But he never forgot how much he had suffered; his past misfortunes had left a leaven of bitterness and hatred in his heart. Wonderful to relate, the remembrance of his poverty and misery, instead of making him benevolent towards those in a similar situation, instead of inspiring him with the desire to come forward to assist them, rendered him cold and hostile to the youthful talents which were seeking to make their way in the world!

It is almost impossible to understand this sentiment of egotism and jealousy in a superior man; yet it is also too true that Ribera was the soul of that association of artists who swore to interdict the entrance to Naples to any foreign painter, and should any be so bold as to brave this interdiction, to use all possible means to drive them out. Annibal Carracci, after him Josépin and Guido, all called to work upon the dome of San Gennaio, were forced to renounce the hopes which their call to Naples had created. The pupils of Ribera, and the partisans of his style, transformed into *bravi*, threatened death to new comers, and thus assisted their master in getting rid of them.

Domenichino alone persisted in remaining at Naples, despite the advice of friends and the prayers of his wife. We have spoken of the persecutions inflicted upon him, and how he died. Ribera cannot be considered innocent of his death : it is a spot upon his glory, and no one can praise his talent without censuring his character.

Ribera gave brilliant entertainments, to which all the Neapolitan aristocracy crowded. He was present himself, but very rarely entertained his guests. He was seen walking alone in his garden, or remaining for hours with his elbow upon a balcony, and no one thought of interrupting his musings, because he was meditating upon the works of the morrow in the midst of the noble crowd attracted to his house by the love of pleasure. It often happened that, struck by the features of some gentleman who was presented to him, he drew his portrait at once, without any person's taking exceptions at the freak of the artist.

The academy of St. Luke received Ribera among its members, and the Pope, charmed with his uncommon talents, sent him the decoration of the order of Christ. His pictures, not less esteemed in Spain than in Italy, were royally paid. It is said that two Spanish officers, going through Naples, wished to pay their respects to him as a countryman. Ribera received them so kindly, that they felt at liberty to ask him if he would not take part in a speculation, which could not fail to be very profitable.

"Trading and art are, in my opinion, incompatible," said Ribera; "but if you will be good enough to explain—"

"We do not ask you, sir, to neglect your pencil," replied one of the visitors: "we wish only that you would associate yourself in a brilliant affair; my friend and I have studied alchemy for a long time, so that this admirable science has no more secrets for us. Unfortunately, the experiments we have made have exhausted our resources, and now we are obliged to give up the wonderful results of our discovery for want of some thousand crowns."

"So, gentlemen, you possess the faculty of making gold?"

"We are ready to prove it to you; and as soon as you shall have consented to unite your interest with ours, no king or prince can rival you in pomp or splendor."

"I am greatly obliged to you for having thought to give me a third in this magnificent affair," replied Ribera, "but I also possess the secret of making gold."

"You, my lord? Is it possible?"

"You shall judge immediately. But allow me, I beg of you, to give a few strokes to this picture, which I was about finishing as you entered."

The two officers seated themselves, curious to see what Ribera promised to show them. In about an hour he called a domestic, and told him to take the picture which he had just finished to a certain dealer, whom he mentioned. The valet obeyed, and returning shortly after, handed his master the sum of four hundred ducats.

"What did I tell you, gentlemen?" said Ribera, pouring the contents of the rolls which he had received upon the table; "behold the gold which I make. Does it appear to you to be of good quality?"

The two officers hung their heads; and understanding that any new attempt would be useless, they went away, filled with admiration for a talent which was well worth the chimerical treasury of alchemy.

Ribera enjoyed much domestic felicity; he loved his wife tenderly, and two daughters, richly endowed by nature, contributed to his happiness. A Spanish gentleman asked, and obtained the hand of the eldest: the artist, not being willing to be separated from her, succeeded in getting the appointment of prime minister of the viceroy for his son-in-law. The love of pleasure and the pride of Ribera lost his second child.

The second Don John of Austria gave magnificent fêtes, to which only the high Neapolitan aristocracy were admitted; but as talent levels all social distinctions, the great painter was invited. Proud of the incomparable beauty of his daughter, he determined to bring her out on these occasions in a manner worthy of her, and obtained permission to present her. The young girl was thought to be charming, but no one was so enthusiastic upon her grace and beauty as the prince himself. Afterwards he came very often to Ribera's studio, affecting much esteem for his talent, and he knew how to flatter his vanity so well, that the painter admitted him into his family circle.

In this Ribera committed a great mistake, which he was not slow to recognize. One day, he went into his studio very anxious: his daughter had not come to give him the morning kiss, and this forgetfulness grieved him, for he idolized the child. Her dear image fell, unwittingly, from his pencil into almost all his compositions. His impatience disquieted him so much that he left his work, and sought his daily kiss, without which his mind was troubled, and his heart filled with anguish. He went to his daughter's apartment, called her, asked for her, and sought her in the house and gardens in vain. The domestics fearing his anger, went away from him trembling. It was not until after many questions, or rather ardent prayers, that he learned the terrible truth: the prince, whom he believed to be his friend, had carried her off!

Ribera, overwhelmed for an instant by this terrible blow, soon recovered all his energy. He collected all his ready money, seized his arms, and followed by a devoted servant, left his house, swearing never to reënter it, until revenged for the odious treachery by which the prince had rendered himself culpable towards him.

He was never seen again, and nothing was ever heard of him or his servant. It is supposed that, despairing of being able to punish his powerful adversary, and unwilling to reappear, dishonored, in the city of Naples, where he had been so proud and so glorious, he put an end to his life by suicide.

We have spoken of the character of Ribera. This character, irascible, haughty, and disagreeable, is found in his works. If he succeeded in painting beautiful angels and sainted Madonnas, one feels that he was not so much pleased as when he reproduced the terrible scenes of the martyrdom of the defenders of the faith. His genius is greatest when guided by his own inspiration: he represents tortured members, faces contracted by sufferings, or looks burning with rage. The *Martyrdom of St. Bartholomew*, to which Ribera owed his sudden elevation, and *Prometheus upon Caucasus*, are the two masterpieces in this terrible style, which he liked best. Besides these two striking pictures, there are the *Twelve Apostles*, and *Jacob's Ladder*, admirable pictures, which are in Madrid; and an *Adoration of the Shepherds*, which is in the Museum of the Louvre.

Although Ribera passed all his career as an artist, in Italy, he never took any of the *chefs-d'œuvre* of the Roman school as models. We do not find in his pictures the types of ideal purity, which we so much esteemed in Perugino and Raphael. Ribera, by the attention which he gave to reproducing nature in all her variety, belongs to the Spanish school. His compositions are distinguished by a wonderful skill in *chiaroscuro*, by a delicacy and vigor of pencilling, which few artists have equalled, and finally, by the inimitable talent with which he represented bald heads, wrinkled faces, and lame, old people.

Ribera was sixty-nine years old when he died, or rather when he disappeared from Naples, for the time of his death is uncertain.

VELASQUEZ.

Don Diego Velasquez de Siloa, born at Seville, in 1599, descended from one of the most noble and most illustrious families of Portugal. His parents, anticipating some career worthy of his birth, gave him a brilliant education, and the young Diego improved in a manner to surpass all these hopes. After finishing his studies, he consecrated all his leisure to painting, until old enough to choose a profession. While the young gentlemen of his acquaintance were running after pleasures, and dissipating their paternal fortunes in all sorts of follies, Don Diego passed his days peacefully and happily in solitude.

He had such a fancy for this occupation, that feeling

he could not give it up, he begged his father to permit him to be an artist, and pleaded his cause with so much eloquence that he was permitted to enter into the school of Francisco Herrera.

Francisco was an able teacher, but a hard, haughty and fantastic man, to whose manners Diego found it very difficult to accommodate himself. Velasquez, brought up with all circumspection in the paternal home, endowed with a gentle and kind character, educated with distinguished manners and polite habits, suffered more than others from the oddities and excitements of Herrera. The love of painting enabled Velasquez to be patient, for a time, but his resignation, far from touching his master's feelings, only caused him to be treated as a drudge. Velasquez left him, and entered the school of Pacheco.

Pacheco, quite as good a teacher as Herrera, was a man of the world. His amiable spirit, lively conversation, the ease and nobleness of his manners, had gained him access to all the learned and illustrious personages of Seville. He became very partial to Velasquez, and taught him with great care. The pupil, filled with gratitude, regarded him as a second father, their mutual affection increased daily, and Pacheco promised to give Velasquez his daughter in marriage.

The first works of Diego were distinguished by a sure and easy pencil, and Pacheco foresaw that his pupil would excel him; however, Velasquez failed in that which promptly develops the sentiment of the beautiful in artists: he had seen none of the immortal compositions, the glory and riches of Italy. Working assiduously, he carefully studied, but he did not know how much genius can add to beauty. Some Italian and Flemish painters coming to Seville, taught him. Seeing that he had much to learn, Velasquez bade adieu to his kind teacher, now become his best friend, and departed for Madrid.

He was then twenty-three years old, and was thought to be a painter of the first order. He was recommended, by his family, to Don Juan de Fonseca, who held a position at court. This gentleman received Velasquez as a relative, and presented him to Philip IV. The king had heard of the talent of the young artist; he received him kindly, and ordered his portrait.

Velasquez, who was very skilful in portrait painting, commenced, full of hope, and the success proved that he was not too much prejudiced in favor of his own talent. Philip was greatly pleased with this portrait, and ordered all the pictures which had been previously made of him to be destroyed, and named Velasquez his first painter.

This position, which Diego was far from expecting, did not make him forget that he had come to Madrid for the purpose of instruction. There were no good masters in this capital; but some beautiful pictures of the best Italian artists revealed the mysteries of the art to Velasquez. By studying them with great attention, he modified his own manner, and made rapid progress. Some time after his arrival in Madrid, the king offered a prize for the best painting, and the subject to be treated was the expulsion of the Moors from the Peninsula. Velasquez gained the prize, and the king, as happy as himself, gave him new honors at court.

Diego gained favor daily. Philip IV., subject to terrible fits of melancholy, had need of distraction of mind; and as he prided himself upon being an artist, it was by artists that he hoped to be relieved from the cruel cares which weighed upon his spirit. The drawings of Velasquez, full of roguery and wit, often made the king laugh; and the verses of Calderon helped to dissipate his sad humors. The painter and the poet lived in great intimacy with the monarch, and both possessed much influence over him. A caricature by Velasquez, a satire of Calderon, sufficed to deprive a favorite of the good graces of the king, or to frustrate projects of the ministers; so that these two artists had numerous courtiers, and more enemies. Velasquez, in the midst of the intrigues of the court, remained true to art and his conscience. He praised only what he believed to be just, good, and useful to the prosperity of his country, and criticised what he believed to be iniquitous or hurtful. He remained what he had been before his elevation, — honest, modest, benevolent, industrious, accessible to all who needed encouragement or assistance.

Velasquez had been in Madrid six years, when he heard that the king of England had chosen the celebrated painter Rubens as his ambassador to the court of Spain. The news created quite a sensation at the court, and was particularly agreeable to Velasquez, who knew Rubens by his works. Rubens, on his part, had heard of the eminent talent of Velasquez; they esteemed and admired each other before meeting, and when they met they loved each other. They spent all the time which was not needed in the service of their respective masters, together. Velasquez showed Rubens the paintings in Madrid and the Escurial, and Rubens told Velasquez all that he had seen in Venice, Florence, and Rome. His warm and enthusiastic descriptions overpowered the Spaniard, who pictured to himself the sublime frescoes of Michael Angelo, the admirable pictures of Raphael, of Titian, and of Leonardo da Vinci. But there came a moment when these descriptions, exact and colored as they were, no longer sufficed; an ardent desire to visit the country of the fine arts took possession of his soul; he lost his sleep, his appetite, gayety, and even his love of work.

One morning Velasquez, who could go to the king at all times, seeing him more lively than usual, threw himself at his feet, and begged leave of absence for some months. Hearing this, Philip cried out, and accused the painter of ingratitude. After he had exhausted his complaints and grievances, he desired to be informed of the motive of this absence.

"I wish, sire, to be worthy of the title of first painter to your majesty, a title, which the king, my master, has deigned to bestow upon me, consulting rather his indulgence than my talent. Sire, I wish to visit Italy: one cannot be a great artist without studying the wonders which the great masters, Michael Angelo and Raphael, have left."

"Say rather that you wish to leave me, Velasquez, because a painter like you has nothing to desire, not even from the illustrious dead whom you mention; and if you wish to give me a better opinion of your heart, upon which I have counted as that of a friend, never speak to me again of this voyage."

Velasquez understood that all his urgency would be in vain, and resolved to wait until some unforeseen circumstance should permit him again to ask leave of absence.

Every time that the king, surprised by some work of his painter, or grateful for the distraction which the lively, and biting pencil of Velasquez procured him, expressed a desire to recompense him, the artist took the opportunity to speak of his favorite dream, a voyage to Italy. Finally, this dream threatening to become a fixed idea, Philip IV., seeing that Don Diego was losing his good humor and his sallies of raillery, consented to his departure, on condition that he should spend no more time than was absolutely necessary to see the *chefs-d'œuvre* which he was so anxious to admire.

Velasquez received this permission with delight; besides, he was anxious to enjoy a little of that liberty, of which those who live near kings are deprived: it seemed to him a great pleasure not to be the favorite of Philip IV., but a simple artist, travelling as he pleased, and stopping whenever he found a beautiful site to paint or a souvenir to evoke. However, he was disappointed in the pleasure of travelling incognito: the king, unwilling that his painter should go like an ordinary traveller, gave him letters of recommendation, decorations, and titles, with a numerous and brilliant suite.

At Venice, the ambassador of Spain received him with every mark of distinction; and desiring to flatter Philip IV. by honoring his painter, he gave Velasquez a brilliant entertainment, to which all the Venetian nobility were invited. When these festivities were ended, Diego commenced to study. The beautiful works of Giorgione, of Titian, of Tintoretto, of Paul Veronese, filled him with enthusiasm. Notwithstanding the king's recommendation to make haste, he would, perhaps, have spent several years in Venice, had he not been forced to leave the city by the war, about the succession of Mantua, which broke out between France and Spain.

At Rome, Pope Urban VIII. received him as one of the first artists of the century. Velasquez saw that Rubens had not exaggerated in boasting of the wonders which the capital of the Christian world contained. It would be impossible to express the admiration with which Michael Angelo and Raphael inspired him. He studied them with the closest attention, and not satisfied with studying them, he copied many of Raphael's pictures, and a part of the immortal fresco of *The Last Judgment.* Having modified his style by this conscientious study, he painted two pictures, which he intended to present to the king on his return to Spain. He received an order to return immediately to Madrid, from Philip IV., who could not accustom himself to his absence; which obliged him to finish the two pictures, — the *Forges of Vulcan,* and the *Tunic of Joseph,* — in great haste. But he would not think of leaving Italy without seeing Naples, where Ribera, his fellow-countryman, was then enjoying great reputation. The two artists, who were already acquainted with each other's works, passed several days together: then Velasquez, fearing that a longer stay would irritate the king, his master, returned to Spain.

Philip was too happy to see him to make any reproaches. He took great pleasure in listening to the recital of the travels of his painter, and hearing his enthusiastic descriptions of the *chefs-d'œuvre* which he regretted having left so soon. The two pictures which Velasquez painted at Rome made the king forget the ennui he had felt during the absence of his favorite: he overwhelmed him with felicitations and rich presents. The court as well as the monarch applauded the flight which the fine talent of Velasquez had taken, and it was but just.

This success made him redouble his efforts. A noble emulation had taken possession of his heart. The beautiful works which he had seen inspired him with the desire of greater improvement, and he succeeded. He almost never left his studio. Philip, who delighted to be with him, was in the habit of going thither, instead of sending for him, as he formerly did. The monarch forgot the cares of royalty during the hours which they passed pleasantly conversing upon the arts.

For some years Philip had been talking of founding an academy of painting in Madrid, and the subject was often discussed in his conversations with Velasquez. The painter, inspired by the love of art, and perhaps some little egotism, urged him to carry out his plan. To endow an academy of painting in Spain, it would be necessary to collect a certain number of antique marbles, of ancient and modern pictures, and of objects of art of all kinds, and Velasquez had no doubt that the king would choose him to select them; in which case a second voyage to Italy would be necessary, and he, under pretext of the exigence of his mission, would be able to prolong his sojourn more than he had ventured to do the first time. The preoccupations of politics caused the postponement of the foundation of this establishment. Philip was obliged to remember that his duty was that of a king, and not of an artist, so that seventeen years passed away before Velasquez could make another voyage to Italy. The most remarkable deeds of the reign of

Philip IV. were represented in the pictures which Velasquez painted during these seventeen years. The uncommon talents of the artist procured him signal favors from the king.

One of the most beautiful pictures which the artist painted at this time is that which represents the family of his sovereign. While he was occupied on this picture, the visits of Philip to his studio were more frequent than ever; he never tired of admiring the astonishing facility with which those beautiful and noble figures, so true to life, were growing under the pencil of Don Diego. The king, wishing to render homage to the genius of him whom he called his friend, desired him to paint himself in the picture. When the picture was finished he showed it to the king, who warmly approved it.

"So," said Velasquez, "your majesty finds nothing wanting to the picture?"

"Have I said so?" asked the king, smiling.

"No, sire; but your majesty has deigned to praise my work in such a manner, that, if I did not know the indulgence of the king, I should flatter myself that I was leaving an irreproachable picture to posterity."

"Be assured, friend Velasquez, that I am not indulgent, but just. Therefore, at the risk of somewhat humiliating your pride as an artist, I beg you to pass me your pallet and brush, that I may remedy what is wanting in your work."

Velasquez was unable to dissemble a certain apprehension: although the king painted tolerably well, he felt that it would be a great pity to spoil his magnificent portraits. Philip easily imagined what was passing in Diego's mind, but he took no notice of it, and, advancing towards the picture, he painted the Cross of St. James near those of the other orders with which the breast of the artist was already decorated. Velasquez, penetrated with gratitude, fell on his knees before him; Philip, raising him, embraced him, and said, —

"Is it not a great honor for the king of Spain to have added the finishing stroke to the painting of Velasquez?"

But to return to the foundation of the academy of painting. Philip was beginning to grow old, and, fearing that death should come upon him before he had given some brilliant evidence of his royal protection of the arts, finally sent Velasquez to Rome.

Pope Innocent X. received him with the greatest favor, and begged him to paint his portrait. The Spanish painter complied with the flattering demand. The public were so much excited by the sight of this picture that it was decided to carry it in procession through the streets of Rome, and afterwards to crown it. Velasquez was not insensible to such honors.

Philip's envoy ordered twelve pictures, from twelve of the most celebrated painters of the epoch: these he was to add to those of the ancient masters, which he had procured at great expense; he bought antique marbles, statues of the preceding century, and being authorized by the king of Spain to spare nothing, that the collection might be worthy of Philip IV. and of Velasquez, he succeeded in obtaining a number of very precious works.

He returned to Madrid with his treasures; and the monarch was so much pleased with the manner in which he had executed his commissions, that he appointed him marshal. With all his riches and honors, he was still modest and industrious. The more he was praised, the more desirous he was to deserve it. His chief pleasure was in the cultivation of his art, and he would have gone from court rather than sacrifice the pleasures afforded by his pencil to the vexatious trials of ambition.

Although he excelled in portrait-painting, he knew how to put much grandeur and poetry into his historical compositions, truth and simplicity into his landscapes, grace and sweetness, beyond all expression, into his small interior scenes; finally, he painted animals, flowers, and fruits as a man for whom Nature had no secrets. Great purity in drawing, a pencil firm, yet light, a good tone of color, perfect knowledge of *chiaro-scuro* and of perspective, distinguish all his works.

Velasquez continued to labor during ten years after his return from Italy; and although his health was sensibly enfeebled, he could not consent to give up his beloved occupation. His talent, far from diminishing, seemed to gain strength daily; his hand was always sure, his imagination full of the generous ardor of youth; age brought him a more profound knowledge of the mysteries of art, of study, and of experience.

Philip flattered himself that his beloved artist, although quite old, would live many years. In the fear of afflicting Velasquez, he insisted less upon the necessity of his suspending his labors than he would have done had he been counselled by his affection alone.

Meanwhile Cardinal Mazarin having concluded the negotiations undertaken with Spain for the marriage of Louis XIV., Philip IV. promised to conduct his daughter, Maria Theresa, who was to be queen of France, to the frontier. Louis, in all the splendor of youth and glory, followed by a numerous and brilliant court, came to Irun to meet his affianced bride. Velasquez left Madrid in company with Philip: in his quality of marshal, obliged to prepare lodgings for the court when travelling, he was ordered to arrange the pavilion where the two monarchs were to meet, and to regulate all the ceremonies of the interview in the Isle of Pheasants. The cares of this journey, the exertion he was compelled to make, in order to see that nothing should be wanting in the pomp displayed by the court of Spain upon this solemn occasion, hastened the progress of his disease. He was taken back to Madrid at the end of the month of March, 1660, and died on the 7th of the following August, at the age of sixty-one years.

The king made a magnificent funeral, which was

attended by the court and the whole city of Madrid. He was interred in the church of San Juan, where his widow, the daughter of his old master, Francisco Pacheco, joined him a few days after.

MURILLO.

The child who became the most celebrated painter of Spain was born the 1st of January, 1618, in one of the poorest houses of Seville. His family name was Murillo, and he was baptized Bartholomew Esteban. His childhood passed in privations and misery, and nothing announced the brilliant career reserved for him. At first his parents scarcely thought of having him learn to read and write; but when he commenced, he manifested so much intelligence and good will, that they were astonished at the progress which he made, and began to hope that some day the little Bartholomew would rise above the miserable condition in which their lot had been cast.

His mother often thought of it; and the more the good qualities of her son developed, the more she was fixed in her hopes. She had a brother, named Juan del Castillo, who was a painter, and who, though he possessed neither fortune nor reputation, was in a brilliant position compared with that of Murillo. She went to this brother, told him of the excellent character of her son, and his aptitude for learning, and begged him to give him some instruction. Juan did not participate in the hopes of his sister, yet he consented to teach his nephew the elements of his art.

When Murillo had a pencil in his hand, and a good sheet of paper at his disposition, — treasures which he had for a long time coveted, — he was happier than a king, and, proud of this happiness, he also began to think of a future career. He saw himself a painter, like his uncle; he had a studio ornamented with fine pictures, a neat and pretty little room, and money, which, while weeping with joy, he poured into the lap of his good mother. Now, in order to realize this fine dream, it was necessary to work diligently; the child did not lose an instant: very soon Juan del Castillo recognized his powers.

Juan was a very bad colorist, but he drew tolerably well, so that his instruction was useful to Bartholomew. Unfortunately, he decided to leave Seville, and establish himself in Cadiz. Murillo would gladly have gone with him; but his parents were unable to pay his board, and Castillo could not afford to make such an addition to his expenses. His departure was a grievous sacrifice to Bartholomew, for all the poor child's brilliant illusions vanished with his master. Then the time which he had spent with Castillo was a twofold loss; for if Murillo had not hoped to become an artist, he would have been apprenticed to some artisan, and now that he was large and strong, he would be able to earn his living. What was to be done? Such was the question which Bartholomew put to himself.

He could not think of going home to his parents, whose labor scarcely sufficed for their restricted wants. Should he give up painting, and learn a trade? Besides the chagrin which he felt in renouncing the career he had chosen, he knew that several years must pass before he could depend upon his salary. Would it not be better for him to try to continue the study of painting alone? He felt no doubt of it, for on that depended his success in life. Yet his poverty presented an almost insurmountable obstacle. He needed time and models for study; he had neither, and the necessity of procuring daily bread would not allow him to choose his labor.

The merchants who fitted out galleons for America were buying great quantities of pictures of the Virgin, for which they received good prices from the newly-converted Christians of Mexico, Peru, and Guadaloupe. These pictures, roughly painted, were called on that account Notre Dame de la Guadaloupe, and were bought by the merchants at a very low price. Murillo, for want of something better, daubed these Madonnas, and thus saved himself from starving.

He had been pursuing this business for some time, when a renowned painter, Pedro de Moya, arrived at Seville. Pedro had studied with Van Dyck, and Bartholomew, who had never seen any more beautiful pictures than those painted by his uncle, Juan del Castillo, was filled with admiration at sight of the paintings of the new comer. He was ashamed of his own work, and determined to imitate, as far as possible, Pedro de Moya. Aided by his own genius, the study of these paintings improved him very much, and his pictures of Notre Dame were quite unlike those which he had previously painted.

Murillo, emboldened by his success, presented himself to Pedro, with one of his pictures in his hand, and begged the artist to assist him with his advice. Pedro examined the picture painted by the young man, gave him some encouragement, and permission to frequent his studio. The joy of Murillo was of short duration: he lost his second master as he had lost the first. Pedro de Moya remained in Seville only a few months, and Bartholomew was almost discouraged at his departure.

What he had seen at Pedro's revealed art to him, so that it became impossible for him to continue painting mechanically, as he had heretofore done. In the midst of the grief and discouragement of the poor young man, an idea, the realization of which seemed next to impossible, occurred to him, and which smiled at his despair. Murillo said to himself, —

"The study of the *chefs-d'œuvre* which are in Italy would make me as able an artist as Pedro de Moya. I will go to Italy, even if I have to beg my way there."

But as begging was repugnant to his pride, unless absolutely forced to it, he set himself to work, day and night, with feverish ardor, and in a few weeks made so many Madonnas, Jesuses, and male and female saints, that he realized a considerable sum from the sale of them.

As soon as he found himself rich enough to go to Madrid, he set out on foot, eating only bread, and drinking water, until he arrived at the capital of Spain. There the paintings of Velasquez excited his admiration much more than those of Pedro de Moya, and he remained to study them while his funds lasted. When he had spent his last piece of money, he sold the copies which he had tried to make from the pictures of Velasquez, to a picture-dealer, and being secure of the means of living for a few days, resumed his studies.

The great desire of Murillo was, to see the author of those beautiful compositions: it seemed to him that one endowed with such a genius was more than a man. He inquired where it would be possible to meet him: he learned that the next day the court would be going to Aranjuez, and he would only have to be where the royal cortége should pass, to see the painter of Philip IV. Murillo was careful not to fail; and touched by the sweet and benevolent face of Velasquez, as much as he had been by his talent, he resolved to try to get an opportunity to speak with him. Eight days of unremitting labor enabled him to remedy the tattered condition of his garments, and no sooner had Velasquez returned to Madrid, than Murillo presented himself at the palace, and depending upon his title of Sevillian painter, he asked admission to the great artist.

Velasquez was always accessible to every one, notwithstanding his elevated position: he ordered the unknown visitor to be introduced into his studio. Murillo fell into a sort of ecstasy at sight of all the artistic riches which met his view; a celestial ray seemed to illuminate his countenance, and tears of joy flowed from his eyes. He had forgotten the artist in the art. Meanwhile Velasquez examined the intelligent face of the young man, his air of frankness, goodness, and resolution, and he felt interested in, and disposed to be useful to him. When the first emotions of Murillo had subsided a little, the painter of the king, seeing him confused and speechless, came to his aid.

"You are a painter, I see, my young fellow-countryman," he said to him.

"If I had believed I was, I shall be disabused, since I have seen your works, sir," replied Murillo. "Alas, no, I am not a painter, but I would be one, if God gave me a protector."

"Explain yourself, my friend," said Velasquez.

Murillo then related his life, his hope twice destroyed, his desire to go to Rome, and the cruel poverty which deprived him of the realization of this desire. Velasquez listened with interest; and although he had never had to contend against misery, he understood the griefs of such a contest.

"Show me some of your works," said he to him, "and if Heaven has destined you, as I believe, to become an artist, you will find in me the protector you are wishing for."

Murillo kissed the hand of the illustrious master, and blushing to bring forth his poor attempts in the midst of so many *chefs-d'œuvre*, he presented a little Madonna.

Murillo underwent the most terrible anguish during the few moments which Velasquez took to study the picture: he dared not interrogate the face of his judge, and awaited his doom with a trembling heart.

"This rough sketch predicts your future welfare," said Velasquez, at last. "Courage, my friend, and a day will come when Seville will be proud of you."

Murillo, suffocated with joy, fell on his knees before him who predicted his glory. Velasquez raised him, and pressed him to his bosom, without the young man's finding a word to express his happiness and his gratitude.

"What is your name?" asked Velasquez.

"Murillo," replied the stranger; "and if ever your grace needs some one to die for you, my life is at your disposition."

"Thank you, my child," said Velasquez; I believe in your gratitude and devotion, but, thanks to God, I hope never to claim such a proof of it. You will not die for me, Murillo; you will live for art. And now, shall I advise you?"

"I listen, my lord."

"Do not go to Italy. Madrid offers you, for some years at least, all that you can ask in Rome. The royal castles, the Escurial, this palace, and my studio, contain a sufficiently large number of pictures from different masters; all these are open to you. Study them, and when you have succeeded in gaining a name, and have created some resources, it will be easier and more advantageous to you to undertake the journey to Rome. Then I shall be able to recommend you to some celebrated artists, whose acquaintance I made when I visited that beautiful country: they will receive you as a brother, while at present I cannot give you an introduction to them."

"What kindness, my lord! Yes, I shall follow your advice, and after a few years I hope you will have no cause to blush for the noble protection you deign to grant me."

The next morning, Murillo received permission to enter wherever he found fine models to copy. Titian, Paul Veronese, Rubens, Van Dyck, were the most seductive to him, and became his favorite masters. His genius developed rapidly, and Velasquez, charmed with having discovered a talent of the first order in his rough sketches, took pleasure in teaching all the secrets of his art to his young protégé. Thanks to these lessons, and his assiduous industry, Murillo, who had commenced by ardently wishing to equal Juan del Castillo, and afterwards aspired to attain to Pedro de Moya, had nothing to desire from Velasquez himself.

He could have entered into competition with his benefactor, and courted royal favor, but, influenced by grateful feelings towards Velasquez, he left Madrid to return to Seville. His fellow-citizens, who had known him as a poor and unskilful youth, paid no attention to his return; he received no orders, excepting for three pictures for the cloister of St. Francis — pictures which the good fathers, having small means, could not afford to order from any artist of renown. But Murillo, habituated to living poorly, and realizing, besides, how important it was to make himself known, was not difficult about the conditions of payment, and set himself to work. When the three pictures were finished, his success far exceeded his expectations. The chapel of the Franciscans was besieged, so to say, for several weeks; everybody was anxious to see the wonderful pictures, and those who had seen wished to see again.

The reputation of Murillo was made. He received orders from all parts of the country, and two years after his return to Seville his name had become so great that he could marry a noble and rich lady, Dona Beatrix de Cabrera, of Sotomayor. Exempt from ambition, and preferring independence to the honors with which he had seen Velasquez surrounded, Murillo settled himself in Seville; and if he did not give up the idea of going to Italy, his passion for work prevented his accomplishing the dream of his youth.

Endowed with a brilliant and fruitful imagination, with a tender and poetic soul, he preferred *those sacred subjects, which permit art to take its flight into infinite space, to all others.* No painter has created more admirable *Virgins*, nor given such divine beauty to his *Christs* and his *Angels*. He comes nearer the Italian school than any other Spanish master. The artists of this school are, for the most part at least, designated by the name of ideal painters, because they have sought beauty even beyond reality, and have often left the care of divining their thoughts to the understanding of their admirers. The Spanish painters, on the contrary, are known by the name of naturalists, because they have tried to be true, and have expressed all their ideas, without leaving anything for the spectator to interpret. Ribera and Velasquez are first among the naturalists. Velasquez reproduced Nature with more naïveté and charm than Ribera, but Ribera painted her with more force and power. Although Murillo has put as much poetry and ideal as the Italian artists into his works, he had nevertheless remained faithful to the traditions of the Spanish school, inasmuch as there is nothing *understood* in his pictures. Thus, when he wishes to represent a saint in ecstasy, he is not satisfied with giving to the physiognomy of the saint the expression which it ought to have; he shows the divine spectacle, which, visible to his eyes for an instant, sheds upon his features a ray of infinite beatitude, the heavens open, Christ is in his glory, and the angels surround the throne of the Eternal.

Murillo's genius was most brilliant during the period which preceded his death. He had all the fresh poetry of his youth at the age of sixty years, and his pencil appeared to obey his noble inspirations more faithfully than ever. Among the great number of works which Murillo produced, the most celebrated belong to his old age. In 1674 he finished his pictures for the Charity Hospital, vast compositions, among which are the *Multiplication of Bread*, *Moses striking the Rock*, *Abraham prostrated before the three Angels*, *Return of the Prodigal Son*, and a *St. Elizabeth of Hungary*, which is considered one of the most precious *chefs-d'œuvre* of painting.

In the interval between 1674 and his death he painted twenty-three large pictures for the convent of the Capuchins; a *Child Jesus distributing Bread to the Poor*, and the *Ecstasy of St. Antonio da Padua*, which are still to be seen in one of the chapels of the cathedral of Seville.

Murillo, invited to Cadiz to decorate the grand altar of the Capuchins, went there in 1681, and commenced the *Mystic Marriage of St. Catherine*. This beautiful composition would have added to his glory, if he had had the pleasure of finishing it. While working, he fell from the scaffold and injured himself severely. At his request, he was immediately taken back to Seville. All the care by which he was surrounded only served to prolong his sufferings, and he expired on the 3d of April, 1682, at the age of sixty-four years.

His fellow-citizens, who had learned to know and to love him, bitterly bewailed his loss. They buried him in the church of Santa-Cruz, in a chapel of which he was very fond, on account of a picture by Pietro de Champagne, which he had many times admired during his infancy and youth. The subject was a Descent from the Cross. One day Murillo remained so long after mass, contemplating the picture, that it was time to close the doors of the church. The sacristan gave notice to the worshippers to retire, but the young man heard nothing; without doubt he would have remained before the altar all night, as he had all day, without observing that the light of a candle had taken the place of that of the sun, if the sacristan, seeing him standing motionless and immovable, had not come to him, and asked " why he did not go."

"I am waiting," answered the youth, "until the holy people have brought our Savior down from the cross."

The sacristan thought he was crazy, and shrugging his shoulders, dismissed him.

Three different manners are distinguishable in Murillo's works; they are what the Spaniards call cold, warm, and misty; he has succeeded equally well in all three. A smooth coloring, a light and gentle pencil, skins full of life and freshness, good understanding of *chiaro-scuro*, a true and piquant manner, and an irresistible charm, render the productions of this artist very precious. His principal works are at Seville; but the

Museum of the Louvre possesses a great number of the paintings of this master, so that one can render him justice without going to Spain. Among the paintings most admired, are a *Holy Family*, an *Assumption*, and a magnificent *Conception of the Virgin*, bought from the heirs of Marshal Soult for five hundred and eighty-six thousand francs.

The life of Murillo was as peaceful and modest as that of Velasquez had been agitated and splendid; a friend of quiet and labor, he was contented with his fate, and rendered himself doubly happy by doing good to others. The qualities of his heart equalled his talent, and not forgetting the misery of his childhood, the griefs and cares of his youth, his greatest pleasure was to give to the poor a part of the riches which he owed to his genius, and to open the path to glory for artists without fortune.

Seville is indebted to him for an Academy of Design, of which he was appointed director, and where he wished to be the first teacher. As a professor, his zeal, patience, and kindness won all hearts. His pupils loved and venerated him as a father; he had a great number, of whom the most distinguished are Antolinez, Villavicencio, Osorio, and Tobar, who, unable to attain the reputation of their master, endeavored, at least, to follow in his footsteps.

Murillo had two sons, whom he wished to become artists. Gabriel, the elder, preferred commerce to painting, and went to America to acquire wealth. Gaspard remained with his father, and became his pupil; but Murillo, seeing that nature had not endowed him with a taste for art, did not encourage him to apply himself to painting, but left him at liberty to enter the ecclesiastical state.

In the space of thirty years Spain brought forth three great geniuses, Ribera, Velasquez, and Murillo, without speaking of Alonzo Cano, who distinguished himself as a sculptor, painter, and architect. Spain produced no more celebrated painters after these.

RUBENS.

Peter Paul Rubens was born at Cologne, June 29, 1577. His family was originally from Styria, and attached to the house of the Emperor Charles V. Bartholomew Rubens, his ancestor, went to Flanders, at the coronation of the emperor, which took place at Aix-la-Chapelle, where he married, and obtained permission to give up his position at the court, in order to establish himself in his wife's family.

John Rubens, father of the great artist, was born from this union; he also married a young girl of Antwerp, by the name of Marie Pipeling. John Rubens was much esteemed in Antwerp; he was elected councillor of the Senate, which office he held six years.

Later he settled in Cologne. Having lost considerable property, he became a silversmith, and bought the house in which Marie de Medici afterwards died.

He had six children when Peter Paul was born, and this family was not only one of the most upright, but one of the happiest in Cologne. The birth of this seventh child was hailed as a favor of Providence, and yet none could foresee how glorious the name of the frail little creature was destined to be.

The Prince of Chimay and the Countess of Lalaing were his sponsors. His first years flowed pleasantly in the midst of the caresses of his relatives, who tenderly loved, and would have spoiled him, if his father and mother, who knew the importance of the first education of children, had not carefully watched over him. Peter Paul was of remarkable beauty, and of so precocious an intelligence, that he astonished by his repartees at the age of five years. He was good-hearted, gay, and amiable, but of extreme petulance, and he could hardly bear the least contradiction.

His father gave the greatest care to his education: he chose a French tutor for him, and as he himself spoke only in Latin with him, and his mother in Flemish, Peter Paul learned the three languages without thinking of it. He was afterwards sent to college, and at the age of ten years could translate Greek authors at sight: he played very well on the lute, was a good horseman, and learned fencing; in a word, excelled in everything he wished to learn.

John Rubens reflected much on the future career of this child; he felt that God had not so marvellously endowed him to be useless in the world, and he prayed that he might be permitted to direct his astonishing faculties aright, that He would show him the career which Peter Paul ought to embrace. The worthy man was deprived of the joy of witnessing the effect of his prayer. One evening, as he was quietly reading by the fireside, he heard a voice in the street calling for help. He rose to run to those who were in danger, but in his hurry he struck his head against the cornice of the chimney, and broke his temple.

This sad loss decided the mother of Peter Paul to settle her property, and return to Antwerp, where she had relations. The young Rubens continued his studies there with the same success as at Cologne: he soon excelled all his schoolmates, and the regular course of his studies not sufficing for his ardor, he learned English, Spanish, and Italian. If it had been a source of disquiet to John to know what profession was best to give his son, one may easily imagine how much this case occupied his widow. The Countess of Lalaing having expressed a desire to have Peter Paul as a page, his mother assembled her family in council, and each member advising her to accept the offer of the noble lady, the godson of the countess left college to live with her.

But the dissipated life of young gentlemen was not pleasing to Rubens, habituated as he was to the austere simplicity of his paternal roof. After an absence of one year, he returned to visit his mother, and amused himself with painting, to occupy his leisure. From a little child he had manifested great taste for drawing, and had resumed his pencil when wishing to escape the ennui inseparable from idleness. One morning his mother found him busy finishing a small picture, with which she was greatly delighted. Peter Paul took advantage of the moment to beg permission to study with some painter of repute.

Madame Rubens was surprised at such a request; she could not believe that a young gentleman like her son, having all that could be desired to succeed in the world, should think of becoming a painter. She told Paul so, but he insisted on representing to her the vacant and useless life which he was leading at the Countess of Lalaing's. The wise lady agreed with him on the latter point, and decided that he should remain at home with her. This was something gained, but it was not all. The taste of Rubens for painting assumed all the character of a real vocation. He often spoke of it to his mother, when she seemed best disposed to listen to him; but she would not consent. Again and again he insisted, and tried to persuade her, that so far from the profession of painting being unworthy of a noble man, it was, on the contrary, one of the most beautiful and glorious of professions. The widow, not venturing to take upon herself either the responsibility of opposing the wish of her son, or of acceding to it, again convoked the members of her family, and after Rubens had expressed his desires and hopes, they judged it best not to contradict him.

Some days afterwards, Peter Paul's tutor conducted him to Adam Van Ort, a painter of great repute in Antwerp, and placed him under his instruction. Adam Van Ort was a coarse, gross, uneducated man. It required great patience on the part of Rubens to bear with his hard and scolding humor, but the love of art silenced his natural vivacity. He remained eighteen months with this teacher. One day Adam entered the studio more intoxicated than usual: after abusing his pupils, he wished to beat James Jordaens, the youngest and most feeble among them. Rubens and some others took the child from him, and resolved to leave such an ill-behaved professor. Peter Paul went home to his mother, who desired him to give up painting as a profession, because people like Van Ort followed it.

Before young Rubens could answer, the visit of Prince Chimay, his godfather, was announced. The prince introduced to Madame Rubens a stranger who accompanied him, who was no other than Master Otto Vænius, then the most celebrated painter in Flanders. Paul, who had long known him by reputation, begged him to take him as a pupil; and Lady Rubens, seeing the respect and esteem in which this artist was held, perceived that there were more worthy representatives of painting than Van Ort. Otto Voenius wished to see some of young Rubens's works before entering into any engagement. A little picture, the Rape of Orithyia, which the young man had made as a gift to his mother, was shown him. The painter uttered a cry of surprise and admiration at sight of the picture: he embraced Rubens, predicting that he would one day be not only the greatest painter of Flanders, but of the world.

Dame Rubens, hearing this from one who was considered as a most skilful painter, made no hesitation about confiding her son to his care. The next morning Otto Vænius returned to Brussels, where Rubens accompanied him. The uncommon ability of the young man, his love of labor, and his charming character, won the affection of his master, who regarded him as a son. Otto Vænius well knew that his pupil would surpass him; but feeling no jealousy, he did all in his power to develop the genius with which Providence had endowed him.

During three years Rubens was the object of his most tender solicitude; and, knowing that it was indispensable for the young man to travel, he encouraged a separation which was painful to himself.

"For a long time I have had nothing to teach you, my son," he said to him; "henceforth my instruction would be superfluous: you must go to Italy, where the study of the *chefs-d'œuvre* of the great masters will perfect you."

Rubens could not refrain from weeping at the thought of separating from his second father, although he ardently desired to go to Rome. He made no objection to following the advice of his worthy master, and Otto Vænius went with him to obtain the consent of Dame Rubens to this voyage. Paul's relations deliberated again, and then gave the young painter permission to leave Flanders.

Otto Vænius had many friends in Italy, to whom he addressed letters of recommendation for his dear pupil; and he charged him to present himself to the Arch-Duke Albert, and his wife Isabella, before leaving. Rubens was most kindly received by them; the arch-duke took a gold chain from his own neck, and put it upon that of Rubens, "in order," he said, "to keep him in remembrance of the ties which ought to attach him to his country." The arch-duchess presented him with a magnificent ring. After receiving the good wishes of his mother, and her blessing, and bidding adieu to his brothers and sisters, he set out in May of the year 1600.

His first visit was to Venice, where he was transported by the works of Titian, Giorgione, and Paul Veronese; he studied them carefully, and tried to imitate what was most striking in the manner of each. A nobleman from Mantua, who saw some of Rubens's pictures, found them so beautiful, that he wrote to Vincent de Gonzaga, Duke of Mantua, in praise of this young artist. Vincent immediately invited Rubens to his court, and finding that his praises had not been exaggerated, named him his painter, made him munificent presents, and otherwise showed him much affection and esteem.

Some differences having arisen between the King of Spain and the duke, the latter, wishing to send some person capable of dissipating the prejudices which the king had against him, chose Rubens as one in whom he could best confide. The young man accepted the mission, and departed for Spain, with a suite of twenty-two persons.

He offered Philip III., on the part of Vincent, a magnificent carriage, with six Neapolitan horses. Although only twenty years old, he exceeded all the hopes of the duke. His loyalty, his frankness, the conviction with which he spoke of the court of Mantua, gained him the most complete success. Philip III. testified his satisfaction that the duke had chosen him for ambassador, and at his departure gave tangible proofs of his kindly feeling towards him. The Duke of Mantua received him with open arms, proclaimed him as skilful a diplomatist as a great painter, and, according to an historian of Ferrara, required that he should pass the whole day in the apartment of the duchess, as *a son of the house.*

A year passed before Rubens could think of leaving Mantua; however, as all the kindness of the duke could not make him forget the purpose for which he had come to Italy, he solicited and obtained his dismissal.

Vincent forced him to accept a large sum of money, and made him a present of a superb gold chain, "although," continues the same historian, "Rubens had received so many since he came to Spain, that there was no more place on his breast for the new one: he wore about twenty thousand ducats worth of gold and precious stones, presents and honorable testimonials of kings, princes, and princesses, whose portraits he had painted, or whose courts he had visited.

Rubens went to Rome, and was received with every mark of distinction by the Cardinal Cynthio Aldobrandini, to whom Duke Vincent had recommended him. Aldobrandini presented him to his uncle, Pope Clement VII., who, charmed with the talent of the artist, endeavored to retain him in Rome; but Peter Paul desired to remain only a few months: he painted three pictures, which had been ordered by the Arch-Duke Albert for the chapel of St. Helena, in the church of the Holy Cross, and then departed for Florence.

The duke, very happy to have a visit from him, engaged him to paint his own portrait, and placed it in the gallery where were the portraits of the greatest painters in the world. After executing some important works in Florence, he went to Bologna, on a visit to the Carracci, and returned to Venice, to enjoy the immortal compositions of the painters who have rendered that city illustrious. The Pope recalled him to Rome; and while there he painted twelve pictures, representing the twelve apostles, for the Palace Rospigliosi. He also painted several pieces for the Princess Scalamara, the Cardinal Chizi, Prince Colonna, and the Pope. Having a desire to return to Flanders, he set out for Milan and Geneva, which he wished to see before leaving Italy.

At Milan he drew the famous *Supper* of Leonardo da Vinci. He stopped much longer at Geneva, which he intended to see in passing only: there he designed, and had engraved, a splendid collection, which was afterwards published at Antwerp, under the title of *Palazzi di Genoa.*

Peter Paul did not wish to undertake anything new until he had seen again his native country, and embraced his mother: it was seven years since he left that dear mother, and during that time he had acquired fortune and glory enough to satisfy the most ambitious person; he had done enough to render the name which he bore celebrated; he felt the need of witnessing the joy of his dear mother at his return, and receiving her maternal felicitations, after so many others. He freighted a small vessel, which was to take him immediately to Flanders, and he prepared to depart. Just as he was about to embark, he received a letter, informing him that this good mother was dangerously ill, and desired to see him before she died. Who can tell the grief and mortal anguish to which he was a prey during the journey? At Flanders he heard that he was too late. . . . Then, instead of going to Antwerp, where his family awaited him, he shut himself up in the convent of St. Michael, where his mother was buried. He remained there four months, giving himself up entirely to his grief, and the pious care of erecting a monument to his beloved mother. He had no wish to leave the cloister; and all the prayers of Otto Vænius, his good master, and those of Arch-Duke Albert, were hardly sufficient to make him resume his pencil.

The arch-duke called him to court, named him his painter, and gave him the chamberlain's golden key. Rubens could no longer resist so much kindness; but fearing that if he remained at the palace he should not have time enough to work, he obtained permission to settle in Antwerp, where he bought a house, and reconstructed it in Roman style, and collected therein all the objects of art which he had bought in travelling, such as paintings, antique statues, busts, bass-reliefs, medallions, and cameos. He arranged a magnificent studio, with a royal staircase leading to it, over which immense pictures could be carried.

Soon after Rubens had settled in Antwerp, he married Isabella Brant, a good and beautiful young lady, the niece of his elder brother Philip's wife. His first child, named Albert, was held at the baptismal font by the arch-duke.

No painter ever rose so quickly, or so high, in the esteem of his fellow-countrymen. Before going to Italy,

Rubens, by the advice of Otto Vænius, had concealed his paintings from public view; since his return to Flanders he had done nothing, and yet was much talked of. His reputation overshadowed that of other painters, who, after giving way to jealousy for a short time, recognized his superiority; and after seeing a *Holy Family*, which the arch-duke had ordered of Peter Paul to ornament his oratory, they became his most ardent admirers.

The fraternity of St. Ildefonso, for whom he painted a picture representing the Virgin seated upon a golden throne, and giving the chasuble to St. Ildefonso, received him as a member. He also painted the portraits of Albert and Isabella upon the two shutters which covered the picture. The admiration caused by this beautiful picture surpasses all that can be imagined. The treasurer of the fraternity offered Rubens a large sum for it, which he refused, saying that he was but too well paid by the honor of being a member of their illustrious society.

Every year that followed the establishment of Rubens in Flanders added to his talent, his renown, and his fortune. He lived like a prince; yet, faithful to art, to which he was so much indebted, he never felt happier than when he was at work in his studio. Peter Paul was not only an eminent painter, but also an architect. The Jesuits of Antwerp wished the plan of a church, in the construction of which they could use a large quantity of different marbles, taken by the Spaniards from an Algerine corsair. The church, which was much admired, was built on Rubens's plan, and he enriched it with magnificent pictures. Unfortunately this church was entirely destroyed by lightning in 1718.

The queen, Marie de Medici, wishing to decorate the Palace of Luxembourg, charged the ambassador to Flanders to invite Rubens to Paris. He went, and, after an understanding with the princess upon the subjects which he should paint, he obtained permission to execute them at his own home. Peter Paul was twenty months painting twenty-four pictures, which contain the whole history of Marie de Medici up to 1620, the time at which they were painted. Rubens took them to Paris, and attended to placing them, to the great joy of the queen, who never tired of admiring the talent displayed in them, and the promptitude with which he had gratified her wishes.

The court shared the queen's enthusiasm, and Rubens was employed to retrace the great deeds of Henry IV. in a new suite of pictures — a task which he accepted with great pleasure. Soon after, discord breaking out between the queen-mother and Louis XIII., Marie de Medici left France, and the work of the great painter was interrupted.

Rubens saw the Duke of Buckingham, ambassador from England, in Paris, and learned from him that Charles I. would willingly renew the old relations with Spain, which had been troubled by various events.

Rubens reported the words of Buckingham to the Arch-Duchess Isabella, daughter of the King of Spain; and she, knowing how much one could depend upon the ability of the artist, empowered him to hold a diplomatic correspondence with the duke, whilst she would undertake to bring the King of Spain to the sentiments expressed by the court of England.

Rubens did not neglect his painting, even while occupied in these negotiations. It was about this time that he painted those of his pictures which he considered the best. Shut up in a castle, which he built near Malines, he painted many admirable compositions for the cathedral and church of St. John of Malines, among which is the *Miraculous Draught of Fishes.*

The death of his wife, in 1626, tore him away from this pleasant solitude; his friends urged him to travel, to divert his grief. He went through Holland, visited all the artists of renown, and enriched his collections with some of their works, for which he paid royally. In this journey he also found the means of being useful to the arch-duchess, by bringing about a good understanding between the states of Holland and the court of Brussels.

Shortly afterwards the King of Spain, Philip IV., wrote to the arch-duchess, his daughter, to send Rubens to him, that he might confer with him upon the subject of the negotiations undertaken with England. He set out for Madrid in 1627: it was there that he met Velasquez, with whom he formed an intimate friendship.

Philip was as much astonished by his penetration and ability in business matters as by his wonderful talent for painting: this prince retained him at his court eighteen months; he then sent him to England, after having presented him with a ring of inestimable value, and six Andalusian horses, the handsomest that could be found. When Rubens arrived in London, Buckingham was dead; he then addressed himself to Chancellor Cottington, who presented him to the king.

Charles I. received the illustrious painter with due honors, and ordered a portrait. But the mind of Rubens was bent upon the mission with which he had been intrusted by Philip IV.: he rendered his conversation agreeable to the king, who, knowing that he came from Spain, conversed upon the difficulties existing between the two countries. Then Rubens told him of the propositions of which he was bearer; and, Charles having accepted him as a mediator, he succeeded in making the basis of a treaty of peace, favorable to England as well as to Spain. Charles was so delighted that he knighted Rubens in full Parliament, put a valuable ring upon his finger, gave him a chain, with his portrait attached, and forced him to accept the bordering of his hat, which was worth thirty thousand francs. Rubens left seventeen pictures in England, a painted ceiling, in the Palace of Whitehall, and an equestrian portrait of the king, under the figure of St. George.

The great artist returned to Brussels, for a short time,

on his way to Spain, charged by the arch-duchess with a mission for Philip IV. This prince, well pleased with what he had accomplished in London, gave him the Golden Key, — a very enviable distinction at the court of Spain, — made him other presents, and charged him with instructions for the States of Holland.

Rubens was delighted to return home to Antwerp, where he recommenced work with a feeling of happiness to which he had long been a stranger. Although he had not abandoned art, he had been much distracted by diplomacy during the four years which had passed. He resolved henceforward to live as a simple citizen, and married, for his second wife, Helena Forman, who, much younger than he, of great beauty, sought only the glory of his name, which she should partake by this alliance. More than once did Rubens regret his sweet and modest Isabelle, who loved him for himself, and never had other care than for his happiness.

The illustrious painter found a great consolation in his labors: assailed by demands for his pictures, he succeeded, through his great facility, in satisfying them. Besides, his pupils, sincerely devoted to his glory, did for him what Raphael's pupils had done: the thoughts of the master sprang up under their pencils, and Rubens, by some wise finishing strokes, impressed the seal of his genius upon them.

His beautiful and glorious career finished but too soon. Peter Paul was not fifty-five years old when violent attacks of gout interrupted his work. At first, sustained by the thought that his sufferings would diminish, he hoped for relief; but they increased so much that he understood that he was past recovery, and resigned himself, calling to mind the virtues of his father, and the pious lessons of his mother. He suffered the most terrible pains, and the idleness they imposed upon him, for six years, without a murmur: finally he died, May 30, 1640, at the age of sixty-three years.

He was buried in the Church of St. James, at Antwerp, where Helena raised a tomb to his memory, the most beautiful ornament of which is a picture by Rubens's own hand.

The principal works of this great master are at Brussels, Ghent, Malines, Antwerp, London, Paris, Madrid, and Rome. There is no museum which does not possess one or more: it is estimated that he left at least thirteen hundred pictures. No kind of painting was unknown to him, — history, landscapes, portraits, fruits and flowers, animals, — all, in turn, occupied his pencil, without one's being able to say in which he excelled. In Rubens were united all the qualities which make great painters, — an elevated genius, vivid and fruitful imagination, varied instruction, a bold, easy, and light touch, true and brilliant coloring. The brilliancy, harmony, and strength which characterize his pictures cannot be too much admired. Nowhere can be found more beautiful ideas, rendered with more nobleness and charm, more varied positions of the head, more life-like, fresher skins, gracefully-thrown draperies, or more truthful and more feeling expression. Some critics reproach him with incorrectness in his figures, and heavy design; but if some of Rubens's works have these faults, it may be supposed that they are not entirely from his own hand; for those which he did himself, with care, are exempt.

Rubens invented so easily, that, if he painted the same subject several times, he always found a new arrangement for the scenes he was to reproduce, different attitudes, and different personages; he made an almost new creation of each copy. He worked with such freedom of mind, that he listened to the reading of celebrated authors and poets, or recited verses himself, while painting. The drawings of this artist are of a firm and wise touch, and replete with spirit and harmony. Rubens also engraved several pieces.

The genius of this great man would have raised him to the first rank in whatever career he might have chosen. As a child, he was remarkable for the facility with which he acquired languages, belles-lettres, and sciences; as a young man, he excelled in arts; at the age of manhood, he conducted the most difficult negotiations with uncommon ability. After the death of the Arch-Duke Albert, Isabella often called upon him for advice and assistance; the kings of Spain and England confided their interests to him, and had no cause to repent their choice.

From the age of twenty, when he was rich and honored, to the time of his death, his reputation and fortune continually increased. He was noble in appearance and manners, his mind was brilliant and solid, and the charm of his conversation caused him to be sought by princes as by artists. He kept up a correspondence with noblemen of different courts of Europe, and kings themselves were happy to be numbered among his friends. His house was a magnificent palace, ornamented with some of his richest pictures: there he received the visits of guests illustrious by their rank or their talent. Rubens lived surrounded by his pupils, as a prince surrounded by his court, or, more properly speaking, as a father in the midst of his children. Among the pupils who became distinguished were Diepenbach, Jacques Jordaens, David Teniers, Juste, Vanmol, Van Tulden, and many others; but Van Dyck eclipsed them all, and inherited the glory of his master.

Although Rubens had studied the Italian schools with great care, he belonged to none of them. He is himself the head of a school which changed the face of painting. We find nothing of the idealistic painters in him; he has imitated Nature, though not servilely; he knew how to express all her power and force without diminishing her grace and beauty. Something great and noble prevents this imitation of nature from becoming trivial; and if he has not obtained his types from the ideal, they are none the less remarkable for their grandeur than for their truth.

VAN DYCK.

Antonio Van Dyck was born at Antwerp the 22d of March, 1599. His father was a glass-painter, and his mother, who painted landscapes very well, gave him early instruction in painting, and he succeeded so well, that they resolved to make an artist of him. When he was old enough to leave his paternal home for the studio of a master, they placed him under the care of Henry Van Balen, who was considered a very skilful painter; he had travelled in Italy, and studied the *chefs-d'œuvre* of that country with great success. He soon perceived uncommon ability in his pupil, which he cultivated with zeal, and after some years passed under his direction, Van Dyck presented himself to Rubens, who was then the king of painting.

Rubens took him into the number of his pupils, for whom he soon became a second master, as he promptly seized the manner of the illustrious artist, and gained his confidence and affection. Rubens, being overburdened with work, left to Van Dyck the care of painting the most unimportant parts of his pictures; then he allowed him to paint the whole, reserving the finishing touches for himself, before inscribing the name Rubens.

One day, when the great master, called away by important business, had forgotten to lock the door of the particular studio in which he loved to paint alone, his pupils, yielding to their curiosity, slipped in to examine his work. The picture was the *Descent from the Cross*, one of his masterpieces. At first the young people respectfully admired the beautiful picture, but soon forgetting where they were, they began to play, and the wildest enticing the rest, they chased each other in high glee through the studio, until one of them slipped, and falling, threw down the easel. *When, raising the picture, they saw that the arm of the Magdalen and a part of the Virgin's face were effaced, a cry of distress resounded through the studio.* What was to be done? They could hope for no indulgence from Rubens for a fault followed by such an accident; he would send the guilty ones away, without doubt; and where could they find another master qualified to take his place?

Van Dyck persuaded his comrades to cease their useless complaints, and offered to try to repair the damage. He set about it, and in a few hours the picture was as Rubens had left it. The pupils went out of the cabinet, shutting the door, and each anxiously awaited the morrow. The master came as usual, followed by his pupils, to whom he distributed their work for the day: he stood before his picture of the *Descent from the Cross*, examined it some moments, then, satisfied with his work, he said to his pupils, —

"How do this head and this arm appear to you? It is surely not the poorest part of what I did yesterday."

The pupils, stupefied, did not answer. Rubens commenced work, and soon discovered that the parts of the picture which he had just praised were not from his own hand, and the pupils were obliged to tell him the truth. The master felicitated Van Dyck, embraced him tenderly, and advised him to go to Italy. The young man anticipated the voyage with pleasure; he made all preparations, and after a few weeks, took leave of Rubens, who gave him a fine horse, a purse of gold, and wished him good success.

Some historians assert that Rubens, fearing that his own reputation would fade before Van Dyck's, advised his departure; but in Rubens's station he had nothing to fear, and we are much more inclined to think that his advice was wholly disinterested.

Van Dyck joyfully set out upon the beautiful horse which his master had given him, yet he did not go far. Captivated by the beauty of a young girl whom he saw in one of the villages through which he passed, he forgot Italy, and installed himself near her dwelling for several months. Rubens, hearing this, went himself to recall Van Dyck to the glory which he was renouncing. Docile to his master's voice, Van Dyck recognized his error, and continued his route. He left a picture in the village, *St. Martin tearing his Cloak in two to cover a Beggar*. Van Dyck, having spent all the money which he owed to Rubens's liberality, offered the curate to make any picture he should choose for his church, provided they would furnish him with canvas and colors. The good curate, who had heard the young man spoken of as the favorite pupil of the great painter of Antwerp, did not hesitate to procure what he wished, and was so much pleased with the picture, which really was one of Van Dyck's best, that he immediately paid him one hundred florins.

This was sufficient for the young man's travelling expenses. At Venice, he studied and copied the compositions of Titian, of Paul Veronese, and of Tintoretto. Then he went to Rome, Naples, and Sicily, thence to Genoa, where he remained some time, occupied upon the portraits of the principal characters of the city. Finally, content with the progress he had made, he wished to see Flanders again. In a few years he attained a brilliant reputation, which was heightened by the following incident: —

The Canons of Courtray ordered a picture for the grand altar of their Chapter House. Van Dyck painted a *Christ on the Cross*, and chose the moment at which the executioners were raising the cross, to which Christ was fastened, to place it in the ground. The picture was admirable: but unfortunately it did not please the canons. They cried out, and said that the painter, who had been so much praised, was good for nothing but a sign dauber. Van Dyck made no reply, placed the picture, and demanded the price fixed, refusing to take less. The canons complained of their misfortune; but, to their great surprise, the connoisseurs, to whom they showed the Christ, declared that they never saw anything more beautiful. The more the picture had been decried, the more it was praised; people flocked to see it, and the canons, recognizing their error, requested Van Dyck to paint two other pictures, which he refused to do.

Jealousy excited enmity among the Flemish painters, and Van Dyck, who loved peace, left Antwerp, and went to establish himself at the Hague, where he was kindly received by the Prince of Orange. All the distinguished persons of the court, beginning with the prince and princess, wished their portraits from the hand of Van Dyck.

From the Hague he went to England, where he was unknown, and remained but a short time. After his departure they learned who he was, and King Charles I. sent a nobleman after him to beg him to return. Van Dyck accepted the invitation of the king, who gave him a flattering reception. His first pictures caused much admiration at the court: Charles, who was passionately fond of the arts, knighted him, presented him with a gold chain, and his portrait enriched with diamonds.

The royal favor enhancing the reputation of Van Dyck, he was overwhelmed with orders. He married into the illustrious family of Count Gowry, lived in great style, had his equerries, pages, and the most beautiful horses in London. The luxury of his table equalled that of his equipage: he was accustomed to invite the nobility, who came to his studio for sittings, and hired musicians played the most delightful symphonies during the repast.

Van Dyck received such large sums for his smallest pictures, that he could have allowed himself all these expenses, if his taste for alchemy had not caused him to sacrifice more gold on chimerical hopes than was necessary for his family expenses. The enormous sums which he spent obliged him to forced labor, which did not fail to prey upon his health. At first he did not perceive this; and finding that he had acquired sufficient renown in England, he went to Paris, to solicit the honor of painting the gallery of the Louvre; but he came too late: the decoration of the gallery had been given to Poussin.

Van Dyck then returned to his native country, but his wife not being able to habituate herself to living in Flanders, he took her back to England. No sooner was it known that he had returned, than he was overpowered with orders: there was scarcely a nobleman in the whole United Kingdom who would not have sold lands, or mortgaged castles, to bequeath his portrait, painted by Van Dyck, to his descendants. The artist resumed his pencil, refusing to listen to the advice of friends who begged him to moderate his ardor. Soon their fears were realized; too much fatigue exhausted the illustrious painter; he sickened and died at the age of forty-one.

He was buried with great pomp in the Church of St. Paul, London, and a magnificent tomb raised to him.

The principles and manner of Rubens are recognizable in Van Dyck's works; however, as a historical painter, he is inferior to his master, although his pencil is often more flowing, and neater, his complexions fresher, and his drawing more elegant. But in portraits, Van Dyck excelled. He could catch the physiognomy of a person, and express his character in his features; in a word, render nature with more grace, spirit, nobleness, and truth than almost any other painter. A brilliant coloring, heads and hands perfect, a wonderful understanding of adjustment, distinguish the portraits of Van Dyck, and place them by the side of those of Titian, which they excel, even in beauty of detail.

This master has become well known through engraving, and he himself reproduced some of his best pieces in this way. We are indebted to him for the portraits of the principal artists of his time, portraits for which he would receive no remuneration, being, as he said, but too happy to be able to immortalize himself by reproducing the features of those to whose genius posterity would render homage.

REMBRANDT.

Paul Gerretz, known by the name of Rembrandt, was born in 1606, in a mill, situated upon an arm of the Rhine, between the villages of Leyendorp and Konkerck, some leagues from Leyden. His father, to whom the mill belonged, called himself Van Rheyn, to distinguish himself from the other members of the family: this name is often added to that of the painter, whose history we are about to relate.

Paul was sent, when very young, to the University of Leyden, because his parents wished to make a learned man of him, and preferred any other than the paternal profession. Their disappointment was very great, when they learned that either through want of intelligence, or of good will, the child made very little progress. Although it grieved them very much to renounce the hope of his becoming a learned man, they took him home, determined to employ him in the mill. Rembrandt felt no regret at leaving Leyden, but his father soon perceived that his assistance would be of trifling use to him. Paul paid little attention to the instructions which were given him, and instead of working, he passed the greater part of the day in copying engravings which he had bought at Leyden, or in drawing the different objects which offered themselves to his view.

"You will never become rich if you spend your time

in such childishness," said his father, who knew that he was much preoccupied with the idea of making a fortune.

"Who knows my father?" replied the young man. "Have you not heard of the fabulous wealth of Master Rubens, the Flemish painter? Why should not I make a fortune as he did?"

Van Rheyn shook his head.

"Try to place me with a painter for some months," said Paul; "and if at the end of the time he does not find that I have a talent for painting, I will return to you, and then I promise you I will work."

The name of Rubens had awakened in the heart of the miller the ambition which he had so unwillingly renounced of seeing his son distinguish himself in some brilliant career: he acceded to Paul's desire, and placed him in the studio of Jacques Zvaanemburg. Jacques was not an able master, but the genius of his new pupil supplied the insufficiency of his lessons. Instead of some months, Rembrandt passed three years under his direction, and left him to go to Amsterdam, where Peter Lastman and George Schooten finished teaching him the principles of painting. When he had learned all that he could from them, he went home, and studied nature with indefatigable ardor. His father and mother, astonished at his talent, advised him to establish himself in some large city, not doubting that he would eclipse the greatest painters. But Paul, mistrusting their judgment in this matter, obstinately refused to allow any one to see his sketches. He worked in this way some time longer; finally, giving way to the entreaties of his mother, he consented to show a small picture, which he had just finished, to some of his friends. They spoke of it to others, and strangers who were in the village wished to see the works of the young miller. Great was their surprise on seeing a finished canvas, that a master of renown would acknowledge, instead of the rough sketch of a beginner: they manifested their pleasure to Rembrandt, predicting a glorious future, and advising him to carry the picture to the city, where amateurs would not be wanting.

Paul took their advice, and was half crazy with joy at having an offer of one hundred florins for his picture. He returned in triumph to the paternal mill, but only to take leave of his parents, for he had already chosen an atelier at the Hague. As soon as he was installed there, he set to work with a zeal which was stimulated by the pleasure of receiving considerable sums for each of his pictures. The young painter made himself known in a short time, and when he had acquired the degree of reputation which he wished, opened a school for painting and received quite a number of pupils. Rembrandt set a good price upon his lessons, was soon in easy circumstances, and in a few years rich.

Differing from those artists who, for the most part, spend their money as easily as they gain it, and who love to surround themselves with all the superfluities of luxury, and all that pertains to an elegant life, Rembrandt adhered to his habits of simplicity and parsimony. He chose a rich country girl for a wife, that she might not oblige him to go into society, for which he had no taste, perhaps because he could not go without expense.

Paul loved money, not for the enjoyments which it procured, but for itself; and if we may believe his historians, he took all means to procure it. He worked night and day to meet the numerous orders which he received. He sold the copies of his pupils as his own work, after having retouched and given them the seal which belonged to him alone. It was in vain that persons distinguished by birth or talent invited him to their society; he paid no attention to them, and continued to prefer the society of the common people to theirs. When asked the reason, he answered, that exempt from all ambition, he only wished to live free and forgotten; but he was careful not to acknowledge that interest had much more to do with his choice than modesty.

The only passion in which he indulged was that for old furniture, old stuffs, old armor, and instruments of all sorts. He filled his studio with them, so that on entering one might have supposed himself in a second-hand warehouse. He called them, jokingly, his antiques, since some connoisseurs, observing incorrectness in some of his works, had advised his going to Italy, to perfect himself by the study of the master-pieces of antiquity.

Rembrandt never thought of undertaking such a journey; it seemed almost that he feared he should lose the repute he was enjoying, by the ardor with which he worked the mine of gold which his pencil had opened to him. He remained the whole day sitting on a wooden bench before his easel in the midst of his old things, and left his work only to partake of his repast, which almost invariably consisted of a salted herring, and bread and cheese, with cold water. He was careful that his wife, the children, and an old servant, his only domestic, should follow the same regimen, or some other of no greater expense. The luxury of clothing corresponded to that of the table; and whoever saw Master Rembrandt, would have taken him for an artisan, in common circumstances, and not for an arch-millionaire painter.

The avaricious enjoy a pleasure unknown to others. When all were asleep in his house, Paul opened the boxes which enclosed his treasures and contemplated them with exultation. Music had for his ears no such agreeable harmony as the ringing of gold. He counted and recounted it, plunged his hands with delight into the mass, which he raised and let fall in brilliant cascades; then trembling with the fear of being seen, he hastily closed his money-box, and kept guard over it.

When some poor farmer, ruined by the unpropitiousness of the seasons, could not pay his rent, he had recourse to Rembrandt, who was said to be rich, very rich; when children, anxious to dissipate the paternal heritage, knocked at the door of his studio, neither farmer nor young gentleman went away empty-handed, if they could give good security, and were willing to pay usurious interest. Rembrandt must be well paid for the privation of the gold which he could neither see, hear, nor admire for a time.

It was well known that Rembrandt was a miser; that he lent money on usury; that he was not scrupulous in the practice of any trick to augment his wealth; yet people thought much of his talent and his works, so that he never failed to sell them, let him ask what price he would. If he imagined that their enthusiasm was in the least abating, he pretended that he would leave Holland, or go to Italy or France to live, and then they would pay whatever he required, thinking that perhaps it would be the last of his *chefs-d'œuvre* which they could obtain.

Very often, when he sent his son to sell his drawings or his engravings, he told him to say that he had stolen them from him, and that he, Master Rembrandt, was saving his collection of drawings and engravings for a foreign prince, and would be furious if he knew that they were being sold singly. And as he feared that the youth might keep a part of the money he received for himself, he never failed, after having taught him so well to lie, to sermonize him upon the horror which one ought to have for falsehood.

The oddest idea which the love of gain could suggest,

was that of feigning death. He confided it to his wife, who, not less avaricious than he, put on mourning, and announced, with tears in her eyes, that Master Rembrandt, her dear husband, who had left home for a few days, was dead. The news quickly spread, and amateurs soon ran to the house of the deceased to trade with the widow for the works which he had left. The studio was well filled with pictures, which were sold in a few hours, at much greater prices than had been offered to the artist himself; for, since he was dead, they could never find paintings to be compared to his for the magic of coloring, the force of expression, and the minute study of details. The traders and the amateurs competed for the possession of the *chefs-d'œuvre*, which became the property of him who paid the most. Rembrandt, concealed behind some tapestry, witnessed the strange comedy, joyfully rubbing his hands, and could with difficulty abstain from interfering in the debates of the purchasers.

When the sale was finished, he came forward, and warmly thanked his admirers for all the praises they had bestowed upon him.

"I had wished," he said, "to know what posterity would say of me, and the proof is so favorable, that when I receive my final summons, I shall, thanks to you, gentlemen, sleep in peace. But thanks to God, I hope to work many years longer, and to satisfy those among you who were regretting that you possessed only a small number of my pictures."

The astonished assembly thought best to laugh at the ruse, and said to each other, that a man of genius is permitted to be a little original. Rembrandt counted his florins, tranquilly resumed his pencil, and recommenced his accustomed life. He worked unremittingly, and painted a great number of historical pieces, interior scenes and portraits. Among the first is a *Tobias*, an admirable composition, in which all the heads appear to live and speak, and where there is nothing to be desired in arrangement, color, and finish.

Rembrandt succeeded astonishingly in portraits. It is said that in order to make his talent in this style known, he painted the portrait of his domestic, and placed it at the window. The neighbors were at first deceived by it, and saluted the old lady, who did not answer. Astonished at such impoliteness, quite unnatural to the curious and talkative old woman, they drew nearer, and recognized their error with bursts of laughter. They told of it to all who would listen, and soon there was not a person in the Hague who had not seen the portrait painted by Master Rembrandt. The nobles and richest people had their portraits taken by him, and nothing could equal the expression, the truth, and the life he gave them. However, he had the fault of not being willing to listen to any suggestion on the part of his patrons; he would neither flatter or make them younger, nor would he allow them to take any other position than he chose. He was the master, and they must do as he said, or give up having their portraits painted by him.

What he wished was not always convenient or agreeable: for example, while he was painting the picture of a family, some one came and told him that a monkey, of which he was very fond, was just dying. Rembrandt expressed his regrets, and continued his work; but, by an odd fancy, he painted the face of the favorite which he had just lost in the foreground of the picture. When the persons for whom he had commenced painting saw this monkey's head, they found it was an ill-timed pleasantry; but it was quite another thing, for the artist declared that he wished to paint this souvenir of the animal he loved, and that he would not erase it. They were angry; then, somewhat appeased, they begged him to take away that grimacing face. Rembrandt would hear to nothing; he preferred keeping the picture, and paying back that which he had received in advance for it.

His pupils, who knew so well to what point the artist carried his love for gold, could scarcely believe that he would make such a sacrifice to the memory of the monkey. They had often amused themselves by painting pieces of money on bits of paper, which they threw on the floor, and which Rembrandt would pick up. His avidity, and disappointment on recognizing his mistake, caused bursts of laughter, in which he almost always joined.

"What are you thinking of, my children?" he would say; "the times are hard, and there is not the smallest bit of money which will not help carry one to the end of the year. You are young and prodigal, I am old and economical; you are foolish, and I am wise."

Thus this man, who lived only on privations, who refused himself not only the pleasures which other men seek, but also the happiness of ameliorating the sufferings of his fellow-creatures, of seeing happiness enter the bosom of poor families, under the form of a little of that gold which he hid away, — this man believed himself wise. A strange effect of the passions which take possession of our hearts: they obscure our intelligence, and falsify our judgment.

Rembrandt died in 1674, at the age of sixty-eight years. He is considered as one of the most celebrated artists. He received from Nature a remarkable genius, which labor alone developed, since he studied neither ancient or modern masters. He is particularly distinguished by a powerful originality; he never imitated, and none of the painters who have followed have been able to seize his manner. Rembrandt possessed the knowledge of *chiaro-scuro* to an eminent degree; he can be compared only to Titian for the freshness and truth of his complexions. His figures appear to stand out in relief from the picture; his faces are varied, full of naïvéte and expression; his old men's heads are particularly good. Looking at Rembrandt's pictures near, they appear carelessly shaded and rough; but seen from a distance, they are all harmony and smoothness. The groundwork is generally black, which gives a wonderful effect. If the beauty of type and the purity of lines which characterize the Italian paintings are not found in his compositions, Nature is found there, given with so much truth and liveliness that we never cease to admire them.

Rembrandt has left many fine landscapes, some drawings, not perfectly correct, but very expressive, and some engravings, which are much esteemed by connoisseurs. The most celebrated of the engravings represents Christ healing the sick. It is known by the name of *the piece of one hundred francs,* because each proof was sold at that price by Rembrandt. The artist had a great number of pupils, among whom were Flinck, Eckoutz, and, above all, Gerard Dow, whose small pictures are marvels of grace, freshness, and truth.

LE POUSSIN.

Nicholas Poussin was born the 16th of June, 1594, at the Castle of Villiers, near Andelys. His father was of a noble family, but his fortune was small, and he married the widow of an attorney. He and his wife differed in their ideas of the education of their children: faithful to the noble recollections of his race, he hoped to make a valiant warrior of his son Nicholas, while his wife ardently desired that he should join the clergy. Neither father nor mother had their wish.

Nicholas early manifested much taste for drawing; to crayon portraits, to paint flowers, trees, birds, had been his greatest amusements. Quentin Varin, a painter of some celebrity in Normandy, having been engaged to restore the Castle of Vernon, made the acquaintance of the father of Nicholas, and, having seen some of the child's sketches, he recognized such a gift for drawing that he wished to teach him the first principles. The progress of his pupil so entirely surpassed his hopes, that he proposed to his friend, with whose precarious situation he was acquainted, to make a painter of his son, rather than a soldier.

M. Poussin reluctantly yielded to this advice; and Quentin Varin, in a short time, was obliged to declare that he could teach Nicholas nothing more. Nicholas, who was then eighteen years old, bade adieu to the castle in which he had passed his childhood, and set out for Paris, where he hoped to find competent teachers, and to make a fortune speedily. But he soon found that he had deluded himself; the teachers were his inferiors, and instead of a fortune, misery stared at him. But men of genius are not cast down by misfortune. Poussin waited hopefully.

He worked with a brave heart; and when he went out of the poor room which served him for a studio, it was to study nature. In one of his excursions through the country he met a young gentleman, with whom he entered into conversation; they separated, promising to meet again, and in a few days they loved each other like brothers. The young gentleman being called to Poitou by his family, wished Nicholas to accompany him, assuring him that his mother would be delighted to receive him, and happy to decorate her castle with some of his works. Poussin accepted the invitation of his friend. However, he was coldly, and almost disdainfully, received in the house which he had promised himself to consider as his home; but his pride equalling his talent, he would not accept such hospitality. He was inspired with a desire to see Rome by the sight of some of Raphael's and Julio Romano's engravings. He resolved to work unremittingly, in order to amass a sufficiency for the expenses of the voyage. To work! But who would give him work? In vain he knocked at the doors of castles and convents; he looked so poor that no one could conceive of his merit, and everybody turned him off: as a last resource, he commenced sign-painting.

This did not pay well, even if he could get enough of it.

Poussin suffered all sorts of privations, and, not knowing what to do to earn his own living, he sold himself to some recruiters; but fasting had rendered him so feeble that he was considered unfit for military service. Again he took courage, and, despite his bad luck, felicitating himself upon the recovery of his liberty and his pencil, he sought work so persistently that he at length found it. Although his wages were very small, he put aside a part every day; for he had not given up the idea of seeing the *chefs-d'œuvre* of Italy. His little treasure increased, and he was already planning for his journey, when, one fine morning, he discovered that the purse, on which he founded all his hopes, had been stolen.

It was useless to be discouraged; it was better to try to forget this misfortune, and begin again to work, and to economize. Poussin thought so, and went back to Paris, which he had left to draw nearer to Italy, painting in every town through which he passed. He was then poor and unknown, when, in 1632, the Jesuits celebrated the canonization of St. Ignatius and St. Francis Xavier. The pupils of the fathers wished to present the church of their college with several pictures, representing the miracles of these two saints; and a great number among them being acquainted with Nicholas, offered him the charge of painting the pictures, which he thankfully accepted. In six days Poussin painted six pictures, in distemper, which were much admired, by amateurs, for their boldness. Among the amateurs was the Cavalier Marin, an Italian poet, who, ready to return to Italy, offered to take the young painter with him. Nicholas would gladly have accepted this offer; but he had promised many works, and, wishing to keep his word, he remained.

As soon as he had finished the pictures he had engaged to paint, he set out for Italy. He was not very rich;

but by working a little on the way, he arrived at Rome, without having entirely exhausted the sums received for his last pictures. He found the Cavalier Marin, who cordially received him, recommended him to Cardinal Barberini, and advised him to study not only the *chefs-d'œuvre* of paintings, but the ancient and modern poets, and the lives of the great men. Poussin felt that he should find noble inspirations in these readings, and followed the advice of his protector. Unhappily for him, the poet died soon after his arrival in Rome, and Cardinal Barberini went to France.

Poussin, left without friends and without support, was reduced to such straitened circumstances that he turned his attention to architecture, sculpture, and all kinds of painting, to obtain a livelihood. Painting was then beginning to decline in the city of the fine arts. The manner of Michael Angelo Caravaggio was substituted for the sublime style of Raphael; and the first pictures which Poussin brought forward caused him to be recognized as an opponent to the new method, of which many amateurs had declared themselves partisans: these pictures were not well received. Poussin, seeing the hope which he had of gaining a name as soon as he became acquainted with artists and connoisseurs, vanish, experienced the most cruel torments which can be inflicted on a man of genius; he doubted himself, and questioned whether he should still continue to struggle, or abandon his pencil forever.

At this time he became acquainted with a French painter named Dughet, who enjoyed considerable reputation in Rome. This painter had a daughter, beautiful and good, and very courageous; she appreciated Poussin's talent, sustained and consoled, and, having married him, made him conscious of his own merit. Nicholas went to work with renewed energy, and perseveringly combated the enemies of good taste. Many *chefs-d'œuvre* from his pencil pleaded the cause of art: the *Death of Germanicus*, the *Taking of Jerusalem by Titus*, the *Pest of the Philistines*, *Eliezer before Rebekah*, the *Will of Eudamidas*, the *Rape of the Sabines*, *Esther fainting before Ahasuerus*, *Moses trampling Pharaoh's Crown under Foot*, and the *Triumph of Neptune*.

The Count Cassiano, of Pozzo, having engaged him to paint the *Seven Sacraments*, was so much pleased with the manner in which Poussin treated the subject that he vowed eternal friendship, introduced him to nobles with whom he was acquainted, and granted a favor more precious still — the use of his cabinet of antiques. It was from the study of the *chefs-d'œuvre* of antiquity that Poussin drew that beau-ideal, which, characterizing his smallest works, seems to make Raphael live again in him.

Cardinal Richelieu ordered pictures for his palace from Poussin; the compositions of the French artist were received with enthusiasm in France, and inspired the cardinal with the desire of bringing back to his native country this genius, of which Rome was beginning to be proud. Poussin received the brevet of first painter to the king, and an invitation to go to Paris to decorate the grand gallery of the Louvre. Poussin hesitated about leaving his dear retreat to take possession of the dignities which were offered him. Louis XIII. wrote a most flattering letter to persuade him to come, and M. de Chanteloup, who was then at Rome, urged the great painter so strongly to accompany him to France, that he consented to go at the end of the year 1640.

Louis XIII., forewarned of his arrival, sent one of his carriages, gave him the most gracious reception, and an apartment in the Tuilleries. The painter paid homage to the king by his beautiful picture, the *Will of Eudamides*, which is now in the Museum at Rouen, and was gratified with a pension of three thousand francs. Cardinal Richelieu was no less friendly to the artist. But Poussin, like other superior men, could not escape envy. Jacques de Fouquers, a Flemish painter, who was protected by the queen, had been promised the decoration of the Louvre: he was displeased with the new comer, who was, he thought, encroaching upon what he called his rights, which he resolved to claim. Lemercier, the first architect of the king, showed himself equally hostile to Poussin, because he had found it necessary to change the compartments of the arched roof, which were too massive for his designs.

Simon Vouet, a painter of note, to whom the French school was indebted for its first glory, was jealous of Poussin's success, which seemed to place him in the second rank of painters. Vouet's pupils took part with him, and Poussin, who valued nothing so much, after painting, as the quiet of a peaceful life, exempt from trouble and intrigue, soon regretted the happy days which he had passed at Rome.

On the other hand, he was continually interrupted in his painting, and occupied with details relative to the decoration of the Louvre, too insignificant for him. However, he finished the *Supper*, and the *Miracle of St. Francis Xavier;* but tired of perplexities and annoyances to which he was continually subject, he solicited permission to return to Rome, under pretext of arranging his affairs, and persuading his wife to take up her abode in France. Permission being granted, he hastened to depart. One thing, however, troubled him; he had promised the king and the cardinal that he would return; but as he did not hurry himself in the arrangement of his affairs, he heard of the death of Richelieu, and soon after of that of Louis XIII. Thus freed from his obligations, he determined not to leave Rome, the country of his adoption and the cradle of his glory.

He continued to enjoy the title of first painter to the king, under Louis XIV., and he justified this title by the advice which he gave to young French artists, who came to Rome to perfect themselves, and by the excellent models which he sent to France. The fine genius of Poussin developed itself in proportion as he advanced in his career. His first works were a little hard and dry, but he corrected these faults, and chose those subjects in which Nature displayed her beauties. Without losing the elevated taste which the study of the antique had given him, he put a grace, a charm, a certain melancholy poetry into his compositions, which touch the heart, and awaken meditation,—*Eurydice stung by a Serpent, while Orpheus, near her, is singing the Praises of the Gods*, the *Remains of Phocion expelled from Attica*, *Diogenes breaking his Cup*, the *Feasts of Ceres and of Bacchus*, *Boaz and Ruth*, admirable pictures, which added to Poussin's glory, were painted immediately after his return to Rome.

This artist never became rich, like many other celebrated painters whose history we have written. He was very simple in his tastes, and preferred easy circumstances to a great fortune. He lived in a modest retreat, which was embellished by the tender cares of his wife, and the visits of sincere friends, whose conversation was his relaxation from labor; and when obliged to mingle in society, he felt ill at ease, and gladly returned to his pleasant retirement. The superfluities of a pompous life had no value in his eyes: he worked for glory, and not for money. He was accustomed to write on the back of a picture the value at which he estimated it, and regularly sent back all that was offered over and above his price.

Poussin loved his art so much that, although he was considered the first painter of the age, he continued to study Nature; and when he left his studio, he went into the country to find some charming site, some smiling landscape, with which to ornament the groundwork of a picture. Very often he brought home stones, mosses, grass, branches of trees, &c, which he had collected in these excursions, because he thought that a painter could not be too careful in the truthful rendering of the smallest details.

Poussin worked too assiduously: his health was impaired, and an attack of paralysis warned him that the end of his career was approaching. After this he finished his fine picture of the *Samaritan*, which he sent to M. de Chanteloup, to whom he was tenderly attached. In the letter which accompanied the picture, the painter spoke of his approaching end, and told his friend that, without doubt, the picture would be the last which he should have the pleasure of painting for him. He worked only a few hours a day, for his hand soon tiring, no longer obeyed his inspirations; which, however, remained as vivid and as luminous as in the prime of his youth. The death of his amiable and beloved companion was a terrible blow, which he bore with resignation, in the hope of soon meeting her in another world. Work was a great assistance to him; and suffering as he was, he finished the *Four Seasons*, which he had sketched during his sickness.

While thus occupied, Poussin seemed to regain new life, and the four pictures finished, he, taking advantage of the last rays of the nearly extinguished lamp, undertook the *Deluge*, a sublime composition, in which he surpassed all that he had previously done. This last was his monument of glory. The *Deluge* was hardly finished, when a new attack of paralysis deprived the illustrious artist of the use of both hands. He languished for some time, awaiting his last hour with calmness and in Christian faith, and consoling his relations and friends for the loss they were about to sustain. He died a few days before he had attained his seventy-second year, and the news of his death cast a shadow of grief over Rome, where he was tenderly loved. The luxury and pomp which would have been so contradictory to the simplicity of his life, were not displayed at his funeral, but the whole population honored him with regrets.

Poussin, one of the most distinguished painters of Europe, was the greatest which France has produced. No master had the glory of teaching him, and he left no pupils. A composition, rich and learned at the same time, correct drawing, ingenuous ideas, an elevated and powerful style, a good tone of color, well-chosen sites, sweetness and poetry, distinguished the works of this illustrious man. His genius was aided by patient study; geometry, perspective, architecture, anatomy, occupied him in turn; then history, poetry, the study of the antiques, and the contemplation of nature, filled all the time not absolutely employed in the culture of his art.

He was equally successful in history, landscapes, mythology, and religious paintings. He modelled statuettes and bas-reliefs, and if he had applied himself to sculpture, there is no doubt that he would have succeeded as well as in painting. Connoisseurs think that his taste for the antique carried him too far, and imagine they recognize some of the statues, which served him as models, in his pictures; they also think that he put too many folds in his draperies, and had not a sufficient variety of positions for his heads; but such defects, if they really exist, do not prevent the name of Poussin from shining among the most illustrious names in the history of art.

This modest and disinterested artist was not less distinguished by his virtues than by his talents. Upright, generous, a friend of justice and of truth, he never courted the favor of the great, nor humiliated himself by honoring their qualities, much less by flattering their vices. He preferred family joys and the pleasures of industry to the intrigues of court. Although he lived modestly, his house was the rendezvous of artists, and persons in the highest stations of life were pleased to visit and converse with Poussin, who was not only an honest man, in all the acceptation of the word, and an eminent painter, but an amiable and witty savant.

One evening Cardinal Mancini came to see him. The conversation was prolonged to a late hour. Poussin was working, and the cardinal could but admire the wonderful facility with which he conversed while his pencil continued to move. Finally the prelate bade adieu to the artist, who took the lamp, and reconducted his noble visitor. The cardinal, confused at having given so much trouble, asked pardon, and said, —

"Truly, M. Poussin, you are to be pitied that you have no valet."

"And I, my lord," replied the painter, "I pity you, with all my heart, that you have so many."

Rome possesses very fine works of Poussin, but the greater number are in France. The great man left no posterity: he adopted the young brother of his wife, Guaspre Dughet, whom he treated as a son. Dughet is sometimes called Poussin: he inherited some of the talent of his brother-in-law for landscape. A delicate and spirited touch, a perfect knowledge of perspective, coloring full of freshness and truth, an uncommon ability to represent storms, the appearance of motion of trees, and well-chosen sites, render his pictures valuable. We are assured that many of the figures which animate his landscapes are from the hand of Poussin.

CLAUDE LORRAIN.

Claude Gelée, better known as Claude le Lorrain, was born in the diocese of Toul, in the year 1600. Though his parents could scarcely support themselves by their labor, they wished to have their son educated, and sent him to school when quite young; but Claude, notwithstanding all the attention he paid to the lessons of his teacher, made so little progress that his father was discouraged in thinking to make something of his child superior to a poor hireling like himself. He then thought he would give him some calling, and put him, at ten years of age, as apprentice to a pastry-cook, who tried to teach him to mix a sauce and prepare a hash.

Claude was no happier there than he had been at school; he had no memory; it often happened that he did entirely the contrary to what he had been told, and his blunders often caused serious losses to his master, for which the poor child had to pay by receiving bad treatment and hard words. The journeymen, his comrades, who thought him an idiot, fit only to amuse them, made fun of him. Claude bore it all with patience and extreme sweetness, or rather he appeared not to perceive that he was the object of their raillery, for his face was always calm and smiling.

However, he was not at all satisfied at the pastry-cook's, but his apprenticeship was to last three years;

the contract had been made, and there were no means of breaking it. As he could neither season a ragout, take charge of a roast, heat an oven, make pastry, or answer a customer, the cook, not knowing how to employ him, sent him on errands, to carry articles which had been ordered, into the city.

Claude had a little more liberty in this way, and less regret that he had no inclination to learn the culinary art. He had no wish to play with children of his age; besides, his little companions played him so many bad tricks, which they called fun, that he was much happier alone than in their society. But in his walks through the city he had found a pleasant amusement; he stopped at the second-hand shops, and was very happy when he saw some pictures in the midst of cast off clothing and old furniture. If by chance he found some landscape, lighted by the sun's rays among these pictures, which were generally very ordinary, it was a perfect feast for the poor little pastry-cook: he forgot himself while stopping to admire, and returned home later than usual, at the risk of receiving a severe reprimand.

One day, when he had a superb dessert to carry to one of the richest houses in the city, he saw two new pictures, which appeared to him very beautiful, on the stall of one of the second-hand shops. He thought to go past and stop on his way back, because he had been told to deliver the pastry quickly; but the temptation was stronger than his courage; he stopped, saying,—

"A few moments will detract nothing from the quality of the dessert; besides, I can walk quick enough to make up for stopping."

Claude had kept the basketful upon his head, but as it troubled him to look at the pictures which pleased him very much, he put the basket on a post near him. He meant to remain only five minutes, but not until standing there a full half hour did he think of his master's orders. What were his surprise and grief, the pastry and basket had both disappeared! Claude knew that he had done wrong, and wept bitterly: but his tears availed nothing, and he returned to his master in despair.

What excuse could he make? For an instant he thought of saying that thieves had stolen his basket, and beaten him; but as he had never told a lie, he felt ashamed to make that excuse, and simply told the truth. The pastry-cook was furious: he had taken extra pains in preparing that dessert, for which he expected to be highly complimented; therefore the disobedience of his apprentice caused more loss than that of the money. He could have forgiven him, perhaps, if it had been in his power to make good the loss, but the time failed, and Claude was driven from the house.

He packed his few clothes in sadness, and went away, knowing no more of pastry-cooking than he did when he entered. The little success he had had, did not encourage him to follow the profession which his parents wished to give him, and he could think of no other which pleased him better. He was then only thirteen years old; but he was large and strong, and resolved to seek a situation as a domestic. Claude was honesty itself, and that was the reason why the pastry-cook had so long borne with his awkwardness: his new masters soon discovered his honesty, but sooner his awkwardness and absence of mind; for he had not the cunning to dissimulate his faults, or to flatter those who could help him in getting excused.

He was turned away; and the poor child, not knowing what to do to earn his living, joined a party of young people, who were going to Italy to seek their fortune. They lived on the way by begging, and sometimes marauding; but this vagabond life did not please Claude, and when they arrived at Genoa, he separated from his companions, saying he would look for work in that city.

By good luck he engaged himself to Augusto Tassi, a painter of some talent. The misfortunes of Claude had not rendered him more active or more skilful, but Augusto, appreciating his sweetness of temper and his good will, was indulgent to him. The young man, touched with this kindness, attached himself sincerely to the artist, who, on his part became attached to him.

Tassi, observing that Claude paid extreme attention to his painting while arranging and cleaning the studio, one day proposed, laughing, to teach him the principles of his art. Claude said he should be glad to paint some nice pieces like his master, but he said it without any enthusiasm. The painter, for amusement's sake, put a pencil into the young man's hand, and showed him how to use it.

At first Claude's intelligence was as rebellious to the painter's instructions as it had been to that of the schoolmaster and the pastry-cook; but without being discouraged, every day, at the appointed hour, he went to the painter, humbly begging him to guide him in his efforts.

At length a ray of light seemed to pierce the thick darkness: Lorrain understood what had hitherto been uselessly explained, and seized by a love for study, as much more ardent as his ignorance was profound, he did not allow himself an instant of repose. He became, as if by enchantment, as active and able as he had heretofore been the reverse: he performed his duties, as a servant in a few hours, and went to the studio, where after having prepared the pallet, or ground the colors, for his employer, he set himself to work, and did not leave until called away. In the evening, when he went to his little room, he took either his books or his pencils, and gave to sleep only the time absolutely necessary for the preservation of his health.

Very soon he manipulated so well that Tassi not only had no fear about his learning, but understood that he would some day surpass him. Nature had enclosed the genius of Claude in a rude and shapeless envelope, as she conceals a diamond in rocks or clay: the envelope was broken, and the precious stone was about to shine forth in all its brilliancy.

But Lorrain was not to be an artist like those of which Italy had produced so many. His pencil was not to produce great historical scenes, nor mythological compositions, nor religious subjects, with their soft poetry, but representations of the wild or graceful sights which met his view: it was the prairie enamelled with flowers, the brook running under the foliage, the torrent bounding in foam upon the rocks, the threatening shadows of great woods, the village situated upon the declivity of a verdant hill, the moon shedding her sweet light upon the sleeping landscape, or the sun pouring a flood of warm rays upon blooming nature.

The first time that Claude saw one of those sites, which he daily admired, come out from his canvas, he was filled with rapture; and when he heard his master say that he would not disown the picture, he was still more delighted, for he had often been jeered at, and distrusted himself. Claude could not be a pastry-cook, or a domestic: he was a painter.

Augusto Tassi had done much for Lorrain, as except for his kindness, perhaps the genius of his poor servant would never have been roused; but up to the time of which we are speaking, Claude's only teacher was Nature. He studied with a patience and love, of which it is difficult to form an idea. Rising before day, he watched the first caresses of the vivifying sun as it drank up its mantle of dew, and compared the different appearances which the landscape takes at different hours of the day. This was no more the young man of sweet and honest face, but unintelligent and distracted, whom Augusto had taken as servant out of pity; it was an artist from whom nothing escaped, and who knew how to make his brush express all he had remarked.

However, whether the distrust which he had of himself remained, or whether he had some real difficulty, Claude worked slowly and hesitatingly: he often painted and rased the branch of a tree, or a stone during a whole day: sometimes after working an entire week, his picture had not in the least advanced; but when it was once finished, it was a jewel worthy of being offered to the greatest kings.

This artist was in the habit of softening his touches, and mixing them in a sort of varnish, which covered all his picture. No painter understood aerial prospective better than he, nor has any one made fresher tints, or succeeded in rendering the soft morning light, the ardent midday heat, or the gentle evening zephyrs, more charmingly or more truly. So Claude Lorrain is considered the best landscape painter in the world.

His reputation grew rapidly; a great number of young people vied with each other for the honor of becoming his pupils. His change in position did not make him forget the misery and humiliation of his youthful days, nor the gratitude which he owed his benefactor. His pictures were sought for by all amateurs, and brought high prices; and if he did not become immensely rich, it was because the recollection of the privations which he had endured, and seen his family endure, rendered him humane and generous. He never saw an old man or a child asking alms without shedding tears, and pouring the contents of his purse, however well filled, into their hands.

Honest, industrious, obliging, full of sweetness and kindness, he was endeared to his pupils, esteemed and beloved by everybody. He often spoke of his sad childhood, of his being continually repelled, of his ignorant and timid youth, without affectation, as well as without shame; and no person knew how to encourage artists better than he.

Claude Lorrain died at Rome, at the age of eighty-two years, without having laid aside his pencil; and his last works are no less remarkable than his first. Besides landscapes, this artist painted marine views very finely; but he never succeeded in figures. He said to his friends, "I sell the landscape, and give the figures into the bargain."

A great number of those which animate his pictures are due to the pencil of Philip Lauri de Courtois, or some other of his pupils. Lorrain was too superior a man not to render to his disciples the justice due them, and he had no fear in confiding to their care the finishing of his admirable pictures. Claude was also an excellent engraver: he has engraved many pieces which are much esteemed.

The life of this celebrated man is one which we love to put before the eyes of the young: it teaches those whose intelligence is not active, that there are no difficulties which patience and perseverance cannot overcome, and it shows those who are highly favored by Nature, that they should never make sport of those to whom she has been sparing of her gifts.

LE SUEUR.

Eustache le Sueur, whose name is placed beside that of Poussin, was born in Paris, in 1617. He passed his childhood in the studio of his father, who was a sculptor, and manifested great taste for modelling and drawing. Very soon he left the clay for the pencil; and his happy inclination for painting strengthening from day to day, they placed him, young as he was, under the care of Simon Vouet, who was then enjoying a great reputation, merited by real talent, and which was undisputed until Poussin returned to France. Simon had a great number of pupils; but Sueur was distinguished among them all, as much by the progress he made as by the sweetness and goodness of his character. He learned so rapidly of Vouet, that in a few years he excelled his teacher.

Some *chefs-d'œuvre* of the great masters being shown him, he studied them with the closest attention, recognized their beauties, and endeavored to imitate them. Then he ceased copying Simon Vouet, and followed only the counsels of his genius.

He had scarcely left the studio of his master when he made himself known through eight drawings for tapestry, in which he displayed much imagination, taste, and talent. He became a member of the Academy of St. Luke, for which he painted a *St. Paul curing the Sick*, which produced great sensation. Poussin, who came from Italy at the time, saw the picture, and predicted a most glorious career for Sueur. Poussin, attracted by the sweet and noble face of the young artist, by his distinguished manners, and by the gratitude with which he received advice, paid particular attention to him during the two years which he spent in France; and when, overcome by ennui and chagrin, he returned to Rome, he promised Sueur not to forget him. He kept his word, sent him valuable sketches at different times, and expressed the most sincere and tender interest in the letters which accompanied them.

Mutual sympathy attracted these two men to each other, whose characters had several points of resemblance. Sueur, like Poussin, loved work, simplicity, and peace; he hated intrigue, and disdained to answer the calumnies of his enemies. He was married at the age of twenty-five: he would have been happy if he could have earned an honorable livelihood for his family by works worthy of his talent; but he had powerful rivals, who were in vogue, and, not being able to obtain orders of importance, he designed frontispieces of books, images of the Virgin, and other current works, which could have been done as well by ordinary artists. However, he did not complain: he waited for better times.

His portraits of Louis XIV., of Cardinal Mazarin, and of the queen-mother, gained him favor at court, and Anne of Austria named him her painter. Some time after this promotion he was engaged to represent the life of St. Bruno, which she wished to present to the Carthusian nuns of Paris.

Sueur, faithful to his habit of studying nature thoroughly, retired to the convent, in order to study the character of the Carthusians, and make his work truthful. He succeeded wonderfully well; and this history of the holy founder, divided into twenty-two pictures, in which the serenity of soul and holy quiet become the portion of those who renounce the world to follow their divine Master, are portrayed with an ineffable charm. These pictures, which placed Sueur in the rank of the first French artists, did not fail to excite the envy of other painters. They were astonished; they were irritated to see a young man go out of the beaten track, and rush into an abandoned way, with no other guide than the luminous train left by the incomparable Raphael.

Sueur had taken Raphael for master and model: his

pure types, beau-ideal, rich arrangement, firm and soft touches, had attracted the young painter, and he became so much attached to the manner of the divine artist, that, although he had never seen Italy, he could have been taken for one of Raphael's best pupils. The Sleep of St. Bruno, his Refusal of Episcopal Dignity, the Death of this pious founder of the order of the Carthusians, were, and deserved to be, admired. The reputation of Sueur increased, and in 1649 he was engaged to paint the picture which the corps of jewellers offered to Notre Dame of Paris on the 1st of May.

Some years previous, on a like occasion, Le Brun had painted a St. Andrew, then a St. Stephen, which were much praised for their beauty. Sueur chose for his subject *St. Paul converting the Gentiles at Ephesus*, and his picture was a *chef-d'œuvre*, very superior to those which had been previously painted. He received the sum of four hundred francs from the fraternity of jewellers. It was very little for such a piece of work; but the price was fixed, and, in point of renown, it was a great advantage to Sueur. The Abbe of Marmontiers, near Tours, desired two pictures in honor of St. Martin, and these surpassed *St. Paul*, of Notre Dame. The *Condemnation of St. Gervais and St. Protais* appeared afterwards; and this picture alone suffices to render the name of the painter glorious. In this composition Sueur displayed all the beauty and richness of his pencil, and all the elevation of his soul. Angels are no purer or more beautiful than those two young people: as they appeared before their judges, their foreheads seemed illumined by a ray of eternal felicity. This picture can be regarded as Sueur's best, and one of the most admirable things which the French school has ever produced.

Sueur was then selected to decorate the mansion of President Thorigny, since called the Lambert Mansion, and he rivalled Le Brun, the first painter of the king. Until then he had only painted church pictures, and Le Brun was thought to be unequalled in mythological painting. This master, who possessed both talent and genius, was surprised and jealous at being surpassed by Sueur, whose grand and fruitful imagination, firm and delicate touch, excited the admiration of the numerous visitors to the mansion. Le Brun feared that the painter would take advantage of this circumstance to recommend himself to the king; but he did not know Sueur, who, satisfied with the glory which he had acquired, loved his independence too much, and was too happy in the modest sufficiency which he owed to his pencil, to desire the favors of the court, to which he knew one must often sacrifice his conscience, and always his liberty.

After having decorated the Thorigny mansion, Sueur returned to painting religious subjects, which he preferred to all others, and produced a great number of pictures of extraordinary beauty. Shut up in his studio, and assiduously devoted to his work, he turned a deaf ear to the calumnies with which his rivals attempted to blacken his character, and answered them only by producing *chef-d'œuvre* after *chef-d'œuvre*. Surrounded by the care and affections of the woman he had chosen, of his brother-in-law, of Peter, Philip, and Anthony Sueur, his three brothers, who worked with him, and shared his joys and his sorrows, cherished by his pupils, esteemed by all who knew him, Sueur found comfort and consolation in their esteem and tenderness. Besides, he hoped that calmness and disinterestedness would at length impose silence upon the envious: he was deceived: the greater he showed himself the more his enemies tried to injure him.

He was animated for the contest, besides incited by his love for art, and the firm and ardent wish to perfect himself; he was never satisfied with his work, but always hoped to do better, and those who loved him vainly begged him to husband his strength, which his great assiduity to labor was visibly injuring. Sustained by his courage, Sueur did not perceive it; besides, his health had always been very delicate, and he paid but little attention to suffering, to which he was accustomed. But sorrow finished what fatigue had commenced. Sueur lost his wife, his brothers married, and the void caused by their absence plunged him into profound melancholy. His enemies, imagining his sufferings, formed new intrigues against him, and the artist, entirely discouraged, fell into a state of languor, which he judged to be mortal.

He died at Paris, the 1st of May, 1655, on the island of Notre Dame, where he had lived, and was interred in the church of St. Etienne-du-Mont.

He is the last of the painters of the French school, who, without having left France, had the talent to resist the academic rules which Vouet and La Hyre, his masters, had substituted for the great Italian traditions, and knew how to preserve, as intact as possible, that elevation of sentiment and that purity of execution which are the appendages of great schools.

SALVATOR ROSA.

Salvator Rosa, painter, musician, and poet, was born in the year 1615, in the village of Arenella, near Naples. His parents, hoping to prepare him for some useful occupation, placed him at a convent school. Salvator was very intelligent, and soon gained the affection of the fathers, whom he astonished by the rapid progress he made in all the studies they gave him. As he grew older, his taste for study seemed to diminish: they no longer saw him with his books in his hands, while his companions gave themselves up to the sports of their age; but they were sure to find him cutting figures upon the trees in the garden with his penknife, or tracing drawings in the sand-walks, or portraits, with charcoal, upon the walls.

The good fathers took this pastime of Salvator for a caprice, which they supposed would not last long, and contented themselves with gently begging him not to neglect his lessons: the child promised to learn them as well as heretofore, and he kept his word. As his memory was prodigious, he required but a few moments for study, and did not cease drawing, as well during the hours of the class as during the recreations.

Antonio Rosa was a mason, and pretended to be an architect; his wife belonged to a family of painters, but ordinary painters, and so poor, for the most part, that Antonio, who earned scarcely enough to carry on his own business, had often been called upon to assist them. No one despised painting more than he did; therefore he was much grieved when he heard that Salvator, in whom he had such great hopes, manifested a decided taste for the profession which could not furnish bread to his uncles. He recommended the fathers to punish his son severely every time he was caught in the act of drawing or painting.

Salvator was ordered to give up his pleasant amusement; and as he continually disobeyed, punishments and imprisonment recalled him to duty. He was indignant at such tyranny, and revenged himself by drawing caricatures of his masters upon the walls. The surprise of the fathers was very great when they saw themselves thus disfigured, and they thought of driving Salvator from the convent; but one of them, who loved young Rosa very much, obtained his pardon, and succeeded in persuading him to study. Salvator promised to submit to the orders of his teachers as well as he could, and again took up his studies. The fathers, satisfied with his submission, abated their severity, and granted him a day's vacation from time to time. Rosa lived only for this day. No sooner was he at liberty, than he ran to the house of Greco, the painter, one of his uncles, and painted, under his direction, until it was time to return to his studies. This lasted a year or so, after which Salvator, although fearing the severity of his father, declared that he had no taste for the career which had been marked out for him, and did not wish to complete his studies. The fathers advised Antonio Rosa not to constrain his son any longer, but to take him home. However, Antonio was not to be persuaded: he obstinately refused to give Salvator what was necessary for drawing and painting, hoping by so doing to make him ashamed of being idle, and that he would return to the books which he had given up. But it was all to no purpose. Salvator, not being permitted to follow his inclination, gave himself up to music and painting.

Some of the songs which he composed became popular in Naples: they promised him fortune and glory, so that Antonio allowed him to do as he wished. Salvator, overjoyed, ran to Greco to get instruction; very soon, however, he perceived that his uncle was only a poor dauber, and he thought of finding some better teacher, when his sister married Francazano, pupil of Ribera. Salvator left his uncle's studio for that of his brother-in-law; yet he was much more indebted to the study of nature than to his new teacher. A painter and poet, he knew how to express all the emotions excited in him by the contemplation of the beautiful sky of Naples, the blue waves which bathe the city, Vesuvius, which threatens it, and the picturesque sites which surround it. He far surpassed Francazano, or rather what he did could not be compared to the works of any other painter, because his manner was all his own; and Antonio, notwithstanding all his prejudice against the art, could not help being proud of the genius apparent in the pictures signed Salvatoriello (little Salvator), he hoped that the young man would enjoy a brilliant position as soon as he became well known. Before this excellent father's dream of happiness was realized, death summoned him to the spirit land.

Added to the heavy loss which Salvator, who was scarcely seventeen years old, experienced by his father's death, was the care of the family, which it was impossible for him to sustain, with all his good will and untiring assiduity. With all his efforts, he only succeeded in preventing his mother, sister, and two brothers, still very young, from dying of hunger. His mother and sister, afflicted at being burdensome to him, and fearing that the necessity of painting rapidly might injure the development of his talent, entered the house of the Viceroy of Naples as domestics, and public charity aided him in the care of his little brothers. Francazano had not succeeded in becoming renowned, and the most frightful misery reigned in this house. Too proud to complain and to beg, the sister of Salvator languished for a time, and died of want.

It would be impossible to express the sufferings of Salvator, endowed, as he was, with a loving heart, a proud and generous nature, and a genius which needed only to expand: the sombre tint, and the sharp and wild sadness, which predominate in his pictures, are to be attributed to these sufferings. He worked unremittingly, and sold his pictures to a dealer in Naples, who did not half pay for them; and when the poor child had laid aside the sum necessary for the purchase of colors and brushes, to begin something else, he had hardly enough left to support himself.

One day the city was in a state of excitement, on account of the arrival of Lanfranc, the celebrated painter of cupolas, who came to decorate the dome of St. Janvier. Everybody desired to see the artist of whom they had heard so much, and Salvator, more anxious than others, tried to find the imprint of glory upon his head. He followed the great painter with the crowd, when he saw him stop at the show window of the dealer with whom he traded. Lanfranc's attention was drawn to Salvator's landscapes, and calling the trader, he conversed with him in an undertone of voice. Salvator, pale with emotion, had crowded so near the speakers, that he did not lose a word of their conversation. When Lanfranc expressed a desire to see the author of the pictures, he could have said "Here am I;" but a glance at his shabby clothing prevented, and fearing that the dealer might see and expose him, he ran away with all his might. However, he did not fail to return in the course of the day, and what he had foreseen, came to pass: the dealer offered him rather more for the small picture which he brought, than he had hitherto done. Salvator became difficult, and boasted of the merit of his picture, and after some conversation, the trader paid him a good price for it. Young Rosa ran immediately to a tailor's, chose a complete suit, and the next day presented himself to Lanfranc. He was well received, and Lanfranc gave him an order for some landscapes, for which he paid him liberally. The dealer in pictures, who had so long disdained his productions, began to be anxious for them. After having suffered so much on account of the poverty of his family, as well as himself, fortune at length smiled upon Salvator. He thought himself rich as soon as his works procured him an honorable living. He asked no more, but Lanfranc advised him to go to Rome, to perfect himself by the study of the great masters. He furnished him with the means, and recommended him to a very rich gentleman, who was much pleased to take Salvator with him, and bear all the expenses of his journey.

The young painter saw, with astonishment, the wonders collected in the city of arts: he could never tire of admiring the masterpieces of Michael Angelo, of Raphael, and the beauties of antiquity; but he fell sick in the midst of his studies, and was obliged to return to Naples. The reputation which Lanfranc gave him in his native city, allowed him to lead an honorable and comfortable, if not a luxurious life. He painted some historic pictures, which were much esteemed; but his combats, marine views, and, more than all, his landscapes, were greatly admired.

Salvator excelled in representing wild and picturesque scenery, mountains, abrupt gorges, torrents, and forests, and he knew how to animate all these with figures, which made his pictures grandiose or terrible. He painted with such facility, that he often finished a picture in a day. When he needed a model, either for attitudes or features of his figures, he placed himself before a large mirror, and studied the changes which joy, laughter, or grief impressed upon his features.

He continued to cultivate poetry, and his house was the rendezvous of the literati of Naples. But it is in the nature of man to be unsatisfied: Salvator longed to be in Rome, which he had seen but imperfectly, and of which he thought continually in his dreams of poetry and art. He readily accepted the invitation of Cardinal Brancaccio to go to Rome. When he left Naples, he thought it would be for a long time, although he loved his independence more than he loved Rome. He had been in Rome only a short time, when he became very melancholy, under the gilded ceilings of the palace Brancaccio, and he returned to Naples.

Fate seemed to drive Salvator from one of these cities to the other; he had hardly established himself in Naples, before he sighed for Rome: this time fortune and glory united with the poetic charm of the Eternal City, in the imagination of the painter. However, he was aware of the obstacles which he would have to surmount, in order to get a name in this capital, where illustrious artists, Italian and foreign, were in great renown. He expected to become known through his poetry, as well as by his painting, and the event proved that he had judged rightly.

It was the time of Carnival. Salvator, disguised as a juggler, ran through Rome several days, dealing out to his rivals epigrams and satires, full of wit and piquancy. Soon this witty dealer in puffs, whose muse could not be embarrassed or intimidated, became the talk of the city. Everybody wished to see and to hear him. He overcame all adversaries by his ridicule, and when he was sure of the public favor, and showed his pictures, he was saluted with enthusiastic acclamations. At first, curiosity caused his paintings to be sought by the nobility of Rome; then, appreciating the merit of them, his pictures came in vogue, and his fortune was made. He lived like a noble, and in great splendor. But this opulence came late, and if it flattered the self-love of the painter, it was far from satisfying his heart; his mother and his dear sisters had died without partaking his good fortune. He had become rich and celebrated; now he wished to go back to Naples, where he had been poor and unknown.

He was in the city when the revolution of 1647, which put the fisherman, Masaniello, in the place of the Viceroy of Philip IV., broke out. The recollection of his past misery, and the love of liberty, threw Salvator into the popular party: he sustained the revolt with all his eloquence of speech, and counselled Masaniello. But a change in public opinion took place at the approach of Philip's troops, and the Fisher King was put to death by those who had proclaimed him their chief. Salvator fled to Rome, where he painted his most celebrated pieces, — *Democritus among the Tombs*, *Prometheus on Mount Caucasus*, the *Death of Socrates*, the *Death of Regulus*, and *Human Fragility and Fortune:* these were allegories, in which the authorities recognized a satire, and signed an order for the imprisonment of Salvator.

Then he took refuge in Florence, where the Grand Duke intrusted him with the decoration of the Pitti Palace. For ten years Rosa enjoyed the favor of the prince, who was charmed by his triple talent of musician, painter, and poet. There was no court festival to which he was not invited, and all the Florentine nobility gathered daily in the sumptuous dwelling of the artist. He tore himself away from his calm and happy mode of living, and went to Rome, where he found the old hatred and envy which had so often pursued him: his enemies went so far as to deny his genius for painting and poetry; but he answered their defiance, by composing the poem of Envy, and painting a magnificent *Battle*, for Louis XIV. This picture is now in the gallery of the Louvre.

Jealousy had nothing to oppose to such proofs, and was silent. Salvator, who was considered one of the greatest artists of his age, showed himself worthy of the homage paid him by producing more beautiful pictures, the most celebrated of which is the *Ghost of Samuel appearing to Saul*, to announce his approaching end.

Salvator was still young, but his years of sorrow had doubled their weight in the balance of death; his eyesight failed, then his memory; the pencil, lately so sure and so bold, trembled in his hand. Disease of the liver caused him great suffering, then dropsy set in, and this great artist died in 1673, at the age of fifty-eight years.

He preserved his good humor, or rather his habit of raillery, to the last. People were deceived by his false gayety, and did not know that he had chosen this iron mask to dissimulate all the bitterness with which the first years of his life had filled his heart. All the artists, and persons of wit and taste, were drawn to his house by the charm of his conversation; and those who sought only pleasure, were also happy to be admitted, for Salvator gave magnificent entertainments and feasts, over which he presided with great hospitality. He decorated the lower rooms of his house, and transformed them into a theatre, where he caused to be played, and played himself, pieces of his own composition. The great prices which were paid for his pictures enabled him to be hospitable and generous as a prince. He who once could scarcely live by the fruits of his labor, now took pleasure in demanding enormous prices for his pictures, and such was his reputation that his pretensions were not considered exorbitant.

Colonna sent him a purse full of gold in return for a picture. Salvator acknowleged this generosity, by another picture more beautiful than the first. Colonna sent a larger purse. The painter sent a third picture, then a fourth, each being paid in the same way. Finally, upon the reception of the fifth, Colonna sent two purses to Salvator, saying that he ceded the honor of the combat to him, and recognized in him an inexhaustible genius.

No painter has ever been able to imitate Salvator Rosa. However, with regard to correctness and elegance, his figures are sometimes wanting; but there is a truth, boldness, and grandeur about them which adds much to the effect of the landscape which they are destined to animate. The battles which he has painted, make the beholder shudder, so true has he represented the fury of the combatants, the sufferings of the wounded, the confused entanglement of men and horses, and all the horrors which seem present to the spectator. The *Banditti* of Salvator are perfectly represented. It is probably owing to this fact that his enemies accused him of having been one of a band of brigands, who had taken refuge in the Abruzzi after the revolution; but nothing is more preposterous than such an idea. Salvator found the greater part of the types which he has rendered in so striking a manner in his fertile and bold imagination.

This great artist was buried in Rome.

ENGRAVERS.

ALBERT DURER.

Albert Durer, the glory of the German school, was born at Nuremberg, in 1471. His father, originally from Hungary, had come to Germany several years previous to perfect himself as a silversmith, and had become very skilful in his profession, which is almost an art. Albert was his second son, and fourteen other children were afterwards born to him. Durer educated this numerous family in the fear of God and the love of virtue, and wishing to give a position to each of his children, he studied their characters and their tastes with great care. Albert soon distinguished himself by his intelligence, sweetness of disposition, and application to study, and was chosen by his father as his successor. When he was sufficiently advanced in his studies, his father began to teach him silversmithery.

The young Durer did his best to satisfy his teacher, and after some years he worked in gold and silver with much taste. But jewellers then being often brought into connection with painters who furnished them with designs to execute upon the pieces of jewelry, Albert, after having admired their talent for a long time, tried to copy some little pictures which ornamented his father's house. At first he did not succeed; but persevering, he was at length not dissatisfied with his own unassisted attempts, and he expressed to his father his desire of leaving silversmithery for painting. Durer, seeing in this wish only the caprice to which young people too easily yield, reprimanded his son, and forbade him to occupy himself thereafter with any other business than that which was given him.

Albert promised to obey, and kept his word for some months; then, one day, when his mother bought a beautiful picture of the Madonna, he forgot the order which he had promised to respect, and passed a part of the night in copying this picture. The light of his lamp betrayed him, and while he was finishing his Madonna in great joy, the door of his chamber opened, and his father entered. Albert, confused by his disobedience, rose, and approaching his father, humbly asked pardon.

"I thought I had a submissive and respectful child in you," said his father, "and see with regret that I deceived myself."

"Take back those words, I beg you, my father: I venerate, I love you, and had no intention of offending you. Since you forbade me, I have not touched a pencil, and

I know not how it was that seeing this beautiful picture, I entirely forgot the promise I made you. You see me ashamed and penitent; pardon me for this once."

"This is no time for a long conversation; your brothers and sisters are sleeping; do as they do: tomorrow I will speak with you."

Albert bowed, and the silversmith had not regained his chamber when the sketch was put away and the lamp extinguished. But, although the young man would gladly have slept, as his father advised him, the thought of the reprimand, which, without doubt, he would receive on the morrow, kept his eyes open during several hours. It was not because Durer was a severe father; he always spoke reasonably with his children; but precisely because he was so good, a severe word from his mouth was a dreaded punishment. Morning came, Albert rose, and after family prayers, he followed his father into his study. But instead of the reproaches which he was expecting to receive, he saw his father reach out his hand to him. He took it, and pressed it to his lips with tenderness and gratitude.

"I have been thinking much of you the past night, my son," said the father, "and I really think that you would succeed as a painter. Come with me; I will take you to Hupse Martin."

Great was Albert's joy: Hupse Martin was in great reputation at Nuremberg as a painter and an engraver, and it had long been the dream of the young silversmith to be admitted into his studio at some future day as his pupil. The young Durer became skilful in engraving, and began to paint under the direction of this master. Afterwards he left the studio of Martin for that of Michael Wolfmuth, who occupied himself more particularly in painting: here he devoted himself to the study of painting and architecture.

He remained with Wolfmuth until he was twenty-one years old, working assiduously, and surpassing all the hopes which this learned master had conceived of him. Not content with simple listening to the instructions of his teacher, Albert daily wrote a summary of them, to fix them in his memory; and, thanks to this precaution, he was able some years after to publish treatises on perspective, and civil and military architecture, — works which added much to his reputation.

In 1492 he went to Colmar, where the brothers Schonganer, astonished to find so much talent in a young man, gave him a friendly reception.

After working two years at Colmar, he returned to Nuremberg, where he married the daughter of an able machinist. Albert Durer had a manner of painting and engraving which was independent of his masters, and people soon perceived that his works were very superior to all which had been done by German artists up to that time.

Albert was happy to have succeeded by his talent in creating a sure position, while he was devoid of the ambition which often torments men of genius: he wished but for one thing; to live in peace, and to have the society of a loving and devoted wife in the hours not spent in work. This wish, however, was not realized: the temper of the companion whom he had chosen was often crabbed and disagreeable, and whatever concessions the artist made, he could not calm her excitement, or free himself from her persecutions.

It was a cruel discovery for Albert: his life was poisoned; he did not complain, but he felt a disappointment and chagrin, which neither fortune nor honors could console. The Emperor Maximilian, having seen some of his pictures, invited him to his court, where he received him with great distinction. He confided the decoration of his palace to him, and his esteem for the man soon equalled his admiration for the artist, and he took pleasure in seeing him work, and conversing with him.

One day, when Albert was drawing a group upon the wall, the emperor observed that the ladder upon which he was standing was not firm, and he made a sign to one of the noblemen of his suite to hold it. The nobleman, surprised to receive such an order, stepped back, and calling a domestic, told him to hold the ladder. Maximilian dismissed the servant by a gesture, and approaching the painter, did not leave the foot of the ladder until the drawing was finished. When Albert descended, the emperor created him a nobleman, and gave him three escutcheons of silver, upon an azure ground.

"Know," said he to his courtiers, "that the title which I give Albert Durer does not raise him in the esteem of any sensible man; for he is indebted to his talent for a grand and illustrious nobility, which none of you possess. An act of our imperial pleasure can make a count or a duke, whilst it is God who makes the artist."

Albert was at court for a considerable time, and made not only fine paintings, but a great number of his engravings, which are much esteemed. Returning to Nuremberg, he continued to seek consolation for his ennui in work: he could scarcely fill the orders which he received; kings and princes disputed for his pictures and his engravings. Charles V., and Ferdinand, King of Hungary, loaded him with presents and testimonies of their affection, and all persons of note in Nuremberg desired his friendship. But, though polite and kind to all, he was far from being prodigal of the title of friend; for he understood the qualities it required, and the duties it imposed. It is seen by the letters which he wrote from Italy to Senator Pirkheimer that he considered this friend as another self, and did not fear to open his entire heart to him.

Let us speak of this journey to Italy, which was the happiest period in the life of our artist. Albert Durer was thirty-four years old when he wished to visit the country of Michael Angelo, of Raphael, and of Titian. Those who truly loved him, had been advising him for a long time to make this artist pilgrimage; but his wife, who took a cruel pleasure in thwarting his tastes, prevented him, as long as she could, from following the advice of his friends. Albert was endowed with superior intelligence, a great and noble soul, and a powerful genius; but he was a friend of peace and tranquillity, and had the habit of obeying his exacting companion. He could not find strength in his heart to shake off his yoke. Pirkheimer was obliged to insist, repeatedly, in order to decide him to go to Italy.

At length he set out, and was received with honor in all the different cities through which he passed; for his name had become popular. His reception at Venice was enthusiastic: all the artists of that beautiful city hurried to see Albert, whose magnificent engravings were well known in Italy. The fraternity of German merchants obtained the preference over all the guilds who requested pictures from the illustrious visitor. Albert painted a *St. Bartholomew* for his countrymen residing in Venice: it was so much liked, that they paid him one hundred and ten florins for it. All the Venetian nobles wished to see the able painter, and disputed with each other the honor of showing him hospitality. Surrounded by so many flattering testimonies, Durer forgot for a time his domestic troubles; so that those who saw him were as much enchanted by his charming spirit, his affectionate manners, and his amiable gayety, as by his rare talent.

Leaving Venice, he went to Bologna, where he met with the same reception. In this city he devoted some time to the study of perspective, and was preparing to go to Rome, when business obliged him to return to Germany. With regret, he bade adieu to the beautiful sky of Italy, under which his heart had expanded and his genius developed, and sadly turned towards Nuremberg. His first work, after his return, was his own portrait, which he sent to Raphael. He had had the pleasure of seeing this incomparable artist, and both had promised to renew their acquaintance at Rome. This portrait, painted in water-colors, upon a very fine cloth, was much admired by Raphael, who thanked Albert in a very friendly letter, and sent him some valuable drawings.

Albert worked unceasingly as painter, engraver, and sculptor, during fourteen years, and his work improved daily. Sincerely religious, he took pleasure in representing sacred subjects. The *Christs* of Albert Durer are so marvellously beautiful and divine, that faith alone could have given them that character of sublime simplicity.

The *Saviour on the Cross*, surrounded by a glory, and having emperors, cardinals, and popes at his feet, is considered the *chef-d'œuvre* of Albert Durer. As to engravings, *St. Jerome meditating upon the Scrip-*

tures, is, perhaps, the most beautiful which art has thus far produced.

Albert Durer made another journey in 1520: this time he went to Holland. Here he became acquainted with Lucas de Leyde, who offered him his house, and with whom he lived for several months, as with an affectionate brother. When they parted they exchanged portraits, and, though separated by distance, never forgot each other. The German artist met with a kind reception at Antwerp, where a large number of painters were united in a corporation. They gave a banquet in his honor, to which the public were admitted, so that every one could see the illustrious stranger. The crowd did not fail to make use of the privilege; and Albert, in his *Journal of Arts*, where he gives an account of his journey, says, pleasantly, that the crowd broke the sides of the tables in pressing to see the celebrity.

Durer went to Aix-la-Chapelle, to be present at the coronation of Charles V. The emperor desired to see Durer, and to manifest the esteem he had for his talent. Emboldened by the kindness of Charles V., Albert offered the Arch-duchess Margarita (daughter of Maximilian, who had so nobly revenged the artist of the disdain of a nobleman) the portrait of her august father, which she refused. Albert was much hurt by her refusal; and, having experienced some other contrarieties, the painter returned to Nuremberg.

There he resumed his chain; for the woman who had

the honor of bearing his name had never learned to appreciate his genius and his excellent qualities; and, never thinking of correcting her bad temper, that she might render his life more pleasant, she grew worse, and as age advanced, became a scourge to him. Albert had need of all the patience and resignation of a Christian to bear the punishment of each day. At first, he had flattered himself that he could get used to it; but it is impossible to get used to being misjudged and persecuted. His trouble wore upon him, his health gave way, and, after languishing for some years, he died, at the age of fifty-seven.

In the works of Albert Durer, we admire his lively and fruitful imagination, elevated genius, firm execution, brilliant coloring, and fine finish. However, he could not entirely avoid the defects of his fellow-countrymen painters — too stiff drawing, and too dry a style. It is to be regretted that Durer had somewhat neglected the study of costume, and the art of perspective in the gradation of his colors. But he was not the less a man of great genius. He was self-made, and balanced the imperfections of his labor by sentiment, energy, and passion, which make dramas and poems of his works, whether they be paintings or engravings.

Albert Durer left a great number of engravings upon wood, copper, iron, and tin, and a multitude of pen and pencil drawings. He succeeded perfectly in portraits and in landscapes, which are admired for piquancy and grace. This artist was the best engraver of his age; and Raphael was so struck by the beauty of his engravings, that he employed Antonio Raimondi to study the manner of the skilful stranger.

Albert Durer has written upon geometry, perspective, and the proportions of the human figure.

CALLOT.

Jacques Callot was born at Nancy in 1593: he was the son of a herald-at-arms in Lorraine, who, designing him to follow the same career as himself, placed him at school to learn to read and write. At first all went on well: Jacques was not wanting in docility or intelligence; but as he grew up he felt a great aversion for the paternal profession — an aversion which came from the desire which he had for another, which, without doubt, he would not be allowed to follow. His greatest pleasure and most assiduous occupation was to draw portraits and figures of all sorts upon his books and his copy-books, which his comrades contemplated with curiosity and astonishment, and to engrave, with the aid of his knife, upon the school tables, or upon the trees in the garden.

This decided taste for drawing disquieted his father, who expressly forbade it, and took away the pencils and patterns which the child had procured. This was a great sorrow to Jacques, who wished to be obedient;

but an irresistible force impelled him: he bought new pencils and new copies, and worked with more ardor than before. For a while he concealed his work so well that no one suspected what he was doing: at length he was less cautious, and his father surprised him. Jacques experienced the harshness and severity which Mr. Callot had acquired at camp. A culpable thought came into the mind of the child; it was to tear himself away from the authority which he could not brave with impunity: he thought and thought, and finally, one fine day, eluding the watch which was kept over him, fled from the paternal roof.

He walked as fast as his twelve-years'-old legs could carry him, and went out of the city, and through the fields, for fear of being pursued. Evening came, and the poor child, tired, hungry, and frightened, began to repent of the step he had taken. He thought of the trouble which his absence would cause his kind and tender mother, and he reproached himself bitterly for the tears which she would shed; and, yielding to a good inspiration, he turned back. But he had walked so much already that he could not hope to regain the city before the next day, unless he should meet some countryman, who would give him a ride in his wagon; in which case he would be obliged to acknowledge his flight, and the motives which induced it. What would his father, who, unfortunately, was then at home, say? What punishment would he inflict on his rebellious son?

Jacques was afraid, and, not knowing what was best to do, seated himself upon the grass which bordered the wood, and burst into tears. Despite his sorrow, despite the phantoms with which his imagination, fed by frightful stories, peopled the darkness, becoming more and more profound, he fell asleep. At daybreak he was awakened by a company of Bohemians, who surrounded him, and who were surprised to find a well-dressed child, at this early hour, sleeping alone by the side of the road. Callot was startled at first by the sight of these odd people, but regaining his courage, told them what he had done.

Instead of persuading him to return to his parents, at the risk of being reprimanded and punished, the vagabonds invited him to go with them to Italy. Jacques, though ignorant as children in general of his age, knew that there were many great painters in Italy; and as his greatest fear the previous evening had been isolation, he joyfully accepted the proposition of the Bohemians. He was strengthened by a frugal breakfast; and without daring to think of his parents, from whom he was going so far away, perhaps for a very long time, followed his strange companions.

The company had more than one resource for getting their living. The old women told fortunes, the young girls sang and danced in the public squares, the children begged, and the men gave themselves up to marauding, or levied contributions upon travellers. All this was far from the honest principles in which Jacques had been educated, and he often regretted his flight, for which he never could forgive himself. However, he never took a part in the reprehensible actions of the Bohemians with whom fate had associated him; when they halted, he drew the most expressive faces of his companions, and the adventurers sold these drawings to the traders in the towns and villages through which they passed.

Finally the company reached Italy. Callot had made great progress without a teacher, and without other models than those which nature offered; and his drawings, imperfect as they were, had such a character of originality and truth, that he found a ready sale for them. He had long been thinking of separating from the Bohemians, but as he was more closely watched by them than he had been in his father's house, was unable to execute his plan. When he arrived at Florence, he was so happy as to gain the interest of one of the Grand Duke's officers, who took him under his protection; and after the departure of the Bohemians, placed him with an engraver of renown, named Remigio Canta Gallina. Jacques was very grateful to this teacher for his lessons, and profited so well by them, that in a very short time he was able to copy from the great masters, — a work which developed his talent and formed his taste.

After some years passed in Florence, Callot set out for Rome, where he hoped to perfect himself in his art.

He was scarcely established in that city, when he was recognized by some merchants from Nancy, who were his father's friends. Jacques was glad to hear from his family, of whom he was thinking continually, and whom he hoped to see again, when, as an artist of renown, he should have a right to his father's indulgence. But the honest merchants did not wish to let the opportunity pass of taking the prodigal son back to the parents who had been so much afflicted by his loss, and when they had finished their business, they forced him to return with them.

The desire of embracing his mother, and obtaining pardon for his flight, which had weighed upon his conscience, prevented his resisting, and sustained him during a part of the journey, but the nearer he approached Nancy the more fearful he was of meeting his father. Although still very young, he had had so much experience since leaving his father's house, that his reason was much matured: his fear was not alone on account of the reproaches and punishment which he expected, but the efforts which would be made by both father and mother to draw him from the career which he had chosen; and the taste which had shown itself in his earliest childhood, had now become an irresistible vocation.

He continued his route for some days in a state of mental disquiet which deprived him of sleep and appetite. At length he left the merchants, and returned to

Italy. Here the thought of those whom he never ceased to cherish, and from whom he had gone the second time, like an ungrateful child, slackened his ardor. About a week after he had left the merchants, they informed his oldest brother, who immediately pursued him. He overtook him before leaving France, and had no difficulty in taking him back to Nancy.

Callot was wrong in anticipating a severe reception: is there not in the heart of a father and mother an inexhaustible source of indulgence and love? Introduced by his brother, Jacques threw himself at his father's feet, weeping. M. Callot, after vainly endeavoring to retain the coldness which he had assumed, opened his arms to the fugitive, and pressed him tenderly to his breast. His mother did not try to dissimulate the joy with which her heart was filled by the return of her beloved boy; she did not think to reproach him for the tears which he had caused her to shed; she saw him once more; all was forgotten.

It is true that M. Callot spoke again of the noble profession of arms; but Jacques, having answered by producing the drawings which he had brought from Italy, his father could not help admiring them, and taking the hands of his son, he said, —

"Be an artist, since you desire it."

Jacques, delighted to have gained the consent of his father, dared not speak immediately of returning to Italy: he felt that it was his duty to consecrate some time to his family, who had been so saddened by his absence; he therefore took lessons in engraving of Philip Thomassin that his progress need not be retarded. Painting had few attractions for him, but he soon excelled in engraving; and when at length he went back to Italy, the Grand Duke of Florence, Cosmo II., charmed by his talent, retained him at his court, and loaded him with honors and presents.

At Florence, Callot began to engrave those small subjects, in which he displayed the fulness and delicacy of his genius. His reputation grew rapidly, and he could not return to Lorraine until after the death of Cosmo, who esteemed him highly, and was very fond of him. Many advantageous offers were made to induce him to remain in Florence, which love for his own country caused him to decline: he returned to Nancy, where the Duke de Lorraine received him with honor, and assured him a brilliant position. Jacques continued to work with as much ardor as if he had yet to make his name and fortune.

Louis XIII., having heard of him, invited him to come to his court, and confided to him the care of engraving the Siege of Rochelle, and taking of the Island of Rhé. Callot acquitted himself of the task in such a manner as to merit the praise of all connoisseurs, and to obtain the favor of the king and of Cardinal Richelieu. Some time after, a war, intended to crush the house of Austria, broke out, and the city of Nancy was taken by the French troops. It is well known that Lorraine was governed by the posterity of Gerard of Alsace, until the year 1735, an epoch in which the treaty of Vienna reunited it to France, on condition that Stanislaus Leczinski, despoiled of the throne of Poland, should reign until his death, over this duchy, erected into a kingdom.

Louis XIII. ordered Callot to represent the taking of Nancy, as he had that of Rochelle and the Island of Rhé; but Callot was not a Frenchman; he was from Lorraine. The defeat of the duke, his master, and the disaster of his beloved city, grieved him, and he had no idea that he should be asked to immortalize this defeat, and this desolation, by his graver. He supplicated the king to excuse him, and explained the motive of his unwillingness to obey. One of the lords present at this interview of the engraver with Louis XIII., thought to please the king by trying to intimidate Callot with threats.

"Sire, here is my right hand," said Jacques; "you can cut it off, and I swear to you that I would cut it off myself, sooner than obey such orders of your majesty."

The king admired the courage and patriotism of the artist, and promised to ask of him nothing which was not in strict accordance with his honor, and offered him a pension of three thousand francs to attach him to his service. Callot thanked Louis XIII., and begged that he would excuse him from accepting these propositions, brilliant and flattering as they were, and allow him to go back to Lorraine, so that no one should accuse him of abandoning his country for those who were its declared enemies, and that he could not reproach himself for having left the Duke of Lorraine, vanquished, to live on the benefactions of his conqueror.

Louis XIII., while he regretted the loss of this artist, could not but admire his disinterestedness and the greatness of his soul, and gave him liberty to leave Paris when he would. Jacques returned to Nancy, and recommenced his work: he died at the age of forty-two. His engravings amounted to six hundred pieces.

No one has equalled this master in the art of representing the grotesque. Old men, beggars, lame people, odd faces, were represented with the utmost correctness. It is supposed that the time which he spent with the Bohemians in his early youth, furnished him with the types which he had reproduced, and varied so happily. The *Fairs, Markets, Punishments, Tavern Scenes, Miseries of War*, the *Great Street of Nancy*, &c., are among the works of Callot which are most sought by amateurs.

The fecundity and fire of his genius, the expression of his faces, the choice and distribution of his subjects, the variety of his groups, in which there is no forced contrast, the facility of labor, the piquancy and newness which he has given to the slightest details, place him in the rank of the most celebrated artists. His conduct at the court of Louis XIII. showed him as a noble and courageous citizen. Finally, his probity, the kindness of his heart, his anxiety to succor the victims of war, his compassion for all those who suffered, recommend him to the esteem, as his talents recommend him to the admiration of posterity.

INDEX.

INTRODUCTORY.

	PAGE
THE FINE ARTS,	1
ARCHITECTURE,	2
SCULPTURE,	4
PAINTING,	9
ENGRAVING,	18

ARCHITECTS AND SCULPTORS.

PHIDIAS,	20
PRAXITELES,	26
POLYCLETUS,	30
LEONARDO DA VINCI,	31
MICHAEL ANGELO BUONAROTTI,	44
BENEVENUTO CELLINI,	79
CANOVA,	88

PAINTERS.

THE FIRST PAINTERS,	95
ZEUXIS.—ARISTIDES,	98
PARRHASIUS.—TIMANTHES,	103
APELLES,	107
PROTOGENES,	114
TITIAN.—GIORGIONE,	119

RAPHAEL SANZIO, ... 142
CORREGGIO, ... 162
PAUL VERONESE, ... 167
GUIDO RENI, ... 175
DOMENICHINO, ... 184
RIBERA, ... 202
VELASQUEZ, ... 217
MURILLO, ... 230
RUBENS, ... 243
VAN DYCK, ... 262
REMBRANDT, ... 269
LE POUSSIN, ... 279
CLAUDE LORRAIN, ... 293
LE SUEUR, ... 300
SALVATOR ROSA, ... 306

ENGRAVERS.

ALBERT DURER, ... 318
CALLOT, ... 328

www.ingramcontent.com/pod-product-compliance
Lightning Source LLC
Chambersburg PA
CBHW030321240426
43673CB00040B/1236